SUE WRIGHT

Peacemaker's Legacy

First published by Sue Wright 2025

Copyright © 2025 by Sue Wright

All rights reserved. No part of this publication may be reproduced, stored or transmitted in any form or by any means, electronic, mechanical, photocopying, recording, scanning, or otherwise without written permission from the publisher. It is illegal to copy this book, post it to a website, or distribute it by any other means without permission.

Sue Wright asserts the moral right to be identified as the author of this work.

Most of the Characters in this book are based on actual people; however, many facts have been lost in the mists of time, and the author has embellished their stories with her imagination to create a work of fiction.

First edition

ISBN: 978-1-7396061-2-1

Cover art by Lee Bogle

This book was professionally typeset on Reedsy. Find out more at reedsy.com

Contents

Acknowledgments		vi
1	VARINA, Virginia 1622	1
2	Heacham Manor, 1622	8
3	A Shattered Dream	13
4	Kokee	18
5	Windfall (London 1622)	26
6	A Dream Destroyed (1632)	30
7	Letters of Hope	35
8	A New Life At Last	38
9	The Journey Of A Lifetime	42
10	A Cruel Beginning	49
11	He Comes	56
12	Land of Hope	63
13	A New Home	67
14	First Day	71
15	Altercation	76
16	Tragedy	86
17	26th August 1635	93
18	Life Must Go On	99
19	Jane	105
20	Weroance	110
21	Kidnapped	113
22	A Different Family	118
23	A Proposition	124

24	Rescue	131
25	Dark Mission	137
26	Saviour	143
27	Back From A Dream	145
28	Back On The Road	149
29	Friends Or Foe	153
30	Whose Side Are You On?	157
31	Release	162
32	Best Friends	167
33	Mission Of Mercy	173
34	Plans	178
35	Peace Or Blame	182
36	Lost Love	188
37	Permission	193
38	Caught	198
39	Broken Hearts	204
40	Back Into The Fold	212
41	A Brother's Plan	216
42	A Team	223
43	The Fire	228
44	The Governor	234
45	Peace Summit	240
46	Family Meeting	248
47	Uncertainty	255
48	My Enemy's Enemy	263
49	Sarah	270
50	Two Sons, One Father	275
51	Unhealthy Alliance	282
52	Bad Heart	284
53	Ambush	287
54	End of Peace	290

55 Bad News	297
56 Another Chance	302
57 Dismantling The Dream	309
58 Home	313
59 The End Of The Legacy	319
60 A Final Score	323
61 Aftermath	328
Epilogue	332
Also by Sue Wright	334

Acknowledgments

The beautiful image of 'Mother and Child' on the cover of Peacemaker's Legacy is the work of Lee Bogle (www.leebogle.com)

The gun and sword at the bottom of the page have been added to the original painting to give the cover context for the story.

One

VARINA, Virginia 1622

It was dark and still like any other March night in Jamestown, Virginia.

John Rolfe, his wife Joan, and their two-year-old daughter Elizabeth were enjoying an evening meal of rich venison stew. The fire crackled in the grate, and the aroma of freshly baked bread permeated their plantation home. The sound of knives and forks scraping plates was all but drowned out by the playful toddler, laughing and banging her eating utensils on the table. The family was warm, comfortable, and safe.

As John and Joan chatted, they looked with amusement laced with horror at Elizabeth's messy attempt at feeding herself. Gravy ran down her chin and her spoon flew into the air, clattering on the floor and spraying the contents far and wide.

Doba, the teenage Powhatan maid, ran to wipe the mouth of the unruly toddler.

Joan shook her head. "Well, Lizzy, I think you have fed the floor more than yourself." She turned to Doba. "It's time for this little lady to go to bed. Could you wash her and get her ready?"

Doba nodded, her silky black hair catching the light. "Yes, Mistress Rolfe," she said as she scooped up the wriggling child and carried her away, both of them laughing. Doba threw the child in the air as the child screamed with delight, her blonde curls and fair skin a stark contrast to the dark complexion of her playmate.

John sighed as he and Joan sat down together in front of the fire, alone at last. His arm reached around her shoulders as he absorbed the peace of the atmosphere, listening to the childish chatter of his little daughter and her nanny in the background. Things felt good.

After the death of his beloved wife Pocahontas, he was a broken man, convinced he would never love again.

Looking at Joan, he felt a pang of guilt. Despite his fondness for her, he was unable to give himself completely to her. She was beautiful, clever, and loving, and she had borne him a beautiful daughter—but Pocahontas still dominated his mind and always would.

Pocahontas would always be his soulmate despite her untimely death. It had been five years, although it seemed like decades, since he had left her beautiful body buried in the cold English earth. Their son, who was only a toddler then, had looked at him with wide, watery eyes full of desperation. John berated himself daily. He had deserted the child when the little boy needed him most. He had handed him over to a stranger as the child fought and screamed for his mother. Thomas's eyes had bored into him like a branding iron, the memory of which scarred him to this day. He had effectively made Thomas an orphan by walking away. Pocahontas's last words to him echoed in his mind: "All men must die . . . at least we have the child." His heart ached with regret.

VARINA, Virginia 1622

Justifications came easily: little Thomas was not strong enough to make the journey, Virginia was not safe enough for him because of the Powhatan attacks, it was all for his own good, it had not been possible to transport him from London to Virginia safely. It was obvious to everyone—he had no choice but to leave Thomas in England. Or had he?

Maybe the truth was that his broken heart could not bear the thought of opening the festering wound of his loss of Pocahontas. To see their child, the symbol of the love of his life, would have rekindled his devastation every time he looked into Thomas's eyes. So he hid from it, making up excuse after excuse, trying to distract himself with his new family and the challenge of cultivating the tobacco that was now the backbone of Jamestown's burgeoning industry. Tomorrow . . . tomorrow, he would start plans to bring Thomas to Jamestown—tomorrow.

Joan squeezed his hand and he pulled himself back from the past with a jolt.

"What are you thinking, my love? You seem deep in thought." She sat up and looked into his eyes.

He braced himself for the lie, pausing to think of a credible alternative to the truth. "I was just wondering about the situation with the Powhatans. There seems to have been fewer hostilities between us recently. Maybe we have made a breakthrough. Maybe Opechancanough is finally realizing the futility of the fight."

Joan snuggled into his shoulder again. "I hope you're right, John, but usually, there is calm before the storm. I wouldn't blame them for rebelling. I don't mean to be disloyal, but if someone took the land I used to cultivate my food, I would not roll over and comply. I would not be surprised if something violent happens soon."

Bang! Bang! . . . Bang! Suddenly, as if on cue, an explosion of gunfire crashed through the night, alien and menacing, shattering the

3

peace like a boulder being thrown into a calm lake.

"Sweet Jesus, John." Joan jumped away from him, her eyes wide, her heart in her throat. "What is happening?" She clutched his arm frantically. "Surely not? Our conversation was indeed premature."

John pulled away from her and ran to the window. The scene that confronted him stopped him in his tracks. At the Homestead of Varina, they were forty miles from Jamestown, so he had always assumed any trouble with the Powhatans would never come this far upriver. But as he looked across the river to Henrico, he realized his false assumption. It was even more terrible than he had imagined.

Shots were fired again, and suddenly, it seemed as if the world had erupted with shot after shot. This was no minor skirmish; this was serious.

As he stood listening, he could now hear in the distance cries of death, the faint sound of women shouting and crying before their sudden silence.

Flashes of orange flickered through the darkness of the tall trees as the gray smoke rose into the air. Although too far to see the details, John had experienced the wrath of the Powhatans before and imagined the brightly painted bodies, their frenzy as they hacked indiscriminately at English bodies—blood soaking into the precious ground that had been stolen from them.

He feared that if it continued on this scale, it would be only a matter of time until they reached Varina. The fact that he was the brother-in-law of the Powhatan leader would not hold him in good stead. It was more likely to make him a prime target. Opechancanough was furious that Thomas had not been brought back to regain his position in his mother's tribe. Anger was running high on so many levels.

He ran back from the window. "Joan, get Doba and Lizzie and escape out the back. You must hide. It will not be long before they are here, and they will kill us," John shouted, agitation in his eyes, his face moist with sweat.

Joan held out her hand. "You must come too, John." Her eyes pleaded with him.

"No, I must distract them while you three escape. It is the only way I can save you."

She shook her head. "Please come with us, John. Lizzie needs her father."

"Joan, please just go . . . you are wasting valuable time, and if you do not go soon, Lizzie will not be around to miss her father." His handsome face was set, and there was determination in his eyes. She knew he had old scores to settle, even if it meant his death. She would never change his mind. She turned and walked away, a tear running down her cheek. Pocahontas, his previous wife and love of his life, would finally have all of him, she thought, her heart aching.

John watched as the two women crept into the woods from the back of the house. Joan glanced back. Devastation was written all over her face as she carried Lizzie like a rag doll, sound asleep in her arms. As their eyes met, his heart sank. Unless there was a miracle, this would be the last time he would see her. His eyes were moist as he nodded, encouraging her to leave. The forest swallowed them up, and he was alone, with only the noise of the approaching violence to keep him company.

He poured himself a glass of red wine and sat down, holding it up to the light, twirling it around, watching the maroon liquid and sighing. He was no longer anxious. He was looking forward to seeing Opechancanough again, even if it meant his demise. Death would take him back to her . . .

Taking a sip of wine, he focused on the fire burning in the hearth, the logs disintegrating into gray lumps of ash as the clock ticked. He thought of Pocahontas's words—"No man lives forever"—as he sank back into the chair, accepting his inevitable fate.

The sounds of the Powhatan warriors screaming and shouting were getting closer and closer. He closed his eyes, waiting for what seemed like hours.

At last, he heard them on the plantation grounds. The guns that had been stolen from Jamestown were being fired into the air as the red mist of adrenaline surged through the veins of the approaching Powhatans, propelling them towards his home . . . his sanctuary.

The door was kicked down, splinters of wood flying, and six natives ran into the house, fired up with excitement, looking for the next head to scalp. He sat watching, breathing slowly. Waiting.

For a moment, when they saw him, they were stunned. They stopped in their tracks. Why was he not running? Why was he not trying to protect himself? One broke ranks, running forward and pulling him to his feet. John looked at the floor, meek and compliant, accepting that his time on Earth was finally ending.

From behind the warriors, John could hear a commotion. Opechancanough forced his way through his men, shouting and gesticulating at them. They all jumped back like startled children, watching as their leader barged his way towards the long-coated man. They were bemused. Why had their great leader troubled himself with just one man? There must be a reason. Maybe he wanted to kill him himself? He must be wealthy from the looks of his large house and acres of land. Perhaps he was a special prize.

Opechancanough stopped in front of John, pushing the frenzied warriors out of the away. "John," he said. "You are the father of Pocahontas's child—a child that we have never seen—a child that should have taken the Powhatan throne. Why did you not bring him to us?"

John looked at Pocahontas's uncle and raised his hands in front of his chest. Maybe the Powhatans would spare his life to bring Thomas to Jamestown and he could finally fulfill Pocahontas's wishes. He started to speak. "Great Opechancanough—"

From behind, a new mob of warriors barged into the room, out-of-control fire in their bellies.

It came silently and swiftly towards its target. John and Opechancanough saw the arrow simultaneously, and as if in slow motion, they watched as it headed straight for John's heart. He felt the pressure in his chest and the sharp pain as it reached its mark.

He fell, blood dripping from his mouth. "Pocahontas . . ." he whispered. The Powhatans watched as John lay, gasping for breath. The gap between each breath became longer and longer as the clock ticked until the spirit left his eyes.

Opechancanough crouched down next to John's body. He placed his fingers over the still warm eyelids and gently closed his staring eyes. "Go in peace, my brother," he whispered, a tear rolling down his face.

At the death of his once-hated enemy, the great leader heard the long-awaited prophecy of what he now must do.

Two

Heacham Manor, 1622

Pocahontas's son, Thomas, was seven years old, and since the age of two, he had lived at Heacham Manor in Norfolk, England, the home of his paternal grandmother and grandfather.

Five long years and Thomas knew that any time now, his father would send for him to come and live in the New World. He prayed every night to get a message to pack his bags. It would happen. He knew it would. He just had to wait a little longer. He was convinced that he belonged in Virginia, and his stay at Heacham, while acceptable, was only temporary until he could be in his rightful place with his father. He might even be able to visit his mother's people.

As he got out of bed on this cold, wintry morning, he looked up at the painting of his mother that hung on the wall above his bed. She was beautiful, with long dark hair and a string of fine pearls around her neck. She sat with her child, looking at him with adoration. He, of course, was the child. The pearls had pride of place on his dressing table, and he looked at them every morning as he rose from his bed, putting them in his pocket so he could feel them through the day.

His mother had died a long time ago, but he often dreamed of her. Well, it seemed like dreams. But sometimes, she came into his room and sat on the end of the bed and they had long conversations. She told him about the faraway lands and Werowocomoco, the village in Virginia, where she had grown up. Her stories of his older brother stirred his imagination and made him want to fly to America on the wings of a bird. His brother and he would be such friends. An older brother . . . maybe he had a painted pony. Maybe Thomas could also have a pony so they could race each other through the fields of corn and tobacco? He could not wait until that day.

He was well looked after at Heacham Manor, but Thomas felt he was tolerated rather than accepted. He could not blame his grandparents; after all, he was half Powhatan, not the usual English grandson that they might have wanted. That is why he was keen to get to Virginia, where he belonged. He would fit in there in a way he never could in England.

He was hungry for adventure; the only adventure he had at Heacham was cantering through the woods on his little pony, Virginia. He glanced up at the picture on the wall once more and smiled. "I will get there, Mama."

He tiptoed across the cold floor in his bare feet, mottled legs riddled with goosebumps from the cold, and looked out the window to see what kind of day it was going to be. A smile crept onto his face as he saw old Mr. Jenkins, his friend, the gardener hard at work already. Mr. Jenkins was special to him. He had known his mother and father, and he was the only one who took the time to regale tales of long ago about when his father had lived at Heacham Manor as a boy.

It was a bright and sunny day in March. The overnight frost tipped the grass and sparkled the vegetation. He could see the misty air coming out of Mr. Jenkins's mouth as he struggled with the wheelbarrow full of manure, the grass crunching under his feet. Thomas jumped away from the window and ran to get dressed. He had to get to Mr. Jenkins before he got too immersed in his work—he was desperate to know everything there was to know about his father and mother. Any chance there was to find out more, he had to take it. He pulled on his breeches and struggled to get his arms in a warm overshirt.

He ran down the stairs, across the large hallway of Heacham Manor, and lifted the large latch to open the heavy oak door. As he ventured outside, the cold air hit him in the face, tingling and harsh but somehow pleasant. Ignoring the cold, he ran down the garden, crunching on the ice-coated lawn and shouting, "Mr. Jenkins . . . Mr. Jenkins . . . it's me. Where are you?" Mr. Jenkins had moved the wheelbarrow and was no longer visible.

"Over here, boy!" shouted the old man from behind a large hedge. His eyes crinkled up as his face broke into a beaming smile. "I have to mulch these roses, so don't distract me. Your grandmother is very fond of her roses and she will not be pleased if I talk to you instead of getting this job done." He sounded grumpy, but his smile told a different story.

"Can't you talk to me while you work?" Thomas pleaded, not ready to give up so easily.

Mr. Jenkins shook his head, the smile still on his face. "You never give up do you, Thomas? You're like your father in that way."

Thomas pounced at the chance. "What do you mean? How am I like my father?"

"Well, your father was a very determined young man. He never gave up on what he wanted, even if it meant hardship."

"What did he want, Mr. Jenkins?"

"He wanted to go to the New World, and even though he had many obstacles, he managed to get there."

"That's what I want too, and I'm going to do everything I can to get there," Thomas sighed. "My father wants me to go to Virginia to be with him, but everyone says it's not safe for me to go. It's just not fair."

Mr. Jenkins stood up from mulching the roses and leaned on the large wooden-handled pitchfork, taking a breath and looking at the youngster. "I'm sure that your father has your best interests at heart, Thomas. He will send for you as soon as he can. You are precious to him. I saw him with you and your mother when they were at Heacham when you were very young. He loved your mother and you very much. I've told you many times how your mother planted that mulberry tree over there . . . It was so sad when she died."

Thomas hung his head. "I can't even remember them. I just want to be with my father. Surely it can't be that dangerous. I'm half Powhatan, so surely the Powhatans would not harm me?"

"Be patient, young man. Things always happen for a reason, even if we do not know what the reason is all of the time."

Thomas scowled. "It's so hard though. You're the only one who talks to me around here."

At that moment, they both heard someone shouting Thomas's name from the manor.

"I think that's your grandmother. You'll have to go and see what she wants."

"I suppose so," Thomas muttered, his mouth turned down at the edges.

"Be off with you, you rascal."

Thomas meandered back to the manor. He opened the large oak door and stepped inside. They had stopped calling him. Maybe he could get away with sneaking through to the kitchen and having breakfast without being seen.

"Thomas, is that you? Can you come here, dear? We want to talk to you."

Thomas was taken aback. His grandmother almost never wanted to talk to him. The only time this happened was when he had done something wrong. What was it this time? He thought of pretending not to have heard her but then thought the better of it. It was best to face it and get it out of the way. Maybe she had seen him talking to Mr. Jenkins and was cross that he had distracted him from the roses.

He walked forward and entered the lavish, worn parlor where his grandmother and grandfather sat. As he opened the door, he saw their faces were unsmiling. His grandmother's eyes looked red-rimmed, and her complexion was gray. Something was amiss. It looked worse than he had anticipated.

"Ah . . . Thomas, my darling boy. Come and sit next to me." Her voice was low and faltering.

This was so unusual that Thomas was starting to get worried. She was rarely this affectionate towards him. He walked over to his grandmother and sat down next to her, looking up at her with wide, expectant eyes.

She bit her lip, put her arm around him and hugged him like she had never hugged him before, silent tears moistening her eyes. "Thomas, I am sorry to say that your father has died . . . The Powhatans killed him."

Three

A Shattered Dream

It took him several seconds to comprehend what she was saying. When he did, the words struck him like a thunderbolt. As reality filtered through confusion, tears welled up in his eyes and he started to shake. It was as if his life was over. The implications of her words started to hurtle through his mind one by one. He would never see his father again. He would never get to Jamestown. He would never ride on a painted pony. His mother's people had killed his father. What would that mean? Would he never meet his Powhatan brother or all his uncles and aunts? How did he feel about the Powhatans now they had revealed this murderous side?

All the imaginings that had taken over his life so far melted into a pool of tears. They were all gone—all his dreams. He was now totally alone. His English grandmother and grandfather were not his people—they had been encumbered with him. What had he done to deserve this betrayal? He should have known that his dreams were too good to be true. How could his father have done this to him? He had been rejected and left once, and now he was being rejected and left again. This time for good. He was Powhatan, he was Virginian—he was different. But the Powhatans had killed his father. How could they? Maybe they were savages like everyone said.

His face turned puce as his thoughts pierced his heart. His eyes were wet and his teeth clenched. He yanked himself free from his grandmother's false embrace and stood up to face her square on, glaring, the heat of his anger flushing his complexion.

"I hate you, I hate my father, and I hate the Powhatans," he screeched. Before she could respond, he turned and ran from the room. His grandparents watched with open mouths as their grandson crashed through the door and disappeared out of view, leaving them in the turbulence of his fury.

He ran outside, the cold fresh air hitting him like a slap. He needed time to think. What was he going to do? How could he get to Virginia? There was no one there who would look after him, no one who would pay for his passage. Did he want to meet his Powhatan family now that they had killed his father? Only heathens could do such a thing.

He thought back to what Mr. Jenkins had said. His father had been determined, had a goal, and did everything in his power to achieve it. But what was his own goal now? He did not even know that anymore.

He looked at the frozen garden. Even it seemed different from a few minutes ago. The sparkling enchantment had morphed into a hard cold wilderness—friend turned to enemy. How could his world have changed so dramatically in such a short space of time? He paused. What could he do next?

He ran back towards the rose garden, his heart beating. He saw the old man still hard at work.

"Mr. Jenkins, Mr. Jenkins . . . something terrible has happened!"

he shouted.

Mr. Jenkins looked up from mulching the roses and leaned on his fork. "What is it, boy—what has happened?" His back bent in a C shape as he stopped, catching his breath, his lungs wheezing clouds of air into the atmosphere.

Thomas looked at the ground, trying to find the words. When he said them out loud, they would become fact, and he hesitated.

"Come on, boy—what is it?"

"My father has been murdered," he said, looking at the old man with tears in his eyes.

Mr. Jenkins dropped his fork and came towards Thomas. "What happened, young master?" he said, concern etched into the lines on his face.

"The Powhatans killed him, Mr. Jenkins."

The gardener was speechless for a moment. The death of the boy's mother had been tragedy enough—some had said she was poisoned. But now his father had been killed at the hands of her relatives. How must the boy feel? His heroes had been his father and his Powhatan warrior relatives. Now one was dead and the others were tainted with his murder. His heart was breaking for the child.

The old man walked towards the garden bench that was underneath the mulberry tree. "Come here, lad." He patted the bench.

Thomas dragged himself over to the bench and eased himself down. Wiping tears from his eyes, he pulled Pocahontas's pearls from his pocket. He rolled them around in his fingers, their soft sheen soaking up his tears.

The crumpled old man and the boy sat silently, absorbing the implications of the tragedy. Mr. Jenkins was compelled to put his arm around the boy, his unyielding old body attempting to cradle him.

Thomas slumped, holding the pearls tightly and weeping.

Mr. Jenkins looked into the distance. "You know you are not alone, boy," he said.

Thomas looked up at him, his face red and moist with tears.

"What do you mean, Mr. Jenkins? I know I have my grandmother, but she's old."

"When your mother and father were living at Heacham, your mother would often come and seek me out. I think she liked talking to someone away from the rituals of the English gentry." He smiled, looking into the distance as if he could see her on the horizon. "Yes, she was beautiful inside and out, your mother. One day I found her by herself in the rose garden. She was deep in thought. As I approached, she called me over."

Thomas sat up, wiping the tears away. "What did she say?"

"Well, I think she was feeling homesick. She told me that she missed her father and her sisters, but she also confided that she had a child that she had left behind in Virginia, and it haunted her that she could not be with him."

Thomas's eyes opened wide. This confirmed what the ghostly figure that came to him in the night had said. It was not a dream. "What else did she say, Mr. Jenkins?" He knew most of the story, but maybe Mr. Jenkins could tell him even more.

"She said that she had been forced to leave him . . . and how grateful she was to have you."

"What's his name? Is he part English like me? Where is he now?"

Mr. Jenkins shook his head. "She told me that she had been married before and had a Powhatan baby named Kokee. She told me that her first husband had been killed. She hoped that one day she could have both of her sons together as a family, and when she returned to Virginia with your father, she would ensure this happened. Sadly, she never made it back."

Thomas nodded his head. "She wanted us to be together." He bit his lower lip, concentration etched onto his face.

Mr. Jenkins smiled. "She told me she would never leave you and wanted you and Kokee to meet and find the peace she could never obtain for herself."

"I must find my brother. It's more important than ever now. Yes, when I am older, I will find my brother . . . I belong with my brother."

Four

Kokee

His mind wandered to another time. He was her first baby, and he remembered his early childhood like it was yesterday. He was a tiny child with inquiring, large brown eyes in a world full of love. His beautiful mother would laugh as his father played peekaboo with his son, the tinkling hilarity resounding through the yehakin.[1] He was the center of their world, and nothing could ever hurt him. He was safe.

Each day was the same. His mother and father were integral members of the tribe. There was always something going on, and there were always people to laugh with and to cry with. There were festivals, there was singing, and there was sadness when someone left for the world beyond life. The skies were always blue, and the gods always protected him. In his world, a cut knee was the worst thing that ever happened to him.

Then things changed. Back then, he was too young to know *what* had changed, but he could see it in their eyes and hear it in their voices. The laughter stopped, and urgent whispers replaced their snatched moments of intimacy. It was like being thrust from a soft cocoon of spun sunbeams into an icy lake. A feeling crept into the pit of his stomach that he had never known before. Then, he did not understand; now he did. It was fear. It was the Longcoat.

Flashing images haunted him to this day. His mother's face as she walked out of the door. He did not understand how he knew she would not return to him, but his childhood sixth sense was rarely wrong. She turned and smiled at him, a tear running down her cheek. Parents never cry; they are always strong. But not in this new reality. His heart broke.

Then, he saw the despair on his father's face. The strong and handsome warrior transformed into a broken man. At the sight of his father's anguish, his childhood was stolen forever. The thief was a new and terrible invader called the Longcoat.

He did not know what was happening, but he continued to watch unfolding events, trembling in the shelter of his aunt Cleopatra's cloak. His father garnered his strength and ran towards the towering ship, screaming his mother's name, his face ugly with distress. Kocoum was mighty in stature, but his strength was nothing compared to the power of the Longcoat. Kokee felt the blanket of doom before it enveloped the world.

The sound. He would never forget the sound. The fire stick cracked a terrifying noise, and his handsome bear of a father crashed to the ground. His strength morphed into vulnerability as the deadly echo faded into the silence. The dust flew, its particles shimmering in the sunlight, as his father, falling as if in slow motion, became a body instead of a warrior. The ensuing silence was deafening.

He remembered (or was it a dream?) running to his father and lying over his warm body, feeling the stickiness of his blood, whimpering. He stared at Kocoum's agonized face, willing his eyes to open, willing his mouth to speak. The world stood still. Nothing seemed to move except the steady stream of warm tears running down his face. He saw Kocoum's spirit rise and felt his last loving spiritual embrace. In that instant, he knew he was alone. The feeling in the pit of his stomach overcame him. He had no one left.

His father was gone, and his mother was gone—all within as much time as it took for a butterfly to flap its wings. Why could he not turn back the clock? Was this just a bad dream? Would he wake up like he did yesterday, and would the day begin as it always did?

He existed in a dreamlike state for two years, waiting for them to return; the feeling in his stomach overtook his whole body and became all there was to feel. To escape, he cut himself off from the world, mute and staring . . . a child existing only with memories and fear.

Like a moth to light, he was compelled to walk into the depths of the river to find them again. Cleopatra watched him day and night, barring his premature union with the gods, so he existed as a shell on dry land in a nightmare that could never end.

When at last she came, his staring eyes could not believe she was there. Was she a spirit sent from the gods? The ship dropped anchor, and she appeared. It was her, but it was not her. She was dressed in the Longcoats' dress and looked hunted and drawn. Could he trust that this vision was truly his mother from a time when the sun shone?

Tension hung in the air as she met each member of the tribe, smiling a vacant smile, looking around her with darting eyes for the part of her that was missing.

He looked on, silent, as if his soul was watching, but his body was not there.

When she came upon him and their eyes locked, there was no one but the two of them. Her embrace was fierce as their tears of joy mingled with their tears of sadness. He clung to her as if his life depended on her touch. Her sobs rang through the trees.

"My Kokee," she whispered as she looked into his eyes, gently moving his hair from his forehead so she could see into him.

"Mama..."

Then, like an axe splitting a log, they were wrenched apart, the mother and child clawing at the air, fighting and screaming, no match for the will of the Longcoats. Finally, as she surrendered, all fight exhausted, they let go of her for a moment, and she escaped, running back to him and crouching down. "Do not hate them," she whispered. "Find your brother... Make peace together. You are my legacy."

They grabbed her arms and carried her back to the ship as her head strained in his direction, her eyes drinking in every last image of her son until she could see him no more.

When she was gone, he hid his head in Cleopatra's skirts, trying to block the scene that would play repeatedly in his head for as long as he lived.

The agonizing sound of her cries echoed through the trees.

***

It had been five years since he had seen her. Now, he sat before his mother's uncle.

"Kokee... I have summoned you here today for a very important reason." Opechancanough drew on his pipe, his eyes dull with sorrow, and looked at the eleven-year-old lad sitting before him.

"Your life has been filled with tragedy, and the hearts of our tribe have held you, as the son of Pocahontas, in high regard. My brother, the great Wahunseneca, lives through you, and I see his greatness in your eyes."

Kokee sat, still as a mouse, eyes wide, listening to every word his great-uncle was saying. An audience with Opechancanough was an honor, and he was curious and apprehensive as to why he had been summoned.

"The Longcoats continue to take our land, and we have had to defend our livelihood. This has led to bloodshed despite your mother's sacrifices for peace."

Kokee nodded. Celebrations for their recent victory were fresh in his mind. Four hundred Longcoats had been killed. While he had replayed his mother's whispered words in his head every night as he drifted off to sleep, he had struggled to understand or comply with her wishes. She had said, "Find your brother," but he did not have a brother. She had said, "Do not hate them"; how could he not hate them? How could he not rejoice at their suffering when they had killed the people dearest to him? He looked at Opechancanough wondering what he would say next.

"Your grandfather, the great Wahunseneca, did all he could to befriend the Longcoats. Your mother gave everything for peace. Until this moment, I never understood why peace was their goal. I wanted to fight; I wanted revenge for all the injustices done to our people.

"Our last attack was a victory . . . But perhaps your mother had more wisdom; perhaps her heart knew the answer was not in the deaths of our enemy."

Kokee frowned. "Surely we did well killing so many?" He was breathless with childish enthusiasm. "I cannot wait until I am old enough to be a great warrior and kill more Longcoats." He looked into the eyes of the old man and saw his sorrow. He paused, confusion flooding his face. "Your sadness tells me you do not share my joy at their destruction."

Opechancanough shook his head. "My son, the scales have been taken from my eyes, and now I can see what your mother saw. It is not about killing. Our goal, the goal of your grandfather and your mother, should be to live alongside the Longcoats. "

Kokee's eyes were wide. "But Uncle, now, after such a victory, can we not take our land back and make them stop stealing from us? Surely my mother would understand after all they have done to us?"

Opechancanough nodded. "We could have wiped them out when their numbers were small and their food was scarce, but the gods spoke to your mother and grandfather, and now they have spoken to me. We cannot question the wisdom of the gods. We must strive for peace. That is the only way to stop bloodshed."

Kokee looked at the ground, his face crestfallen, hearing the echoes of his mother's cries in his head. "But how can we make them listen to us? They do not want peace; they want us to give them all we have. They took my mother and father, and my heart is broken and bleeding with hatred."

Opechancanough paused. He leaned over the boy and took his hands in his own. "Your mother had another life when the Longcoats captured her. She was married to a Longcoat."

Kokee pulled his hands away. "No . . . she would never do that!" he shouted, the vision of her being dragged away still as vivid as the day it happened. "She loved my father . . . and she wanted to stay with me! They forced her to leave me!"

He covered his eyes with his hands and sobbed, his shoulders moving with the force of his emotion. Since he was a baby, he had struggled with the loss of his parents, and now loss combined with anger flooded his senses once more. Was she forced to abandon him . . . or was it a choice?

Opechancanough moved closer and put his arm around the boy. They sat together, the old man and the young lad. The embers of the fire were growing dim, but Opechancanough did not move. The boy needed him, and while he could not foretell the end of his unfolding tragedy, his brother's grandson would be treated with the respect of a future leader.

Finally, Kokee's shoulders became still. He sat with Opechancanough, staring at the blackened embers of the fire, all energy expended. His face was moist and red with crying, and his breath came in quick bursts.

A sense of calm descended. "Your mother was a great woman. She loved you more than life itself," Opechancanough said, breaking the silence.

The boy looked up at him with red-rimmed eyes. "Why did she leave me?" he whispered.

Opechancanough sighed. "The world is very cruel, and sometimes the gods cannot protect us from pain. Your mother was forcibly taken from us. She suffered greatly in captivity and nearly died from ill-treatment at the hands of the Longcoats, but also from the heartbreak of losing you and your father. She was only alive because a Longcoat called John Rolfe rescued her. The only way he could save her was to marry her."

Kokee looked at the floor. "But why did she not take me with her?"

Opechancanough put his finger under the boy's chin and lifted his face so their eyes met. "She knew it would not be safe for you and that we would care for you. When she visited that last time, she wanted to see you to make sure you were being cared for with us. She wanted you to grow up as a Powhatan, to be a great warrior and leader of the tribe, so you and your brother could continue working towards peace."

Kokee blinked, and he sat straight, looking at the old man. "My brother?"

Opechancanough nodded, a smile creeping onto his gnarled face. "Yes, my son. One good thing to come from your mother's captivity was a child."

Kokee blinked, looking into the cold embers of the fire, thoughts ricocheting around his head. She had whispered, *Find your brother.*

"Where is my brother . . . How old is he . . . What is his name . . . Can I meet him . . . ?" His voice was high-pitched and urgent; he was desperate to know about the one remaining connection to her.

Opechancanough put his arm around the boy. "You have many questions. I have few answers. John Rolfe is your brother's father. Your brother is Thomas Rolfe, and he is four years younger than you. No one has seen him in Virginia since your mother sailed to England, but we know John Rolfe was planning to bring him from England when it was safe. Sadly, it has never been safe enough, and John Rolfe was killed in our recent war."

Kokee looked earnest. "Is my brother still alive?"

Opechancanough nodded. "The gods say he is still alive, and one day he will return to us. Part of the heart of this child is Powhatan and part is Longcoat. He has been sent into the world as a peacemaker. It is prophesied that you and he will be united as the sons of Pocahontas, and the fate of our tribe will be in your hands. Thomas will marry and together, you will continue the work that your mother started."

Kokee looked at his uncle, his heart beating faster as he absorbed the meaning of what he was being told. "I must find my brother, and we will make peace together." He put his hands together and bowed his head.

[1] Powhatan house.

Five

Windfall (London 1622)

"So, Henry, first of all, I would like to extend my heartfelt condolences to you on the tragic loss of your brother," said Sir Charles Buckingham, solicitor, as he held out his hand to Henry Rolfe. Sir Charles was an elderly man with white hair and an air of authority. His clothes were immaculate, his ego very large, and his body odor overwhelming.

Henry Rolfe bowed his head solemnly, nodding as he shook Sir Charles's hand. "Yes, Sir Charles—it was a tragedy," he said with pronounced solemnity. Henry was tall and slim, with a large pointed nose and piercing blue eyes. He paused, bowing his head as he sauntered into the room, arrogance emanating from every pore. He was here for a purpose, but he had to be careful not to divulge it.

Henry shook his head. "Yes, and the poor little lad is all alone in the world now." He stared out of the window as if empathizing with his nephew. He hoped the charade would not take too long. It was tiresome. It just needed to be sorted. He had an appointment in an hour with a very willing lady, and he did not want to keep her waiting. If this meeting was successful, he might even be able to give her a bonus.

Sir Charles nodded. "Indeed, indeed. Thankfully the lad has you though, Henry. That is a godsend. It must be a real bonus for you having the lad around when you have no children of your own."

Henry hesitated a fraction too long. "Yes, yes, of course, that is true, although he lives at Heacham at the moment, so I do not see that much of him. He looks very Powhatan unfortunately, which would make it difficult for him to mix in London. We have kept him in Norfolk for that reason."

"Oh, I see . . ." Sir Charles gave Henry a knowing look, scratching his chin. "I understand that John also had some land and assets in Virginia. You must be aware these will not be covered by this will. Correspondence with my colleagues in Virginia indicates that he split those assets between Thomas and his Virginian daughter, Elizabeth. His wife, Joan, is the executor of his Virginia property until the two children come of age. It is only his English assets that we are dealing with today."

Henry's attention returned to the room, his thigh bouncing up and down as an indication of his impatience. "There is not that much to discuss, Sir Charles. John left Thomas with me, and I have had to pay for his upkeep all these years. Therefore, I assume that all of John's money will be coming to me in recognition of what I have had to do." His eyes were staring, his manner condescending. "I will have to continue paying for Thomas's education and upkeep until he reaches majority. I think anything John left should contribute to that, don't you agree?"

Sir Charles sighed. The patches of dampness under his armpits were getting bigger, beads of sweat turning into rivulets that ran down his plump face. "Indeed, Henry, that would make sense. However, the law is not quite as simple as that. Thomas is John's heir, and Thomas has a right to all of John's assets—a considerable amount. Your brother has been sending money back from Virginia for several years to pay for Thomas's keep. That money, technically, is Thomas's—not yours, even if your intention is only to use it for the benefit of Thomas."

Henry stiffened. He paused. He had to approach this differently if he was going to get access to that money. He needed that money. He had debts that he had to pay. He sat back in the chair and smiled. "Of course, but Thomas is only a child. He will need an adult to look after the money for him in trust until he comes of age. As his uncle and someone very close to his father," he lied, "I should be the person to manage the money in trust."

Sir Charles's eyes glazed over as he absentmindedly rubbed a stain on his jacket, remnants of his overindulgence of the previous evening. He knew where this was going, and he did not care. He wanted to get home and pour himself a large glass of ale. He had had enough for today. These issues did not interest him. "Well, Henry, John specifically requested that I, as a reputable man of the law, manage Thomas's inheritance, and I have a small retainer for my efforts. I have to earn a pittance, you know, old boy." He smiled, his agenda quite clear.

Henry knew he had to be careful. He could not be too obvious. Incentives could be given without resorting to bribery.

"I know you're a busy man, and it seems a shame to lumber you with such a small matter. I could easily manage Thomas's inheritance on an ongoing basis. Of course, the retainer would still be paid to you, plus a little extra. I could do the irritating day-to-day management to save you time. After all, it's not like I'm a stranger. I am Thomas's uncle, and I can be trusted, can't I?"

Sir Charles was tired. It was time to close this thing down. He would have a substantial retainer for doing nothing. Why not let this odious man have control of the money and be done with it? Who would ever know? He clasped his hands in front of his ample belly and looked down his nose at Henry.

"It's very unusual, Henry," he said, eking out the suspense, milking his power. "However, if we keep the arrangement between ourselves . . ." He preened himself. "I suppose I could make an exception." He took his time. "I have known your family for many years, and you are very close to the boy. It makes perfect sense for you to have access to the money. I'm sure we can come to a mutually acceptable agreement for how we take this forward." He winked and tapped the side of his nose.

Henry smiled. "Thank you, Sir Charles. You will not regret this decision. I will always have Thomas's best interests at heart." Inside his calm exterior, Henry was jumping for joy. He could pay off his debts with money to spare. The lad would not go hungry, and mother and stepfather would look after him as they had done for the past five years. No harm done. John owed him for looking after the brat—well, he had made sure he was looked after at Heacham, had he not?

Six

A Dream Destroyed (1632)

"All my father's money is gone? I have nothing to my name?" Thomas's dark eyes stared wide with disbelief as he looked at his uncle Henry sitting in a comfortable armchair while he sat on a functional wooden chair opposite. The room was dark and somber. Thomas had traveled to London excited by the prospect of negotiating with his uncle to receive an advance payment to get himself on a ship to Virginia. Now, as he looked at the smug face smiling at him, his world, once again, seemed to crumble.

Henry, sitting in his armchair like the cat that got the cream, steeled himself as he looked at his sixteen-year-old nephew. "It is a shame, but you have nothing left, young man . . . and do you know why? Who do you think has fed and clothed you for all these years? Who has kept you in the lap of luxury? Where do you think the money has come from?" He paused and took a deep breath, raising his voice. "You don't belong here, you never have. We have suffered your presence out of charity, my boy. If it were up to me, you would be in the workhouse." His voice was strong and uncompromising. His cold blue eyes flashed with superiority. He was a master of bullying and his victims usually caved in.

Thomas's body visibly tensed as he heard his uncle's words. If his father's brother felt this way about him—his flesh and blood—he never stood a chance. They both knew the truth of what his uncle had done, but it would not change the fact of his half-caste heritage. Tension hung in the air as Thomas digested his new situation.

Henry sat, confidence emanating from his pinched and arrogant face. It had been so easy, like taking sweetmeats from an innocent child.

As he looked at the boy before him, a Rolfe with heathen appearance, he started to feel an uncharacteristic pang of guilt. Maybe he had been a bit harsh. The boy was only sixteen, and he could not fight back, even if he wanted to. The word of a heathen against the word of an upstanding member of the community? Maybe appearances dictated that he should relent a little. He would make sure his generosity was well publicized.

He relaxed and softened his voice. "Look, Thomas, your father made a terrible mistake marrying your mother; we all know that. You, as the bastard son, will now have to survive as best you can. So far, to our credit, we have supported you, but in all honesty, you cannot expect the Rolfe family to continue paying out for your every whim." He sighed and looked at Thomas, shaking his head. "You will have to find work now that you are coming into adulthood. Sadly, with your heathen background, there will be few choices open to you. I can try to help you find laboring work, and maybe, one day, you can save enough to go to Virginia. It may take a few years, but you never know, eh?" His smile did not reach his hard-staring eyes. "I am so sorry, Thomas. We have done what we can, but your father is the only one that you can blame for your unfortunate circumstances." This was going well, he thought.

Thomas's calm exterior belied the volcano in his head. In the space of a few minutes, his father's brother had demolished everything that he held dear. His hopes and dreams were crushed once again; his future was made bleak. With every word his uncle uttered, his heart raced more, and he struggled to restrain the words that were bursting to wipe the smile off Henry's face. He had very few options, though, and impulsive retaliation was a luxury he could not risk. He paused, staring at the floor, organizing his response.

"Uncle Henry, with respect, surely you are mistaken. My father left enough money for my childhood expenses with an even bigger sum to start me off in whatever adult endeavor I should choose. So, the fact that there is none of my inheritance left comes as a great shock to me."

Thomas noticed Henry flinch as he instinctively started to tap his toe on the floor. "Oh, Thomas, I'm afraid that is just not so. I was given sole responsibility for all of John's money, and I assure you, there was not much, and it has all been spent." He shook his head, a glum look of sympathy radiating towards Thomas. "You will just have to accept the facts, old boy. I am sorry, but apart from helping you to find employment, there is little I can do. I am sure your grandmother would continue to support you at Heacham until something more permanent is found."

Thomas sat tall. "I have a letter from my stepmother, Joan, given to her by my father before he died, detailing exactly what my father left, and what his instructions to you and the solicitor in charge were." His voice was controlled and confident, devoid of emotion. "Before he died, my father gave Joan details of all his finances—including those he had put in place for me here. He was concerned about his safety and that he might not live to see me again. Joan promised him that if anything happened to him, she would make sure that I would receive my inheritance."

A Dream Destroyed (1632)

Henry looked around the room, buying himself time. "She must be mistaken, young man. How can a woman halfway across the world know the details of what has been spent here? It is preposterous." He laughed a fake laugh, his eyes remaining steely and condescending.

"My father also lodged details of my inheritance with the Virginia Company." His dark brown eyes bore into his uncle. "So . . . I would be grateful to receive some of that money now, to start organizing my trip to Virginia." Thomas's face showed no emotion.

Henry turned a dark red as he resorted to his usual way of handling his affairs. He launched himself from his armchair and charged towards Thomas with his eyes flashing. "You heathen vagabond! You are suggesting that I stole your money! I will not take allegations like that lightly." He lunged, with fists raised, towards a bemused Thomas, who jumped from his chair. The chair crashed to the floor, the sound of wood on wood vibrating through the room. With Thomas removed, gravity took its toll, and instead of Henry's fist colliding with Thomas, Henry fell into the empty space and landed on the floor with a loud thud.

It was a bad fall, and Thomas looked on in horror as his uncle lay prostrate on the floor, whimpering with pain, his arm extended in a contorted angle. Blood oozed from a large gash on his head caused by the corner of a coffer that had broken Henry's fall. Thomas knelt to help his uncle. "Uncle Henry, are you all right?" he whispered, putting his hand out tentatively, knowing full well there was nothing right about this situation.

His uncle raised his head and turned to look at him. "You are finished now, you heathen bastard. You will be charged with assault for this attack on your defenseless and benevolent uncle. The courts will not be lenient - I will make sure of that.

Peacemaker's Legacy

Seven

Letters of Hope

My dear Stepmother,

 I am forcing my hand to write to you as my circumstances dictate that there are no other options left open to me. I crave your indulgence and goodwill as I write to you in secret as the only person connected to my father who might be able to alleviate my plight.

I understand from previous correspondence with your good self and my elders, that my father, who I did not see after he left me as an infant in the good care of his brother Henry, always intended me to return to Virginia. His devastating death did not dim my ambition to see the land he held so close to his heart.

Through a series of misunderstandings with my Uncle Henry, I have been left without the financial resources my father bequeathed to allow me to carry out this aim. At present, I am working on the farm at Heacham to earn my keep, with no prospect of that changing in the future. My grandparents have been kind, but my guardian, Henry Rolfe, no longer feels empathy towards me.

I know that my father left land in Virginia to me and your daughter (my sister) Elizabeth in equal measure. I also understand that my Powhatan grandfather left me an inheritance of which I have no details.

I hope you can imagine my frustration at being penniless in England when my inheritance and my family lie elsewhere.

In the hope that the deep feelings you bore my father might allow you to relate to the part of him that flows through my veins, I am writing for your help.

Is there a way that money for my passage could be raised on the understanding that it will be repaid out of my Virginia inheritance when I can access it?

Forgive my impertinence in writing to you in such a manner. My choices are few and any advice on who I might contact, or what I might do to realise my ambitions would be received with gratefulness.

Your stepson
Thomas Rolfe

Letters of Hope

My Dearest Thomas,

Your father spoke to me many times of his regret at being unable to have you by his side. Be in no doubt that his heart ached as the dangerous situation, (that finally took his life), made it unsafe for him to bring you here to live as part of our family. Your name was on his lips the last time that I saw him alive and I promised that I would look after your interests.

The colony continues to grow, and the tobacco industry that your father started with your mother so many years ago continues to thrive. However, the governors are concerned that the numbers in the colony are not as great as they would desire. They have instigated a new scheme to encourage migration to Virginia that may help us to achieve your goal.

Successful members of the Virginia colony are being granted plots of land in return for bringing valuable new colonists with skills to the Colony.

My father, Captain William Pierce, (who incidentally, travelled with your father to Bermuda on the 'Sea Venture') at my request has volunteered to apply for this scheme to bring you to Jamestown.

There are several hurdles to cross, and this may take many months to come to fruition, but, my dearest stepson, this could be the answer to your prayers.

We will keep the details of this to ourselves at present, and I would ask you to be patient while we negotiate details and practicalities.

I live in the hope of meeting you, as my beloved John lives on through you and our daughter Elizabeth.

Yours in anticipation,
   LOVE
   Joan

Eight

A New Life At Last

He stood stock-still, taking in the sights and sounds, a smile fixed on his dusky face. He had grown a beard, as at twenty years old, the rugged outline made him look older and more competent. He was tall and lean, but despite his youth, he had a commanding air about him, of which he was unaware. His dark good looks made him stand out from the crowd of ordinary people swarming the quay. Against all odds, he was standing next to the ship that was to finally take him to his dreams. He imagined how his father had stood on the same quay experiencing feelings similar to his own.

Horses and carts rumbled across the dirty cobbled street, and sweating men shouted to one another as they tossed the final provisions for the long trip to Virginia from cart to hold. The fog shrouded everything in a damp, gray mist that chilled to the bone. It was grimy, smelly, and loud, but to Thomas, it was paradise.

He could see other passengers emerging out of the mist and walking toward the gangplank for embarkation, looking around in anticipation. As a mother holding the hand of a small boy passed him, he smiled, before overhearing their conversation on the wind.

"Mummy who is that man? Is he one of the heathens? His skin is dark . . . but he looks nice. Is that what they look like in the New World, Mummy?"

The young mother glanced in Thomas's direction, meeting his gaze. A spontaneous smile touched her lips. He noticed her bright red hair and green eyes and thought he had never seen such a vibrant woman.

Suddenly her eyes turned toward the ground, her face fixed and brows furrowed as she hurried past, yanking the boy forward.

"But Mummy, I wanted to see the heathen . . ." The voice faded as the child stumbled and was herded up the gangplank, looking back in Thomas's direction, disappointment on his face. The mother glanced back momentarily, attempting to disguise her curiosity.

Thomas nodded at the child. It was always the same. He had vowed that he would stop being hurt by the comments and gestures and remember that his appearance was only a reflection of his likeness to his beautiful mother, something he was proud of. Some people said he was handsome, some said he was foreign and odd looking; whoever was right, he could not change who he was. However, despite all his efforts, the disapproving looks never failed to hurt. Why did appearances matter so much to people? Why had that mother pulled her child away? He had been brought up as English. The only difference was that he had some Powhatan blood. Their bigotry was the reason he had to go to Virginia. He had to find his place in the world, and he hoped that his mother's people would open their arms to him.

He looked up at the sky and breathed in the smoke-filled air, imagining how different things were going to be. As he turned back, he took a sharp involuntary intake of breath as he saw a familiar figure in the distance in animated conversation with a rather portly looking man who was nodding his head, his face lined with concentration. It looked as if orders were being given. What was Henry doing at the docks? He saw Henry passing the man something. Thomas frowned.

What was going on? There had been no love lost between them since Henry had banished him and refused to give him money for the passage to Virginia.

When Jane's father, William Pierce, had put up the money for his passage, Henry had been furious. His plan to keep Thomas hidden from view, a disgraced member of the Rolfe family whom no one would take seriously, had backfired.

Thomas had been powerless to defend himself against his uncle's deceit. Henry had vowed to bring an assault charge if Thomas made public his accusations of his uncle's fraud. Pleas of innocence from a heathen would never have been taken seriously. Nevertheless, the truth hung over his uncle like a bad smell. When Thomas saw him plotting, his blood ran cold.

Against all instincts, he took a deep breath and headed in Henry's direction. He needed to try and find out what was going on. As he grew closer, he saw Henry's face darken, his eyes shifty.

"Well, if it isn't my beloved nephew," he growled. "Thought I would come and give you a send-off . . . Make sure you got on the ship. At least we won't have you draining the coffers any more, old boy." Henry winked and chuckled.

Thomas held a straight face. "What are you doing here, Henry? We both know it's not to wish me well."

"Well, truth be told Thomas, I have a friend on the ship. I have asked him to make sure your journey is as comfortable as one befitting a man of your status." He smiled again and patted Thomas on the back.

Thomas flinched, his frown deepening.

"You cannot let me live my life, Henry, can you? My father would turn in his grave if he knew how you have treated me. I have never said a word against you as you are a blood relative, but you continue to make things difficult for me. Do you never think of your brother?"

Henry put his hands on his hips and stood firm. "I do not know what has ruffled your feathers, old boy, I am only trying to help. I cannot see the harm. I must admit we have not seen eye to eye in the past, but I do not think anyone can blame me for that."

Henry looked around to see who could overhear. As he turned back staring at Thomas, his voice became a growling whisper. "You look like a bloody heathen. How do I know you are even John's son? He was my brother, but he was obviously prone to mistakes. Why he took that bitch, your mother, and her brat under his wing, I'll never know." Henry was getting into full flow, his eyes staring and his face red as he continued."I would stake my life that you are not my brother's son. It was common knowledge that the squaw was a whore, so who knows? I can only imagine that John married as a political move to create peace with her people. Good for his career. Why else? Under those circumstances, I think the Rolfes have looked after the cuckoo in the nest rather well."

Thomas was shaking, quelling the volcano of emotions in the pit of his stomach. "I'll not respond to such vile accusations. To do so would validate them. Maybe one day, Henry, everyone will realize who is the bastard in this family." Thomas turned away from him and walked toward the gangplank, gritting his teeth and forcing one foot in front of the other to stop himself from turning back to wipe the smile off Henry's mocking face.

"Have a good trip!" Henry shouted. "My friend William Penhaligan will give you what you deserve!"

Nine

The Journey Of A Lifetime

Thomas's head was spinning as he walked up the gangplank. He had wanted to savor the moment, but his uncle Henry had succeeded in ensuring that only bad feelings accompanied him as he reached the deck. Usually, he was strong and independent, but at that moment, he felt like a small orphaned child. He was alone. He was different from everyone, and no one understood him. He felt in his pocket, and the smooth round pearls of his mother's necklace deepened his feelings rather than comforted him. Why had his parents left him? Everyone in the whole world had parents except him. His English family hated him. His only hope of a loving family lay in Virginia.

He charged to the opposite side of the ship, trying to get as far away from England as he could. But as he looked out to sea, the rippling waves below him were a blur. His uncle's cruel words overwhelmed his consciousness.

Suddenly, he saw her image swaying in the wind. He was startled as he felt warmth surrounding him. His anger started to melt. The red throbbing tension was overtaken. He saw the sparkle of her eyes and her long black hair as it blew in the wind. How could he, for even a moment, forget that she was with him?

"You must never be ashamed of who you are. No person on this earth is perfect, but each has unique value, regardless of race, color, or creed.

"You are on a journey that will teach you many things, but the greatest wisdom you will find is that your difference is of great value. The uniqueness of each individual contributes to the glory of the world.

"I say this not because you are my son but because every sentient being is special in their own distinct way, from buffalo to bee.

"Your journey may seem daunting. See it as an adventure rather than a battle. Learn all that you can about yourself and the world around you.

"There will be fear in your strange new world, but remember that fear never kills; face it with determination and it will hone your instincts and make you stronger.

"You are torn between two worlds like I once was, struggling to fit in.

"Be yourself, without striving to please or stifling the views of others without due consideration, and your place in the world will become clear. **Different does not mean inferior.** *With this self-knowledge, energy accumulated in anger towards those who despise you will morph into acceptance of their shortcomings and pity for their ignorance.*

"Peace comes in many guises, and you will find yours."

She smiled softly, bowing her head and placing her hands together over her heart.

He felt a rush of panic like the one he had felt all those years ago when she disappeared from his childhood. A tear ran down his cheek for the love and the loss of this remarkable woman and for the small boy who had had to fend for himself since he was two years old.

He looked up at her once again, and as she enveloped him in her mystical arms for the last time, he felt calmness descend.

As her image floated away, he wiped the moisture from his face and, with it, any of the remaining self-pity that blighted his resolve. He was the lucky one. He was her son. The universe had given him his cards; he would use them well, not despise them. He would make her proud.

The sights and sounds of the ship started to penetrate his consciousness, replacing his mother's shimmering image. Only elation was left. The hustle and bustle, the shouting, stomping, stinking ship that would be his home for the next six weeks, again instilled excitement. How could he allow his uncle Henry to spoil things? His life was ahead of him; he would use it well and follow her words to peace.

As he was about to turn around to explore the ship, he felt a tiny hand in his. He looked down and saw the small boy who had stared at him as he was boarding the ship. The child looked up at him with large blue eyes, smiling, innocence glowing in his face.

"What are you doing, Mr. Heathen?" he said. "Who was that pretty lady? She was very nice."

Thomas's heart leapt in his chest. The lad had seen Pocahontas. Animals had the sixth sense, but he never realized that children were also at one with the spirit world. If the child described what he had seen, an accusation of witchcraft was a very real possibility.

"What do you mean? I did not see a lady." Thomas said, looking around.

The child's face crumpled with confusion.

"Well, she was talking to you, and you were nodding your head. She said something about 'your peas'?" He looked up at Thomas, eyes wide.

Thomas laughed and crouched down, taking the boy's hands in his. He resigned himself to the child's unwavering curiosity. "What is your name, little lad?" Thomas smiled.

"My name is George Fitzgerald the Second." The tiny tot stood as if to attention, pulling his hands back.

"And how old are you, George Fitzgerald the Second?" Thomas stood up, mirroring and respecting the child's formality.

"I am four years old, sir."

Having given his credentials, Thomas could see the child's eyebrows drawing together. "But who was that lady talking about peas?"

"Do you know what, my little friend? That lady can only be seen by very special people. Most people cannot see her, so we must not tell others we have seen her."

The boy's brows drew together, large blue eyes wide. "But who IS she?"

How could he explain? The lad was so young that the cynicism of the world had not touched him, and his true nature and senses had not yet been repressed.

George would not be satisfied with patronising excuses, but the truth was a dangerous thing.

Thomas crouched down again looking at the boy eye to eye, his face showing the seriousness of the situation. "You and I have seen something very special, George Fitzgerald Second. That lady was a spirit of the universe. She is part of the wind and the sea; she lives with the fish and the animals.

"Spirits are not people who live on the earth, but sometimes they can guide the people who live in the world. Her name is Pocahontas, and she is a spirit for good. You are lucky to have seen her. If you see her again, do not be frightened, she is a good and friendly spirit that will look after you. You must be special to have seen her. There is one thing, though . . . she must be our secret. If you tell others, they will not believe, and they might think badly of us. Do you understand, George?" He smiled at the lad and took his hand as he started to stand up. "You and I will be firm friends, I can tell."

George looked up at the tall man standing next to him and smiled. "We have a secret," he said nodding, breathless with conspiracy. "George Fitzgerald Second always keeps secrets."

At that moment, they both heard a whisking sound above them as the sky took on an erie hue. When they looked at the clouds above, they saw the image of Pocahontas smiling. She put her finger in front of her mouth and whispered "Shhhhhh . . . our secret . . ." She smiled, her eyes twinkling, her hair swirling in the wind. Then, her image gradually started to fade like a beautiful sunset.

They stood like two children in the thralls of conspiracy, looking up hand in hand and trying to savor every last drop of her image as she merged into the universe, swallowed up by the sea spray and the wind.

When she had disappeared entirely, Thomas looked down, and George looked up, their eyes meeting as they grinned from ear to ear at the shared experience. Hand in hand, they looked upward together at the space where her image had been, breathing in the salty air.

Suddenly, their moment was shattered by screaming and shouting permeating the air like a boulder landing in the middle of a still lake.

Scrambling feet on the wooden deck and voices screeching at different tempos, competing and drowning each other out. One voice stood out among the others.

"Where is he? Where is my son? I turned my back for only a moment, and he was gone! Maybe he has fallen overboard . . . please . . . please, somebody do something . . . find him!" Her voice went up an octave. "George? George?" She hollered his name repeatedly, her voice becoming hoarse with the effort.

George looked up at Thomas, his eyes moist, mouth trembling. Thomas picked him up and held him firmly.

"He is here with me," Thomas shouted. "He is safe." He carried George towards the sound of his mother's voice.

When she saw her little boy, she rushed forward and snatched him from Thomas's arms, her face tear-stained. Her body was trembling with emotion. She could only have been about twenty years old.

"What do you think you are doing with my son, you filthy heathen?" she shouted. Her flaming red hair, neatly arranged when she boarded the ship, was now loose and straggly, flying in the wind. Her green eyes flashed wide open with fear as she clasped her child, forcing his face into her dress as if protecting him from a monster.

Thomas pulled back, startled by her rebuke and the look of hatred on her previously beautiful face. At that point, he knew things were going to turn nasty.

Most of the passengers were now assembled on the deck, curious to see what was happening, necks craning, shuffling to get to the front for a clearer view of the unfolding drama.

Thomas looked in horror as he saw the portly William Penhaligan in front of the clambering crowd, standing still and glaring with a self-satisfied look on his face. He winked at Thomas and shook his head, raising his right hand in the air for silence like a thespian quelling an audience. The crowd responded at once, sensing his power and authority, willing the situation to increase in drama, hungry for the blood of a filthy heathen who had harmed an innocent child.

Someone in the back of the crowd hollered "Jail him! Jail him!" The crowd clapped and shouted in agreement.

William paused, lowering his hand, staring at Thomas, the echoes of angry voices filling the air once again. "Order, order!" he shouted, continuing to stare, directing his dialogue at the object of the crowd's displeasure. "Gentlemen, we are civilized people. We must find out what has happened so we can deal with the situation appropriately. Indeed, although we all know these types have criminal tendencies, we always seek true and fair justice in our superior culture. We are not a lynch mob after all, are we?"

Anyone hearing little George's cries of anguish assumed the child had been abused. None of them took the time to register that his cries were proclaiming Thomas's innocence; his face was crumpling with frustration that he could not save his friend from persecution. He knew the mood of the crowd, even at his tender age, and collapsed with exhaustion into his mother's arms when he realized how powerless he was to deliver the truth. They did not want to know.

Penhaligan faced the crowd. "As we are about to set sail, we have little time to deal with this matter with due diligence. I suggest we arrest this man and incarcerate him in the hold until the captain is able to deal with this matter."

He pointed to two burly sailors. "You and you—take the prisoner to the hold where he can be prevented from further misdemeanors. We will organize a trial to determine his guilt or innocence once we are safely at sea."

Thomas was propelled forward. He glanced over at George and gave him an encouraging nod.

So began Thomas's new life.

Ten

A Cruel Beginning

It was so cold. Thomas could hardly feel his feet in his damp hose. The grimy makeshift jail was dingy and cramped. He crouched, making his body as small as possible to try and retain whatever heat there was.

Food and water were thrown at him at random intervals with a grunt from burly sailors who, more often than not, landed vicious kicks at his helpless body as they laughed at his plight. He had lost all sense of timing as day and night faded into one, like a dark cavern of timelessness.

How long had he been there? It could have been days, weeks, or months. Thomas's delirium was sporadic. When it came, it was a retreat from pain into an even darker place of frightening images pooled from the depths of imagination.

Then, through the fog of his agony, he sensed a presence. It was not the loud brash sailors, the aura was quiet and gentle. He shook himself, forcing his swollen eyes to open as he saw her flaming red hair through the bars.

She stood looking at him, tears running down her face. "I know the truth, Mr. Rolfe," she said. His head was spinning trying to organize his thoughts. What truth? Who was this woman? Red hair . . . it must be George's mother. Had George told her about the vision? Fear struck him like an icicle into his heart. Witchcraft held a death sentence.

"You have done nothing wrong. A great injustice has been done to you." Her voice faltered as she saw relief flood his battered face. "George told me that you found him wandering around the ship and your only concern was to return him to me." She turned her eyes to the floor avoiding his gaze. "I'm responsible for your being arrested—I jumped to conclusions." She whispered the words, her face drawn with shame.

Thomas could feel hope flooding his body. It gave him the strength to grab hold of the iron bars that were confining him and pull himself up to standing, his face pressed against the bars.

"Can you get me released?" His voice was hoarse and faint, filled with emotion.

"I have been trying for weeks, ever since George told me what had happened, but no one will listen to me. The captain refuses to see me, referring me to William Penhaligan, but he has avoided any requests to see him. I keep insisting that I am not pressing charges, but to no avail. I think there is some kind of conspiracy going on as I saw Penhaligan hand money to the captain. But it was I who started it all, and I feel so guilty that I thought the worst of you." Her green eyes were framed by moist, luxurious, dark lashes.

He could feel no anger towards her as he looked at her standing in front of him with earnest frustration written on her pretty face.

"Believe me, I understand," he said, his voice harsh with the memory of his uncle and Penhaligan. "This is not about you or George; it's far more complex. I'm being punished for things that happened at another time and another place. There is nothing that you can do, dear lady."

"I am so sorry," she whispered, coming closer.

He reached through the bars and took hold of her hand. It felt warm and delicate as he raised it to his lips and gently kissed it. "My lady, have no fear. The blame lies not with you. If the incident with George had not happened, there would have been some other manufactured crime for them to mete out their revenge." He tried to smile.

The sound of footsteps approaching caused them to pull apart as the portly figure of Penhaligan approached. "Mrs. Fitzwilliam, this is no place for you," he bellowed, glaring at Thomas. "You should be nowhere near disreputable heathens." He looked down his nose at Thomas as if he was a piece of dirt.

As Thomas watched, Sarah Fitzwilliam seemed to grow in stature. Her previously grief-stricken eyes flashed with anger as years of aristocratic authority rose to the fore. "Sir" she barked, "what do you mean 'disreputable heathen'? This man is guilty of no more than returning my child to me. You have refused to listen to me, you have refused to grant me access to see him and both you and the captain of this ship are guilty of holding a man in prison without trial."

Penhaligan stood with his mouth hanging open. He shuffled his feet, as he tried to regain his composure, but small as she was, Sarah Fitzwilliam retained the upper hand as she continued. "Be in no doubt, sir, I will not let this injustice go. If Mr. Rolfe is not released, my husband, the Honorable Sir George Fitzwilliam the First will bring this matter to the attention of the governor of Virginia." Her face was as stern as a schoolmistress as, with a rustle of silk, she turned away from the two stunned men and marched away, shouting over her shoulder, "It is Lady Fitzwilliam!"

Thomas smiled to himself. Penhaligans's face was a sight to behold. His eyes were wide, and he was trying to respond, but the words just did not come.

"Looks like you have bitten off more than you can chew with that one, Penhaligan," he said winking.

Penhaligan shook himself, regaining his composure. "No woman will tell me what to do, sir! I am the one that holds the key, and I am the one that will decide when you are released." His rotund face was flushed and sweating.

Thomas nodded and smiled. "I know who I would bet money on winning this one."

Penhaligan grunted and turned, refusing to look in Thomas's direction as he stomped away swearing under his breath.

***

He had been confined for five weeks. However, following Lady Fitzwilliam's intervention, he was released without further ado. No comment had been made about the reason for either his imprisonment or his sudden release. He let it rest. There was little point in stirring up a hornet's nest when his allies were few and far between.

At last, he stood on the deck, the strong wind blowing through his dark hair. The salty smell of the sea was fresh and invigorating after the stale dampness of his prison cell. The weakness in his body was starting to leave him from the countless times he had paced up and down the deck over the past few days of freedom, determined to be strong and healthy when they landed in Jamestown.

As he stopped and stared out to sea, he heard the patter of small feet on the wooden deck. He saw George hurtling towards him, followed closely behind by his mother. George threw his arm around Thomas's legs as he screeched, "Heathen!" pleasure and innocence written all over his face.

Sara's mouth opened with shock. "George, you must not call Mr. Rolfe a heathen," she chided.

The child looked up at her, eyes wide. "Why not, Mummy? That is what everyone calls him."

She paused and took a breath, looking at Thomas as she struggled to find words.

Thomas smiled and bent down towards the child. "You're right George," he said, "but those people are not my friends. My friends call me Thomas, and you are definitely one of my friends. Why don't you and your mother call me Thomas from now on?"

The child nodded vigorously, looking back and forward from his mother to Thomas.

Thomas smiled at the beautiful woman before him, her delicate frame masking the strength of character that had saved him. He had seen her from a distance since his release but had refrained from approaching her, as he felt it unseemly. Now she was here, he could convey his thanks.

"Lady Fitzgerald, I am greatly indebted to you for your intervention in my incarceration." He bowed slightly.

She smiled. "No need for the 'Lady' . . . 'Sarah' will do. I was only ensuring that the injustice that I had bestowed on you was revoked. George put me right. I should have known, but I was out of my mind with worry about George's disappearance and was not thinking straight. I hope you can forgive me." Her eyes bore into him in a way that held a certain intimacy that was new to him, causing him to look away.

When he had partially regained composure, he returned her gaze.

"My lady, there is nothing to forgive. The fault did not lie with you. Let us put it behind us with the proviso that I am your servant from now on." He bowed lower, sweeping his arm in front of him in an exaggerated gesture of subservience, that he hoped would cover his blushes.

Her face lit up with amusement.

***

"Land ho!" the young sailor shouted.

It was what they had all been waiting for these past seven weeks. Thomas had been looking forward to it since he was two years old.

All he had wanted since that dreadful day was to get to Virginia, the home of his closest blood relatives. Fate had intervened to leave him an orphan, but his resolve had never wavered. Now as he strained to catch the first sight of Virginia, the tears percolated silently down his face. At last, he was coming home—he was going to meet his Powhatan family and his half sister and stepmother. Now it was going to be alright, now he would feel part of something, and now he would not be alone.

"Thomas, Thomas!" He looked behind him as George ran towards him. "We are nearly there! I am going to see my father!"

Thomas smiled and gave a slight bow as Sarah approached.

"My lady. Our journey is almost at an end," he said.

" Or just beginning," she said, looking towards the approaching shoreline. "I have not seen my husband for nearly four years. George does not even know his father. He was called to duty soon after George was born."

"We are all being reunited with loved ones, then," said Thomas. "My stepmother and sister will be waiting for me . . . and I hope to visit my Powhatan family as well." His voice wavered with the words he had longed to say for many years.

Sarah sighed. "Letters from my husband tell me that relations with the Powhatans are not good, Thomas." Her face was grave. "Sadly, no one is allowed near the natives, as they have looted and murdered so many of our people. Please be careful."

She saw his face drop, and quickly added, "But they are negotiating peace all the time." Her voice was hurried. "I am sure it will only be a matter of time before the Powhatans are controlled and you can meet your family."

He looked towards the shore, hiding his shock at her words. She had described his people as murderers who had to be "controlled." She was the wife of a military man and was only repeating what she had been fed about the Powhatans. She was not to blame, and he was still grateful for her part in his release, but it gave him a hint of what was to come, and his heart sank. He turned back to her. "My lady, let us hope that both our journeys are fruitful."

He stooped down and picked George up. The three of them watched, as the land and the trees grew larger and larger. As they gazed, each of them wondered what their futures would be in this foreign land. Each wondered what they would find behind the high wooden balustrade that protected Jamestown from its foes.

Eleven

He Comes

Since hearing of his brother's existence, Kokee had woken up every day, hoping it would be the day Thomas would arrive in Virginia. When John Rolfe was killed in the massacre of 1622, it seemed unlikely to many that Thomas would come, but Kokee always clung to his dream.

And now, after all this time, his instinct proved correct; the day was finally coming. Opechancanough had received the message from the gods and shared it with Kokee before today's public announcement.

Thomas Rolfe was coming.

At twenty-four years of age, Kokee was no longer a child, and neither was Thomas. Many years had been lost, and now they would meet as men ingrained with differing cultures, not boys pliable and open to change. But they had the same blood flowing through their veins; nothing would change that.

Kokee had made it his mission to find out as much as possible about his brother's English family—their daily routines, who the different people were, and how Thomas might fit in.

He had memorized the route from the port at Jamestown, where his brother's ship would drop anchor, to the Varina plantation where he would live. He had scouts strategically placed along the coastline to send word when there was a sighting of the ship so he could position himself ready to observe his brother's arrival.

He sat waiting, looking at the gray river, thoughts of the future crowding his mind. Would he be able to meet Thomas? What if Thomas wanted nothing to do with his Powhatan family? Conflicting images of embracing a man with a blank face, and turning away from the same blank face, competed for space in his mind . . . What would he look like? Could they carry forward the work of their mother?

"Kokee! Kokee!" It was Nikkiti and her brother Nectowance. "What are you doing down here? We have been looking for you everywhere and now we are late. It is almost time for Opechancanough's speech!"

Kokee stood up, startled out of his excited musings, and sprinted to join them.

Nikkiti grabbed his hand. "Opechancanough will be furious if we are late again."

"Your father will forgive you; he always does," Kokee said, smiling.

Nikkiti pulled harder on his arm. "Come on, Kokee. Rumor has it that this announcement will change our lives," she shouted, her eyes wide.

He allowed himself to be pulled away from the river towards the quioccosan.[1] The tribe had gathered to hear the latest proclamation of the gods, and the quioccosan was warm and silent. As the three young people entered, all eyes turned to see the commotion. "Shhhhh" came from every corner.

Kokee, Nikkiti, and Nectowance crouched down, bowing in apology, and made their way to the front, waiting for Opechancanough to enter.

The drums began with a long and slow beat as Opechancanough glided in, sagely nodding in every direction as his audience stood respectfully to acknowledge his authority and wisdom. Despite the years having hollowed his cheeks and wrinkled his skin, he was still an imposing figure. His eyes were bright, and his aura of determination and strength were equal to a man half his age. He sat down and signaled with his hands for everyone to follow him. Silence reigned.

"My brothers and sisters, I have asked you to gather here today as the gods have decreed that a great change is coming. Soon, we will welcome a long-lost son into our midst." There were gasps from the crowd.

"Our legendary daughter, Pocahontas, died many years ago, but she left a legacy—the desire for peace. She was blessed with two sons, and this legacy has been passed to them. Her first son, you all know." Everyone turned to look at Kokee, who smiled weakly, uneasy with his sudden notoriety. "Her younger son, whose father was a Longcoat, was left in England when his mother died there. For many moons, the gods have told me he will return to us. Now that he is a man, this prophecy is coming true." The crowd mumbled as they digested what Opechancanough was saying.

"When this son—Thomas Rolfe, by name—comes to Virginia in the next few months, he will want to know his mother's people. I have seen in my dreams how he will walk among us and take us to his heart. I have seen how his loyalties will be divided between Longcoat and Powhatan. But I have also seen the deep connection that will grow between Thomas and his mother's people.

"When the time comes for me to fade into the forest of the gods, Thomas and his brother Kokee will take my place. Having leaders such as these, one of whom has Longcoat blood, will ensure our successful future when living in peace alongside the invading colonists. The legacy of Pocahontas will live on for as long as her sons are on this earth. They will bring Peace." Opechancanough looked around the quioccosan, his eyes scanning the faces. Silence reigned as the tribe digested these momentous revelations.

"Opechancanough—I mean, my venerable leader." Askook cleared his throat, and all eyes turned to see who dared to address the Powhatan chief. "I hear your words, but my heart sinks when, once again, we are the ones working for peace. Why is it that for years, even when our numbers were the greater, we did nothing to force the Longcoats to respect us as legitimate overseers of this land?"

He paused, taking a breath. "It is our land, and it has always been our land. These Longcoats are not interested in sharing anything peacefully. History has already shown that they steal everything from food to land from us, while we benevolently assist them in doing so." His words were laced with hatred. "I am disgusted with this pretence, this image of a peaceful land with native and Longcoat living and working side by side. It is as if Kokee and Thomas Rolfe are emissaries of the gods just because they are the sons of a dead squaw who unsuccessfully worked for peace, and you have dreamt of them!

"You must do something NOW to end this insanity. You must wipe the Longcoats off the face of the earth before it is too late. Future generations will curse you if you do nothing but rely on a flawed dream."

There were mumbles of horrified disbelief and sharp intakes of breath. To speak like this to Opechancanough was unprecedented.

But Askook ignored the gasps and stares. "My father gave his life to save you from the heathen's gun, and instead of honoring your promise to him on his deathbed, you are giving away our land to his murderers by relying on some half-breed to save the day!" He turned and spat on the ground with revulsion.

His words hung in the air as the ensuing silence conveyed the shock of the disrespect shown to their great leader.

Opechancanough paused momentarily. Askook's father, Amaru, was at the forefront of his mind.

Amaru had been his best friend—a hero who had taken the bullet that would have ended Opechancanough's life. As Amaru had gazed up at him on the battlefield, his plea was for Opecachancanough to be a father to his soon to be orphaned son, Askook. It was a debt Opechancanough had paid daily since Amaru's last breath.

Sadly, Askook had turned into a deranged misfit. Whether his anger and cruelty had resulted from the loss of his father, Opechancanough would never know. But a pledge was a pledge, and everyone knew that Opechancanough always treated Askook with more leniency than that afforded even his own offspring.

Opechancanough rose from his seat. His eyes were steely, and his face was lined with anger. "Askook, come here and kneel before me," he shouted.

Askook was propelled out of his trance of fury to crouch down as he started to tremble in front of his leader. He feared he may have gone too far this time.

"You have always worried me with your anger and your impulsive ways. I cannot have members of my tribe disrespecting me in this way. It is treason." Opechancanough was staring at him, beads of sweat on his forehead. "Never speak to me that way again, Askook."

Askook looked up at him with pleading eyes. "Please, please do not hurt me," he wailed, trying to shrink into the ground, pathos seeping out of every pore.

It was the same old pattern. Everyone knew what would happen next. Opechancanough always pulled himself back from chastising his adopted son. The vision of the man who had saved his life, Amaru, always stopped him in his tracks.

Opechancanough paused as his eyes took in the pathetic man before him.

"Askook, the Longcoats took the life of your father. But that is no excuse for the disrespect you have shown me today. I understand your distress, but you must respect your leaders and your Gods. You must swear that this will never happen again and that you will support Kokee and Thomas for as long as you shall live."

Askook nodded and crossed his heart. "This will never happen again, my lord," he said.

"Get up, my son. Embrace me, and talk no more of these things."

Askook stood up, visibly relieved that he had gotten away with it once again. "I am so sorry, my esteemed leader. My emotions got the better of me," he said. "I miss my father so much." He hung his head, a tear in his eye, as he embraced the old man.

As Opechancanough pulled away, he looked at Askook. "Your father was a hero . . . You must try to be the son he would have been proud of. He would not be proud of you today."

Askook was on the verge of defending himself when he realized the folly of doing so and nodded with fake compliance. He had almost gone too far again, but he knew how to manipulate the old fool. It was a game, and it was fun to instill emotions in others that he could not feel himself. Opechancanough thought he missed his father; nothing could be further from the truth. Feelings were for losers, manipulation was for winners.

"I am sorry, my great leader." He looked upwards as if addressing his dead father. "Forgive me, my blessed father," he said, tears silently falling.

Opechancanough nodded, sympathy in his eyes, and signaled for him to sit down.

As he did, out of sight of Opechancanough, Askook smiled. He was untouchable as he whispered under his breath, "I will get that bastard

Thomas Rolfe. No Longcoat will ever rule this tribe."

[1] A large building used for ceremonies.

Twelve

Land of Hope

The huge wooden gates of the town rumbled and screeched back as the ship approached. Townspeople could be seen gathering around to inspect the newcomers, eager to be first in line for the provisions that had been brought from England. A motley mixture of men and women, dirty and desperate, with native Indians among them, pushed and shoved.

Thomas had no idea what to expect. He looked frantically at each face in the crowd, hoping that somehow he might recognize his stepmother, Joan, and his fifteen-year-old sister, Elizabeth. William Pierce, Joan's father and the benefactor who had arranged his passage, might also be there.

As he scanned the crowd, he caught sight of a young girl, tentatively waving at him. She was short, with shiny brown curls that bounced up and down as she moved. She was as unsure as he was, but he guessed from her age, that this must be Elizabeth.

"Elizabeth, Elizabeth!" he shouted. Her eyes widened and she jumped higher and higher and prodded the woman who stood next to her, who then also started to wave, a broad grin filling her face.

He picked up his small bag and weaved his way through the crowd to reach the two women. Standing in front of them, he hesitated. What should he do—should he embrace them, shake their hands, bow? He did not have to wait very long before Elizabeth flung herself at him, shouting, "Thomas! Welcome!"

Everything was a blur to him. He was shaking, mute with emotion. His family.

He glanced over at his stepmother. Her eyes sparkled as she came towards him. She was petite with long black hair streaked with gray. Her simple clothes could not hide her inbuilt elegance, and Thomas immediately warmed to her.

"Thomas. I am Joan, your stepmother. Welcome to Jamestown," she said.

It was more than he could bear. He forgot about niceties and pulled Elizabeth towards her mother, embracing them both.

"You cannot know how long I have waited for this moment," he said. He noticed Joan's tired eyes and the wrinkles around her eyes that told a story of sadness. There was much he had to learn about this new family of his.

Joan extracted herself gently, looking at him, her eyes earnest. "Thomas, your father longed for this moment too. There was not a day that went by that he did not think of you and speak your name. I am sorry that he did not make it to see you put your feet on this land. But you are John Rolfe's son, and this land is your land, make no mistake. He wanted you to carry on what he started." She smiled and touched his shoulder. "But you must be exhausted," she said. "We must go home so that you can rest."

"Resting is the last thing on my mind," Thomas said. "I need to explore and see this land. I need to make arrangements to see my Powhatan family as well." His concern for her quelled, his excitement returned.

Joan and Elizabeth looked at the ground, suddenly solemn. Something dark and unspoken was hanging in the air. Had he said something wrong?

Joan looked up. "Thomas, I'm sorry to tell you, but relations with the Powhatans are at a boiling point. Going beyond the fortified part of the town is dangerous. Even getting to Varina, we have to be on our guard. Your meeting with your Powhatan family at a time like this will be out of the question. It is forbidden."

"But they are my family as much as you are . . . even more. I have to meet with my mother's family. They would not hurt the son of Pocahontas, surely?"

Joan shook her head, her eyes soft. "At least leave it for now, until you can judge for yourself what danger you may be putting yourself in. Please, do not make any rash decisions. I owe it to your father to make sure that you are safe."

Thomas felt like he had been punched. For so long, he had wanted to be here, imagining a life with his two families. Now it seemed half of his dream had been taken from him. Anger welled in him like a hot coal, but as he looked into Joan's kind eyes, the desire to vent it was smothered, although not extinguished.

He took a breath and paused. "I must be guided by you, Joan. I've yet to find my feet and I am grateful for your advice. I cannot say it is welcome advice . . . but I'm sure it is wise." He managed a half smile.

A booming voice echoed through the crowd. "This must be Thomas. So good to meet the man that I am sponsoring!"

John turned to see a large portly figure approaching with outstretched hand. "I'm Joan's father, and I cannot express enough how welcome you are." He grinned from ear to ear and shook Thomas's hand, almost crushing his fingers with his strength and enthusiasm.

"Thank you, sir. I am extremely grateful for what you did for me. Without your help, I would never have been able to get to Virginia. I know my father would also be thankful to you."

"Ay, lad. Your father and I were the best of friends. I would do anything for that man. We survived countless perilous adventures together. At some point, I will have to tell you some of the stories of Bermuda and the starving time. Yes, your father was quite a man . . ."

William Pierce smiled when he noticed Thomas struggle to hide a yawn. "But for now, lad, we must get you home, get you some food, and allow you to rest. There will be lots of time for gossip when you have settled in." He patted Thomas on the back as he picked up his bag and led him through the crowds. Lizzie and Joan walked arm and arm with him towards the horse and trap.

Family.

Thirteen

A New Home

The journey to Varina seemed to take hours; this new country had not had time to develop the sophisticated roads Thomas was used to. The horse and cart rumbled unsteadily over rough paths that had been well-worn over the twenty-odd years that the plantation had existed. It was a wooded land. Trees surrounded them, reaching up to the sky, dense and dark for mile upon mile. After a while, among the trees could be seen large tracts of land that had been cleared and were growing healthy crops.

"Elizabeth, what is being grown here?" he asked.

She smiled. "That is your livelihood . . . that is your new life . . . that is tobacco."

Thomas shook his head in disbelief. "Of course, I knew of our father's business, but I could never have imagined the scale of it."

There was so much land in Virginia. He had never seen trees so tall, and where the land was cleared, he could now see cultivation on a scale that he could never have previously imagined. Native tribes' people mingled with English workers as they picked the tobacco.

Thomas was pleasantly surprised to see men and women who shared his complexion, and he grew excited as he saw more and more of them along the way, hard at work in his father's fields. Maybe he would not stand out any more. Maybe the stares would stop and the whispers would die down.

They turned off the main pathway and headed down a smaller track through the fields and forests. As they rounded the bend, the Varina plantation came into view. Thomas stared at his father's house, trying to imagine what his father would look like standing on the large veranda. If only his father could have survived to greet him. But no image came, and a wash of sadness descended through his body. His shoulders slumped. He breathed, trying in vain to free himself from darkness. Then, he remembered the words of his mother's spirit. A smile crept onto his face.

Thomas refocused on the house. It was imposing, if not as grand as an English house. It was made of a brick foundation with a wooden upper structure with clay infill, as few local houses boasted brick exteriors. Thomas assumed brick was not yet a plentiful commodity in this new world, as he had seen only a few in Jamestown but none in the surrounding countryside.

A large welcoming veranda surrounded the front of the house, and steps led up to a heavy wooden door. All around the house was a thriving kitchen garden full of vegetables. Pens of chickens and pigs were off to one side. There was a stable, a large barn, and a covered area for the cart. A cow looked up lazily as they approached. John sighed with satisfaction. It was no Heacham Manor, but it warmed his heart as Heacham could never do. It was his home; and because of that, it was the most magnificent house he had ever seen.

Joan pulled the horse and cart adjacent to the steps and secured the brake. Elizabeth climbed down and took her mother's hand as Joan gingerly stepped down from the stationary vehicle. Thomas jumped from the cart and pulled his bag of belongings after him. They all turned to the door as it opened, and out came a teenage girl and two boys aged about twelve years. Thomas was surprised. He had no idea who these youngsters were.

"Thomas, come and meet your two stepbrothers and one of our greatest friends." Joan put her arms around her two boys, hugging them tight and smiling at them. She looked to the taller of the boys. "This is John." John had sandy-colored hair and a freckled smiling face.

Joan then turned towards the dark-haired, shorter lad. "And this is Francis." Francis made a mock bow, feigning a salute.

Thomas stepped forward and shook their hands. "And who is this lovely lady?" he asked.

Thomas looked to the one person he had not been introduced to. She stood demurely watching the proceedings from the sidelines. Joan rushed forward and pulled her to the front. "This is Jane Poythress. She is a dear friend, and her parents have a plantation not far from here," Joan said. "Jane and Elizabeth are inseparable friends, so be prepared: where there is one, there will probably be another lurking behind the corner!"

Jane stepped forward, her blue eyes looking at him through thick, dark lashes. She smiled as she held out her hand. Thomas hesitated. He sensed a fragile connection between himself and this girl with white-blond hair. He took her hand, and instead of shaking it, on instinct, he raised it to his lips and gave it a feather-light kiss. He did not smile; he just looked at her with wide, unblinking eyes before standing back, gaze unbroken. "Pleased to meet you, Jane Poythress," he said. She nodded as she scanned his every feature.

"Likewise," she said.

Joan bustled forward, placing herself between them. "Well, what am I doing? We must get you inside and get you something to eat." She put her arm around Thomas's shoulders and propelled him up the wooden stairs.

Thomas allowed her to lead him. He was overwhelmed. He had no idea that he had two stepbrothers. He had been expecting to see Captain Smith, Joan's second husband. Maybe he had been called away. No doubt he would find out in due course.

As for Jane Poythress . . . what had happened there? He blinked himself back to reality. This was like a dream. All these people had welcomed him with open arms, and he still had his Powhatan family to meet. It was beyond his wildest imaginings. Finally, he had somewhere he belonged. After all these years of being alone, his hopes and dreams were finally coming true.

Fourteen

First Day

"So, Lizzie, how much of this land do we own?" Thomas looked down at his little sister briefly before looking up, his eyes scanning the acres and acres of land stretching before him.

Lizzie smiled, standing proudly. "As far as you can see . . . Our father did so much in cultivating the tobacco industry before he died. He saved this colony from extinction with these plants. Can you believe that most of this was forest when Father first came here? Not a tobacco plant in sight. Of course, some of it was Powhatan land already cleared, but most was virgin land. He was a great man, our father. I wish we had both known him for longer." She sighed, reaching for his hand, a moment shared between newly found siblings as they pondered their loss together.

Thomas stood, silent and still, feeling not only the loss of his father but the gain of a sister. A sister that he could share feelings with, even if they were sad feelings. He squeezed her hand and smiled at her. "I am no substitute, but you have me now. I will do all I can to carry on from him." He looked down at his freckled-faced fifteen-year-old sister and saw the pain of years of trying to survive in this inhospitable place.

She squeezed his hand in response and smiled up at him. "I am so relieved that you are finally here. Mother has tried to keep things going, but it has been so hard for her since my stepfather passed."

"I did not like to ask what had happened to Captain Smith yesterday as there was so much going on, and I thought it best to wait for the right moment."

Her face clouded over and her eyes became moist. She paused for a moment. "It was the most terrible thing that happened to him, Thomas. I don't know where to begin . . . I know you have family who are Powhatan, but unfortunately, they may not be who you had hoped them to be." She stared at the ground, tragedy written on her face. "There have been so many violent things that have happened, so many people killed, that I hold hatred in my heart for those people."

Thomas was stunned. "Are you saying that the Powhatans killed your stepfather?"

She nodded slowly, raising her eyes to meet his. "That is exactly what I am saying, Thomas." He bit his lower lip and took a deep breath. His first thought was that the captain must have provoked them in some way.

She let go of his hand and stood back from him; the sadness in her eyes was replaced with rage. "The Powhatans killed him when he was merely going into town for provisions. It was wretched what they did to him. I cannot even begin to describe it." She looked away. "I despise those people. They killed both my father and my stepfather. I fear that they will kill you too." She slumped, despair and helplessness

First Day

replacing the energy of her anger.

Thomas walked over and pulled her to face him, drawing her in and holding her in a protective embrace. He did not know what to say. She was vulnerable and small as he felt her shaking. Simply a child who had lost so much.

At that moment, he felt hatred for the people who had taken away her two fathers. He knew his father had been killed by the Powhatans but had convinced himself over the years that it must have been a sad accident. Doubt was creeping into his mind, clouding his hope to reunite with his mother's family. But then . . . Maybe Lizzie had gotten it wrong? Maybe the Powhatans had been fired on first on each occasion?

His head was swimming. He had so much to learn. All those years fantasizing in Heacham, his head full of images of friendly Powhatans on painted ponies. He had been innocent of the complexities of this country.

He remembered the picture of his gentle mother. Her people were good people, surely?

He kissed the top of Lizzie's head and released her. "I am so sorry," he said, looking deeply into her eyes. "I had no idea what it has been like in the colony. I have a lot to learn. I am here for you now, Lizzie; I will not let you down. I know that Powhatan blood runs through my veins, and the Powhatans have done some terrible things. But I hope that, in some way, I might be able to make a difference. Our father and my mother tried so hard to bring peace. There must be something that can be done."

She looked at him and shrugged.

"Thomas, I know I am young, but I am old enough to realize the difficult position you are in. Your mother was in two worlds, and she was a brave and heroic woman. She has left you with her dilemma. But I cannot sympathize with those people, and I pray you will take our side in this horrible war."

He struggled for words but remained silent, clinging to the fading dream of his Powhatan brother and English sister embracing.

He put his arm around her again and hugged her. "Let's make our way back; Joan must be wondering where we are." He looked toward the house and looked back for one last moment, scanning the acres surrounding them, sighing. He reached out to take her hand, and they walked with leaden legs, hand in hand, back to the house, each with their own thoughts, neither wanting to make eye contact.

As they walked through the door, Thomas smelled the comforting aroma of a beef stew bubbling in the hearth. The room was warm, but he was still freezing, so he walked over to the fire, rubbing his hands, shivering before the warmth gradually brought the feeling back into his fingers. Joan was at the sink peeling potatoes, and her two boys were cleaning carrots. A peaceful domestic scene, he thought. Warmth permeated through him, not solely emanating from the fire. He had gone from being an only child to having a stepmother, two stepbrothers, and a half sister. It was a lot to take in, not least the pain that lay under this harmonious scene.

"Ah, the wanderers have returned," Joan said, smiling at him. "Did Lizzie give you a good tour, then?"

"Yes, she showed me the tobacco plantation. It is bigger than I ever dreamed it would be. I will have to try and understand how everything works so that I can help you with it."

"For now, why don't you and Lizzie just sit down and have a mug of ale? There is plenty of time to think about your life in Virginia. I must say, though, the timing of your coming could not have been better for me." She sighed. "I have been struggling these past months since Richard was killed." Her words were whispered as if she could hardly utter them. The ensuing silence hung in the air. The boys looked down at their hands. Lizzie hovered in the background.

An air of darkness seemed to descend on the previously happy scene. Thomas looked from one to the other, trying to gauge the best response. They all avoided his gaze.

Thomas walked towards Joan grim-faced. "I am so sorry for your loss. Being so far away, Richard's death had not been communicated to me." She turned towards him, trying in vain to smile, and held her hand out to him. He squeezed it gently, his eyes full of compassion.

He took a breath. "I know I am coming into a situation of which I have little understanding, but you are family, and while I cannot replace those that have sadly gone, I promise I will do all that I can for this family." Sincerity shone on his face.

Joan looked up at him. "I ask only one thing of you, Thomas: do not get involved with the Powhatans. You will be killed just as your father and Richard were."

Fifteen

Altercation

Thomas was left in no doubt that there was a taboo surrounding contact with the Powhatans. His heart sank, but he had to hide his disappointment until he fully understood the implications. The evening had been magical. He was starting to get to know the two boys, Lizzie, and Joan. He was over the moon to be part of this family. They were kind and welcoming. He had been with them for only a short time, but it felt like years. It filled him with joy that they had accepted him as part of the family already. His only regrets were the years spent in Heacham apart from these lovely people and, of course, not having been reunited with his father.

Today, Lizzie and Jane would take him into Jamestown to familiarize him with the town and introduce him to the people of the colony. Francis and John had tacked up the horse and trap and were waiting for Jane to arrive. Thomas had not seen her since his arrival when he had sensed something between them. There was so much going on that he had banished it to the back of his mind, putting his feelings for her down to "new acquaintance" nerves.

Then he saw her in the distance walking the muddy path through the trees. She was skipping and jumping—a young girl unaware of his eyes on her. Her long blond hair flew in the wind as she danced along, singing to herself. She kicked the puddles as she passed, droplets of water spraying through the air. The mud collected on the bottom of her dress, but she seemed oblivious. He absorbed her sense of fun and smiled to himself, having observed the real Jane behind her quiet and demure exterior. His experience of girls and women had been limited to sipping cups of tea with them in silence while his grandmother entertained their elders in the parlor at Heacham Manor. They had seemed like a foreign species—untouchable and aloof. This new world showed a side of many things he had previously been unaware of.

Lizzie caught sight of her friend and ran towards her. "Come on, Jane!" she shouted. "We've been waiting hours for you!"

Jane hurried forward and took her hand, laughing. They dashed toward the waiting horse and trap, absorbed in their friendship, almost forgetting the handsome dark-haired newcomer standing in awe.

Lizzie jumped in the back of the trap. She glanced at her friend and took the role of organizer. "I'll be lookout on the way there." She looked at Thomas. "Thomas, come in the back with me so I can show you what you must do." She grabbed a rifle from Francis, who held two rifles. "Thomas, you take the other rifle, and Jane, you drive the trap. Francis, hand me the tobacco." Francis passed her a large sack.

Thomas's eyes were wide. Girls with rifles and sacks of tobacco. What was going on? He glanced at Jane. She looked at him, their eyes locking for one intimate second before she smiled, nodded, and took the reins.

They all took their places in the trap and started jiggling down the uneven track towards Jamestown.

"So, are we protecting ourselves from wild animals?" Thomas asked. Lizzie was crouched next to him, eyes scanning the terrain.

Her eyes very briefly met his, eyebrows raised. "No—Powhatans, of course," she said. "I can see you do have a lot to learn, Thomas."

Thomas felt rebuked. "Oh, I see. I had not realized it was that bad." His face fell.

"Yes, it's that bad . . . and worse. We take our lives in our hands every time we leave the plantation. Powhatans take any opportunity to attack. They want the tobacco we have as currency on the way there, and the corn and provisions we have on the way back. We tried to hide the situation from you when we brought you to Varina because we did not want to alarm you . . . but the reality is that we live in fear all the time. It's a way of life for us."

Thomas was stunned into confused silence as he processed this new reality.

Now and then, Lizzie or Jane shouted, "Movement!" and Jane pulled up the horse while they scanned the woods, eyes peeled. Today, it had been the movement of nature as they saw a baby wolf dart through the trees.

After traversing many miles, they approached a high palisade stretching as far as the eye could see. The large wooden gates were shut, and men with rifles stood on a high platform, keeping watch for enemies approaching. They saw Lizzie coming, and she waved, indicating they should open the gates.

"Hello, Miss Rolfe," one of the guards shouted as he pulled back the large gates. "Welcome to Middle Plantation."

"What is Middle Plantation?" Thomas asked Sarah.

"We built the palisade across the land between Queens Creek and Archers Creek to protect Jamestown from the Powhatans. Most colonists live inside the palisade between here and the center of Jamestown. There is another palisade around the center of the town. The whole triangle of the town is now as secure as we can make it. The outlying plantations are still vulnerable, so we must keep vigilant and protect ourselves as best we can." Lizzie sighed.

The gates swung open, and before him, Thomas could see an area of cleared land through the trees, dotted with wooden dwellings along a road that stretched into the distance. As they continued down the road, another palisade appeared.

Further large wooden gates were guarded by two fierce-looking men, who smiled as they facilitated entrance to Jamestown. "Morning, Miss Rolfe!"

The town lay before them. Thomas had been so excited when he landed that he had not taken in its characteristics.

Developed in a triangle with one edge facing the river, it was relatively small, with a blacksmith, military buildings, a church, a town hall, and a few merchants' stores dotted along the other two edges. People milled around, and Thomas was surprised to see a few Powhatans among them.

Lizzie jumped from the cart. "We are going to Grandad Pierce and Grandma Joan's shop. We need a few things, and Grandma Joan wants to meet you." She smiled at him, seeing his eyes wide as he tried to process the sights and sounds of his new capital town. "You wait till you try some of Grandma Joan's fig jam . . . it's sublime." She licked her lips.

Thomas walked with Lizzie and Jane to a small shop. Most of the buildings were wooden, and compared to an English town, it looked very primitive.

As they approached the general store, the door swung open, and an older lady with white hair, who looked remarkably like his stepmother Joan, rushed forward to greet him. "You must be Thomas," she said as she hugged him.

He returned the embrace. "So nice to meet you," he said.

"And this is Angelo." She gestured toward a dark-skinned lady of about thirty years of age.

Thomas nodded. The only dark-skinned people he had seen before were slaves. He was uncertain of the status of this quietly smiling person.

"Nice to meet you too." Angelo nodded.

Lizzie stepped forward, noticing the confusion on Thomas's face. "Angelo came to us with the other slaves, but she has become one of us. She is only indentured now, but we feel she is one of the family and has been the inspiration for the fig jam."

His brows were still furrowed, as he looked around. It was all so new, he could find no words.

Jane laughed. "Don't worry, Thomas," she said. Her eyes were shiny, and her voice was soft. "It will take you a while to get to know us all." Thomas looked at her and smiled, his stomach somersaulting before he turned away to look at Lizzie to calm his emotions.

"I think I am well outnumbered here. Not a man in sight," he said, his eyes dancing.

Granny Joan laughed. "Some might say you are lucky."

"Some might say you should be very afeared!" Angelo hooted with laughter and clapped her hands.

Lizzy giggled. "Enough of this frivolity; let's get the groceries we need before we show Thomas around."

He looked at the shelves stocked with provisions from candles to jam. The shop was cozy and comforting, and the musty aroma of wooden floors and fresh vegetables was not unpleasant.

After they had acquired all that was on their list, Lizzie took one of Thomas's hands, and Jane took the other. "Come on, big brother, let's show you around."

Thomas was speechless. He had never touched a girl before, and now he was holding the hand not only of his newly found sister but also of a girl who made his heart race.

They walked down the street hand in hand, laughing—Thomas, Lizzie, and Jane.

Suddenly, they heard a voice: "Heathen, Heathen . . . I mean . . . Thomas! It's me, George!"

Thomas felt a small body colliding with his legs, nearly toppling him over.

"George Fitzgerald the Second!" shouted Thomas, picking the small boy up and twirling him around. His two girl companions stood back in amazement.

Thomas put the boy down as he saw George's mother approaching very demurely, accompanied by a stern-looking military man.

"George, come here at once. I have never seen such behavior," bellowed the man. His eyes scrutinized Thomas with a condescending glare. He grabbed George by the arm, pulling him away from Thomas. "Sir, please be on your way. Be in no doubt that my son will get the appropriate punishment when we are behind closed doors. Good day to you." He stomped away, dragging the wailing child behind him.

Thomas stood open-mouthed for a moment. Then he braced himself, turning to call after him. "Sir, the boy has done no harm. I made the acquaintance of Lady Fitzgerald and George on the ship from England. We are good friends. He was just greeting me, and I was very pleased to see him again. There is no need for punishment, is there, Lady Fitzgerald?" he asked with formality as he saw her trying to look away.

Sarah looked at the ground. The strong, authoritative woman he had come to know, the one that rescued him from prison, seemed absent, replaced by a shell of her former self. "My husband knows what is best for George and myself, sir," she mumbled. Her eyes did not raise, and her pretty face remained a blank canvas.

Thomas's heart was breaking. He had become attached to this feisty young woman and her little rascal of a son. But what could he do? She was this brute's wife, and protocol dictated that he was not at liberty to question what was going on to bring about such changes in her, especially in the middle of the street.

He walked over to her. "My lady," he said. "It is an honor to make your acquaintance once more. Perhaps you, George, and your husband would like to visit our plantation when time allows. We are in Varina, just a few miles from Jamestown." He tried looking into her eyes as he had before but received no response.

"Heathen, Heathen! Yes, we will! We will come and visit you!" George yelled with delight.

The general pulled little George almost off the ground in an attempt to get him away from Thomas. "Boy, in the name of the Lord, behave yourself. We do not talk to filthy heathens. And you . . ." he said, glaring at Thomas. "Be on your way."

The child called out in pain; his arm was nearly wrenched from its socket as his father dragged him farther away. The little boy was crying with misery, tears running down his cheeks, but fear prevented a sound from passing his lips.

Thomas felt like he had been punched. He could feel the blood rising in his face, and he trembled with rage. He was unsure if his anger was for himself, George, or Sarah, and he clenched his teeth in frustration.

Just as he found the strength to control himself, his heart sank when he saw another familiar figure walking towards them. William Penhaligan.

Thomas froze. Uncle Henry was out to get him through this reprobate. He wondered how much money had changed hands to ensure his downfall. It had been too easy to think he was safe after

Sarah had rescued him.

"Sir George," said Penhaligan, bowing with deference to the general. "I see you have met Thomas. He is the heathen I was telling you about. Your good wife rescued him from the dungeon." Penhaligan smirked at Thomas and ignored Lady Sarah. "Perhaps, now that we are on dry land and you have authority over your wife, we can see that justice is done. After all, we cannot have the natives assaulting our children, especially your children. We need to set an example."

"Indeed we do." Sir George pumped himself up, becoming more incensed as he considered the situation. "We should have this man arrested at once," he proclaimed.

Thomas saw Sarah look up, and for a fleeting second, he detected the feisty fire in her eyes, ready to defend him once more, until her husband glanced menacingly at her, and she returned her eyes to the ground. It was then that Thomas saw the bruises.

Lizzie, standing next to Thomas, saw the look in his eyes go from anger to rage. She reached out and took his hand firmly. "Thomas, Jane has gone to get Grandad Pierce; please do not do anything you will regret before he comes," she whispered.

Thomas looked down at her, barely hearing her words, dazed by the unfolding events. He blinked and looked around him. A crowd was gathering, sensing there would be some violent entertainment to break the monotony of the day.

He looked at little George, an innocent child whose joy had been beaten out of him. He could take this injustice no longer, and he moved towards the general. Lizzie grabbed him tighter.

Then he saw Jane running towards him, followed by Joan's father.

William Pierce approached Sir George smiling, his hand stretched out in friendship. "Sir," he said, "I think there may have been some misunderstanding here. I have sponsored this young man to help with his father's plantation."

Sir George looked at him. "And who might you be, sir?" he said, looking down his nose.

"I am Captain William Pierce, lieutenant governor of Jamestown. I own Mulberry Plantation. Thomas is a relative of mine. My house is just over there, sir." He pointed to one of the few brick houses in Jamestown. Sir George looked at it and realized that this beautiful house signified more than mere words could ever do: the standing of Captain Pierce.

William Pierce stood waiting for a response. "Perhaps you and your wife and son would like to join me for a refreshment, and we can discuss this sorry situation civilly."

Sir George's face turned from scornful dismissal to subservient compliance in less than a breath. Well-versed in the need for superficial political alliances, he moved away from Penhaligan, ignoring his pleading glances, and reached for the lieutenant governor's hand, shaking it vigorously.

"Most kind of you sir, most kind . . . I am sure there has been a terrible misunderstanding. I would be delighted to join you," he fawned.

Captain Pierce led the three of them away, leaving the dejected Penhaligan standing with a face like thunder.

"This will not be the end of it, you heathen," he growled, staring at Thomas.

"Oh, I think you will find it is," said Thomas. Penhaligan turned and walked away.

Thomas turned to watch as Sarah meekly followed her husband, holding George's hand. The spirit seemed to have been removed from both mother and child as they plodded behind the two men who were now in animated conversation. Sarah glanced back over her shoulder and caught Thomas's eye for a split second. In that moment Thomas saw the hopelessness on her face. His heart ached that he could not rescue her the way she had rescued him.

Lizzie saw the sorrow on his face and took his hand. "Come, big brother. I think we have had enough excitement for one day."

Thomas was ashamed of his powerlessness to help Lady Sarah and angry at having been seen, yet again, as a heathen. And this time, it had been in the presence of his new family and Jane. He let go of Lizzie's hand, pulled himself together, and marched back to the horse and trap, his face contorted with anger. Would he ever be accepted? Could he ever truly be a part of this family?

As they followed him back to the horse and trap, he searched their faces, expecting to see the usual condescension of white man to Powhatan. All he saw was warmth. No questions were asked, and no doubts were expressed. He had been accepted as one of them, no matter what.

His eyes watered as he nodded, acknowledging their support, holding Jane's gaze for a moment longer than the others.

Sixteen

Tragedy

An eerie light filtered through the dark green trees. The smell of damp earth clung to the air as the wind whispered through the leaves. He wandered in a daze, looking up at the shafts of light that danced above.

This was a foreign land, about which he knew next to nothing. With each day that passed, things became less, not more, clear, and his ambitions became increasingly thwarted. He was starting to question everything he had ever pursued. His goals had been clear when he first arrived and met his new family. Problems of color and race had become a distant memory, and he'd reveled in the unconditional warmth he had found at Varina.

But Uncle Henry had seen to it that this mirage of acceptance had been removed and replaced by stark reality.

Tragedy

Grandad Pierce had done his best to smooth over the public altercation with Fitzgerald, but somehow, things would never be the same. Thomas felt he had been found out. He was an intruder with dusky skin, no matter how much his family tried to ignore this fact.

He wandered through the woods, trying to organize his thoughts. Thoughts of Joan and Lizzie were painful, but thoughts of Jane were unbearable.

Had he seen a hint of disdain in her eyes when he had been called "heathen"? What did she think of him? They had never been alone and spoken only a few words together, but the connection when their eyes secretly locked surely meant something. Maybe it was wishful imagination.

No matter. He could not bear to hope that Jane's feelings for him—if they existed—were any more than a girlish crush. And if she did have strong feelings for him, he could not subject her to the humiliation of being associated with a man shunned by society.

He knew, without doubt, that he must put her out of his mind. She was out of his reach. He must think of her only as a friend.

Now he understood how his mother must have felt. She had loved a man of a different race and had paid the price. How had she coped? How had she stood the humiliation of being Powhatan in an English world?

He must put Jane out of his mind—she deserved better.

***

Having made his mind up about Jane, Thomas had to distract himself with other concerns to ensure he did not waver from his resolve.

He saw his sister in the distance feeding the chickens. "Lizzie, can I talk to you for a moment?" he shouted.

She turned and walked towards him. "Why don't you go inside and warm some ale for us, Thomas? I need to finish what I am doing. I've had a hard day and I could do with sitting down. Mother has gone into town for some provisions and should be back any time now to put on the dinner. I can have a quick talk with you before I have to help her."

Thomas wandered into the cozy and inviting kitchen. His brow was furrowed as he warmed the ale. Thoughts darted around in his head about his future without Jane. Meeting his brother would give him something else to think about to distract from the loss.

Lizzie had always been on his side. Surely, no matter how she felt about the Powhatans, he could convince her to help him? He could never know all about himself and the world around him as Pocahontas had advised, without exploring his Powhatan roots. He must go on this journey, this adventure . . .

He heard thumping as Lizzie jumped up the steps two at a time, and the door swung open.

"Well, big brother, what is on your mind?" she boomed; her curls bounced and her smile was wide.

"Here." He passed her a steaming mug of ale. "Sit with me. I want to ask your advice." His voice was quiet, his face drawn as he looked at the floor. The light of the fire flickered on his lightly bearded face, showing shadows of apprehension.

Her bouncy mood was dashed as silence reigned. "My goodness, Thomas." She faltered, his mood enveloping her. "It sounds very serious."

"It is serious, Lizzie." His eyes were glued to the floor as he bit his lip. "I would like to meet my Powhatan family, and I would like you to help me," he gushed, raising his dark brown eyes to meet hers.

She looked away, and when she looked back, there was tragedy on her face. "Thomas, you do not know what you are asking. They killed our father. They killed my stepfather; they have killed so many people. Relations with them have deteriorated even more since they massacred so many of us thirteen years ago." Her voice got higher and louder as memories were triggered. "I was a small child, but I remember the pain of that time. I remember seeing our father for the last time and how my mother and I ran for our lives. I have told you these things before. How can you ask me to help you meet them?"

"I know, Lizzie. I tried to force the thought of my mother's people out of my mind. You and the rest of the family have helped me do that with your love and kindness. For a while, it was more than enough. But I am struggling, especially since that incident in Jamestown. I am condemned for being part of a race I know nothing about. I am not saying that I want to live with them, but I need to know who they are."

Lizzie's eyes softened. She could sense the pain of his conflict. "Thomas, even if I did agree to help you, I have no idea what I could do. It is punishable by law to meet with Powhatans. We have a new governor, John West, and we don't know what he will be like yet. Certainly, his predecessor, John Harvey, was a brute and was sent back to England because of that. It may be that things will get a bit easier now, but there are no guarantees."

Thomas looked away, sipping his ale, deep in thought. "So I would have to do it in secret?" he whispered, looking back at her, his brows raised.

"Indeed you would. You could petition the governor for special dispensation, but I honestly don't think the time is right to do that. All you would do is highlight your connections to the Powhatans, which would not be helpful if you want to become a serious member of the colony. It would also put our family's reputation in jeopardy."

Thomas looked her straight in the face. "I appreciate that, and I know it is a lot to ask, but please, would you help me do it in secret?"

She looked at his puppy dog eyes pleading with her and paused. "If there were anything I could do, then maybe I would think about it, but honestly, I don't see how I could be of use."

"You know the landscape, you know where the tribes are, you could show me where I have to go. You could point out ways I could get there without being seen." He sensed her wavering, and his dialogue increased in speed. "This is your land; you know it so well. I know nothing, Lizzie." He held out his hand to her. "Please," he begged.

Just then, the door was flung open. John and Francis crashed through, out of breath and staring.

"Is she here?" Francis cried.

"Who?" asked Lizzie, panic in her voice.

"For goodness' sake—Mother, of course," shouted Francis, his eyes staring, looking around him as if he was a madman.

John rushed up to Lizzie. "She asked us to ride shotgun with her this morning, as she had to go into town. We got held up, and she must have gone into town on her own. We went to find her, and she wasn't there," he said, breathless with emotion.

Francis looked into the fire, breathing heavily. "If she is not on the road to Jamestown or in Jamestown, and she is not here, those bastards must have done something to her."

***

"We've looked for hours. Maybe the Powhatans took her back to their village." Lizzie looked at Thomas, John and Francis, who were now beginning to believe the worst had actually happened. Their faces were long and their movements slow as they began to run out of options for their search. They had scoured every inch of the path to Jamestown, and no sign of Joan was evident. It was like she had disappeared off the face of the earth.

"Maybe she diverted off the track. Was there anywhere else she might have gone?" asked Thomas, hope in his voice.

"The only place she might have gone would be to visit Jane's family. It would be unusual for her to do that on her own, but it is possible. There is a track just a few minutes from here that is a shortcut to the Poythress plantation. Why don't we try and retrace the steps she might have taken to go there before darkness sets in?" said Francis.

After much searching, they discovered the overgrown trail that led to the plantation home of the Poythress family.

"Someone has passed this way quite recently," said Thomas.

It was wooded and overgrown, but it was definitely a path.

"Hold on, I think I see the carriage. Look over there to the left," shouted Francis, who pointed through the trees.

All three of them rushed forward.

"Stop!" screamed Thomas, who was in front. "Don't come any farther." His face was crumpled with angst. "She has been killed . . . mutilated." He turned his face away from the bloodied sight; his body doubled up with revulsion.

John was just behind him, and when he, in turn, saw his mother, he cried out in pain. "Don't look, Lizzie," he cried. "You do not want to remember your mother like this."

Lizzie could not bear it. She ran past them. "Mother! Mother!" she shouted.

When she saw the scene before her—the blood and bones in her mother's torn dress—she fell to the ground sobbing. "What have those bastard Powhatans done?" She picked up an arrow that was lying on the ground next to the mutilated body of her mother, and she viciously snapped it in two. "I hate you bastards with every fiber of my body!" she screamed at the top of her lungs, looking around her through the trees and up to the sky. "Why? . . . Why? . . . Oh my God, why?"

Thomas looked at the body of his stepmother and retched. How could one human being destroy another to the extent that she was hardly recognizable? If this was the work of his Powhatan family, they were inhumane, and he wanted nothing to do with them.

He walked over to Lizzie and stooped to put his arm around her, both of them weeping.

Seventeen

26th August 1635

The sky was the blackest any of them had ever seen. The morning of the funeral had started with pouring rain. It gradually eased, replaced by a ferocious wind that tangled the black clouds as if being stirred in a cauldron of putrid smoke. The water of the James River tossed and turned, crashing against the pier in a frenzy of power.

They stood in a line, heads bowed, shivering, as the strong late summer gale started to turn uncharacteristically icy. Reverend Burke's voice droned on and on, but the words, hardly audible through the gale, were being drowned out by Mother Nature's distress.

The rain started to fall from the clouds in icy needles.

Thomas looked to the skies, wondering how God could be so cruel. First, taking his kind and gentle stepmother in such a violent way, and then sending a storm to prevent them from paying their last respects in a manner befitting her. He looked along the line of people. The rain beating down mingled with their tears and soaked them to the bone.

One set of eyes was raised, gazing at him. Jane.

When their eyes met, he looked away, trying to smother the affinity that he felt so strongly with her. Even at a time like this, when his mind should have been solely on Joan, seeing Jane made his stomach lurch. He was disgusted with himself but was compelled to look back.

However, having instinctively felt the change in him, she was now looking down at the open grave, hurt and confusion on her pretty face. Her blond hair was plastered to her face, and she was shivering. How he would have liked to comfort her, but he had to put her out of his mind. She deserved better than a half-caste Powhatan whose people had killed the wonderful woman they were all now grieving. Seeing her confusion, he knew he would have to be open and honest with her; he was not prepared to blight her life by taking their friendship further.

Lizzy stood beside him, putting her hand in his, noticing the interchange between him and Jane. Thomas looked down at Lizzy's tearful face and squeezed her hand, wrenching his mind from thoughts of Jane to what he now must focus on. He had a family to look after. He was the eldest. He could not let them down. He owed it to Joan and his father to protect the family and the business the way they would have wanted him to. He had no choice now.

Everyone looked around in panic as the rain and wind increased to the point that it was difficult to hear or even stand without falling over. The reverend hastily threw a clod of earth into the grave to signal the end of the service.

What had been a storm was developing into a hurricane, the likes of which even colonial veterans had never seen before. The atmosphere slowly started to morph from somber respect to terror as the realization of the impending danger hit. Each person looked around in confusion, wondering what they should do. What could they do? This was no ordinary storm.

The waves in the harbor were now high and mighty, spraying over the whole town. The sound of the sea roared in the ears of the terrified inhabitants.

The mourners in the churchyard all moved away from Joan's recently dug grave, looking around frantically as parts of the fence and roofs became detached and hurtled through the air. Captain Pierce shouted at the top of his lungs, but no one could hear him, his mouth moving seemingly without sound. He gestured towards his house, which stood not far away outside of the inner palisade. It was made of brick, and its imposing structure was one of the few buildings able to withstand this onslaught.

Thomas signaled to John and Francis and raced forward, almost pulling Lizzie off the ground to get her to safety. But he couldn't help himself; he stopped for a second and looked frantically around, searching to ensure that Jane was not left behind. He saw her running with her family and breathed a sigh of relief. She was looking backwards, forwards, and sideways, her eyes wide with fear as she ran. She was trying to find someone. Could it be him? He forced himself to look away.

He had to stop thinking about her and get his family to safety. Jane had her mother and father. He was not responsible for her.

The rain was like sharp icicles beating down. They were completely exposed to the ferocious wind and flying debris, and they all ran, frantic to find shelter. There was shrieking and yelling, but it looked like they were only mouthing silently, as nothing could be heard above the roar of the wind and the pelting of the rain.

Thomas made it up the front steps of Captain Pierce's house and threw open the door, pulling Lizzie behind him, followed by John and

Francis. He collapsed on the floor as Captain Pierce shut the door behind them.

"Please keep it open, Captain Pierce," Thomas said, his chest rising and falling, his damp hair hanging down as water droplets rolled onto the floor, "just for a moment—Jane and her family are following us. They should not be far behind." He closed his eyes, catching his breath.

A few moments passed. Thomas opened his eyes, brows furrowed. "They should be here by now." He jumped up and ran over to the door, peering out. "Where are they? They were right behind us."

Then he saw them. Jane's father was carrying her dripping body in his arms. Her neck hung limply over her father's arm as if she were dead. Her mother's face was screwed up in agony as she followed behind. Thomas saw a large gaping and bloody gash on Jane's forehead. Blood was dripping and mingling with the rain streaming down her face as her father struggled to battle the strong winds that were holding him back from getting her to shelter. He waded through inches and inches of rain that had created a mini river and finally staggered up the steps.

Thomas rushed forward, taking Jane from him and running through the entrance to the house, laying her gently on the sofa. Everyone gathered around; concern was etched on their faces as they observed the young woman, eyes closed and head bleeding.

Angelo, the maid, ran forward and picked up Jane's wrist. Everyone held their breath.

Angelo nodded her head. "She is alive, thank the good Lord."

Granny Joan rushed forward with a bowl of water and some rags and knelt, gently bathing Jane's blood-drenched head. Her white-blond hair was pink with blood.

Her mother, pain etched on her face, knelt beside her, taking her hand.

"My poor baby," she whispered.

"What happened?" asked Thomas.

"We were running after you, and a large piece of wood from one of the houses blew off and crashed into Jane. It tripped her up, and she fell, banging her head on a large rock," said her father, shaking his head.

Thomas stared helplessly as Jane was surrounded by her mother, father, Granny Joan, and Angelo. He had no place, but he felt he was closer to her than any of them, even though no words had been spoken to this effect.

He had to remind himself that he had decided to distance himself from her, for her sake. His heart was breaking at this decision, but his feelings were not important to her or anyone else. He turned away, but as he glanced back, he saw her eyelids fluttering.

Angelo started. "She is opening her eyes!" she cried.

Jane's eyes slowly opened. She looked around, squinting as she raised her hand to the gash on her head, wincing. Angelo helped her to sit up.

Jane's face was expressionless. "What happened?" she asked, looking at the blood on her hand.

"You were hit by flying debris and fell, knocking your head," her father answered.

She continued to scan the room, holding her injured head.

Thomas could not allow their eyes to meet; hiding his overwhelming feelings would be too difficult. He abruptly turned tail and walked into the kitchen, trying to look purposeful.

Lizzie watched him disappear and saw the strained look on his face.

After scanning the room to see who was there, Jane said, "Where is Thomas?"

Then Lizzie understood. She followed Thomas into the kitchen. He was sitting at the kitchen table, his head in his hands.

"Thomas, she is asking for you . . . why don't you go to her?"

He looked up, shaking his head. "Lizzie, I am a half-caste heathen. I cannot blight her world with a man like myself. I will never tell her how I feel. She deserves a decent man that is worthy of her."

"She wants only you. I saw the look on her face. Does she have no say?"

"No. She will find a good Englishman." He put his head in his hands once again. "Please leave me alone, Lizzie. I have made my mind up."

Eighteen

Life Must Go On

The storm had caused chaos with the loss of many lives and the destruction of crops and buildings. As a result, the "Great and the Good" of Jamestown were meeting to discuss storm damage and the concerted communal effort to make repairs. As a new landowner, Thomas was about to set off for one of the most important meetings of his life. This was his chance to make an entrance to this new society as the heir to John Rolfe.

As he prepared himself to leave, he thought of lovely Joan. He would not be going to the meeting if she had not been killed. She would have gone. How could his mother's people have killed her? His heart ached at her loss, even though he had known her for such a short time. He was the Rolfe in charge now, and he needed to step up to the demands of his new role.

He mounted the horse and clutched his rifle. He waved goodbye to

Lizzie as he moved along the track, looking back at her smiling face.

"Take care," she shouted as he gathered pace. "And good luck," she yelled louder, rising on her toes to catch a last glimpse of him. He lifted his rifle in the air in recognition, and soon he was out of sight of the plantation house, moving slowly and deliberately through the trees.

Every movement of a leaf, every crack of a twig caused his sinews to tense, his eyes to dart. He was at the ready.

He heard the snap of wood and stopped his horse, ready for battle, remembering the sight of Joan's mangled corpse. The horse snorted and backed up, steam emanating from its flared nostrils, sensing a presence. His spine tingled as he peered through the darkness of the trees.

A glimpse of black and white . . . it was a badger. He breathed a sigh of relief.

But he was not relaxed; thoughts like messages appeared as whispers in the wind. The dictum was clear. Yes, he was scared. Scared of all he now had to face. At the age of twenty, he had to take on a job that he was ill-equipped to do. He had to be a father to Lizzie, John, and Francis, and he had a plantation and many acres of land to manage. Grief, fear, and anger were his constant bedfellows, but he had the determination to push through. He was in the place of his dreams and he would do his very best for those who relied on him.

How scared must his father have been when he battled the seas and the wrath of the Powhatans. How fearful must his mother have been as she entered a world so foreign to her own!

Being scared is integral to survival. Fear does not kill; it hones the instincts. Being scared was something he had to accept in order to grow.

Thomas smiled as he looked up at the sky. He could not see her, but he knew she was there. He nodded and placed his hand over his heart.

With renewed energy, he patted his horse and gently dug his heels into its sides to spur it on.

***

Thomas looked around him. He could see that these men were gentry. They were in command and a force to be reckoned with. He was younger than most, and once again felt out of his depth, but his fear did not phase him.

The tobacco smoke in the room was almost suffocating in its density, and the murmuring hum of conversation filled the air.

Governor West stood up behind a table at the front, flanked by two of his councilors. His chair scraped on the wooden floor. The room became silent as all eyes watched the man they had elected to replace the governor they had ousted. He was a tall man with a presence of authority. His steely blue eyes were unflinching. He was more than ready to crush dissent.

"Gentlemen, first I would like to thank you for attending this emergency meeting at such short notice. We are in crisis." He looked around the room, pausing, his face long and drawn. "Time is of the essence. This storm has rendered us not only vulnerable to food shortages, but the damage to our defenses has made us, once more, vulnerable to heathen aggression."

The audience was still; only an occasional cough could be heard.

Gratified, he continued. "The palisade has been blown away in several places, and in areas where it is standing, it is extremely weak. The Powhatans know we are vulnerable, and we must repair this damage as soon as possible. They will watch our every move and can easily take advantage of the situation. Opechancanough is an angry and unpredictable individual, and we cannot allow him to move in on us now. Few of us will have forgotten the massacre of 1622. We have gained superiority since those days, but we must not sit on our laurels. We must act."

The room erupted with cries of "Hear, hear." They stomped and clapped their approval.

The governor raised his arm, moving it slowly up and down to signal for silence.

He continued, "The heathens themselves have, no doubt, lost a lot of crops and homes, and what food we have left is very attractive to hungry natives. Their numbers still outweigh ours. They could easily eradicate all of us and take back their land."

Thomas listened, face set, gleaning as much information as he could. The atmosphere in the room was tense. He was surrounded by hate for the Powhatan aggressor, and since Joan's death, he had absorbed the enthusiasm to defend by killing these enemies if necessary. This, indeed, was a war of survival of the fittest. Despite his familial connections, his heart was turning against his mother's people.

An anonymous voice shouted, "Let's attack them once and for all. We need land; the storm must have weakened them, as it has us."

The room erupted with voices shouting support. Fists were raised in the air, and chanting began. "Kill the filthy heathens! Kill the filthy heathens!"

Thomas felt the emotion in the room, and thinking of Joan, he almost raised his fist in support before the governor banged a gavel on the desk.

"Order . . . order!" shouted the governor. "Gentlemen, please. We are lowering ourselves to their level." He stood at attention, scouring the audience, his face inscrutable.

"For a few years now, we have managed to coexist with the Powhatans. To reignite hostilities at this point would be folly. We need to trade with them until we expand our resources. It is only by becoming self-sufficient that we can finally take over this land and make it our own without pandering to these damnable Indians. Until then, unfortunately, we have to rely on the manpower and resources of the Powhatans. No matter how distasteful that may be."

There were rumblings of discontent.

The governor leaned over the table, looking at them as if they were naughty children. "There is little point in becoming rich producing tons of tobacco if we starve in the process." He stood staring into the crowd, daring someone to contradict him. There was silence.

He sat down, taking a sip of water. "Now, if you don't mind, I think we should get back to the matter in hand. Our first objective is to repair the damage done to our defenses. We will start repairing the palisade from tomorrow. I want all men and boys to gather at the main gate at six o'clock in the morning. I will allocate teams to cut wood and teams to erect the fences. When that is complete, we will move on to Jamestown buildings, the outer palisade, and any individual plantations that need our manpower. Have I made myself clear? Anyone who feels they are above a working party will have me to deal with."

The governor stood up to end the meeting and walked towards the exit. As he caught sight of Thomas in the audience, he came to a halt, staring in his direction.

"On a final note, we have a newcomer to welcome in our midst. John Rolfe's son, Thomas, has joined us to farm his inherited land." He put out his hand in Thomas's direction. "My sincere condolences for the loss of your stepmother." Thomas smiled and bowed his head. "Thank you, sir."

The governor turned to the colonists. "Please make Thomas welcome, and give him all the help and support that he needs."

There was a ripple of applause. "Stand up, Thomas, so everyone can see who you are," said Governor West. A broad grin lit up his face, lightening the mood in the previously somber atmosphere. He hoped this would make a good end to a difficult meeting.

Thomas stood up, smiling at the faces around him, and nodded and bowed to acknowledge their appreciation. He was on top of the world. He was accepted.

Suddenly, a voice from the back shouted out.

"He may be John Rolfe's son, but he is half Powhatan. We have a bloody heathen in our midst!"

Nineteen

Jane

They had been as kind as they could have been under the circumstances. Governor West had chastized the heckler, and everyone around Thomas had stood up and patted him on the back, shouting encouragement. "Welcome, young man!" said one. "Pay no attention to ignorant hecklers!" said another. "Any son of John Rolfe is a friend of mine," said a third.

He had been accepted superficially, but in reality, he would always stand out. Why should they trust him? He looked like a Powhatan, and he had Powhatan blood in his veins. How could they know where his loyalties lay? In their shoes, Thomas would feel the same way.

He left the meeting accepting the reality of his position. As he rode up the track towards the plantation, he saw a familiar pony and trap tied up outside. His heart did a lurch. He was still raw from the comments in Jamestown, and now, to have to see Jane, knowing he would have to reject her, he almost felt physically sick.

There was no hiding. Lizzie came to the front door when she heard him trotting up the path. She ran down the stairs, holding up her long skirt to stop her tripping.

"So . . . how did it go, big brother?" She was smiling, her brown curls bouncing as she skipped towards him.

He pursed his lips. "Everyone was very kind." He looked at the ground. "I almost got away with it until someone pointed out that I was Powhatan."

She reached up to take his hand and help him down from the horse. "Oh, Thomas, I am so sorry. Some people are so ignorant."

As he jumped down, she pulled him towards her and hugged him. "It just takes some folk time to get used to things. Granny Joan always says that if people do not understand something, it makes them scared and defensive. There is a lot of fear in this colony, Thomas . . . and with good reason. When they get to know you, I'm sure it will be fine."

He looked down at his cute little sister and realized how much harder things must have been for her, an orphan relying on a brother she had not known for long. The girls sipping tea in his grandmother's house in Heacham would never have come up with such a profound statement or even considered fear and survival. Now that he was here, he would look after his little sister, no matter what.

He stood straight, determined not to wallow in self-pity. "Come on, let's go inside. I see we have visitors."

She gathered up her skirts and darted up the stairs before him, opening the door and signaling his entrance with her arm outstretched as if he were royalty.

As he walked in, Jane was sitting at the kitchen table with Francis, deep in conversation. At first, they were not aware of his presence.

Thomas bathed himself in the sight of her. She looked so beautiful.

Jane

Her flaxen hair was pulled back into one long plait that fell down her back. Her blue eyes were wide as she concentrated on what Francis was saying. She still had a large bandage on her head and minor cuts to her face.

She turned and looked up. Her porcelain complexion flushed as their eyes met.

Lizzie felt the awkwardness in the room. "Francis, can you please go and chop some more wood for the fire?" she said.

Francis looked around, oblivious to the tension permeating the warm kitchen. "Oh, for goodness sake, Lizzie, there is plenty out there; I will do it tomorrow. I was just talking to Jane. Anyway, I want to hear how Thomas got on in Jamestown," he whined.

Lizzie put her hands on her hips and glared at him shaking her head. "Please just do as I ask."

He got up from the chair and shrugged his shoulders. "Yes ma'am," he said, saluting her in mock obedience. Then he turned and walked out.

"I just have to go and put the chickens away," Lizzie said as she followed Francis out of the door.

The two of them were left alone.

"You have been avoiding me, Thomas," said Jane, her voice wavered, but her resolve did not. Her straight talking threw him off guard, and he stood mute, unable to respond, emotions paralyzing his response.

She continued, her face flushed. "I thought that we were friends." Her large blue eyes stared at him, leaving him no room for avoidance.

He walked over and sat down at the table next to her. His heart was beating so loud he thought she might be able to hear it. He slowed his breathing, trying to regain control. He had to stick to his decision.

He paused and returned her gaze. Then he looked away momentarily, steadying himself before facing her again. "Jane, I am your friend. I will always be your friend." He reached over and took her hand. "But that is all that we can ever be. I am half Powhatan . . . I'm not good enough for you."

A silence hung in the air as she digested what had been said. She pulled her hand away from his, her eyes welling up. "I don't know what you mean, Thomas." She looked at the floor, then looked him straight in the eye. "When I look at you, I see Thomas. I do not see someone who is half of anything. I see the whole of someone who is special to me." Her voice was shaky as she looked away from him again towards the window, brushing a tear from her eye. "I mistakenly thought you felt the same about me."

Moments passed, and nothing was said.

"Jane, I—"

"There is no need for further explanations, Thomas. You have made everything very clear." She bit her lip, the sobs suppressed.

They sat together but apart. He looked at the dusty floor. A part of him wished that he could turn the clock back and that instead of rejecting her, he could have taken her in his arms and kissed her. But the other part of him knew what he was doing was for her. He wanted her happiness more than anything. She deserved more than a man with Powhatan blood. He could never make her happy. Today's meeting in Jamestown confirmed that he was tarnished, and he could not inflict that on her.

The silence was broken as Francis and John crashed through the door pushing and shoving each other, completely unaware of the emotions in the room. They laughed and swore at each other, playfully punching and hitting.

Thomas moved away from Jane.

Then Lizzie waltzed through the door. She looked at Thomas and Jane and saw the tragedy in their faces. Francis and John were still larking about, shoving each other with good-hearted banter.

"Will you two just stop?" Lizzie shouted at her young brothers.

Jane

They looked at her with wide eyes, blank faces confirming that they were in their own world, oblivious to the undercurrents in the room.

Jane cleared her throat. "Actually, I think it's time that I went home, Lizzie," she said.

"But you were going to join us for dinner. Why don't you stay for a bit," Lizzie pleaded.

Jane's face fell as she struggled to contain her emotions. "Thank you so much, Lizzie, but I feel I must go. I'm not feeling very well." She glanced at Thomas.

Their eyes briefly met. Thomas got up from the table and walked towards her. His eyes were full of sadness as he gave her a brotherly kiss on the top of her head.

Twenty

Weroance

~~~

Opechancanough was weary. He sat in the quioccosan, smoking the pipe, pondering steps he needed to take. He knew the world was changing, and his time on the earth was running out. The old days were gone, when conflicts were confined to intertribal skirmishes over land and power. Now, with the invasion of the Longcoat, the survival of not only the Powhatans but all Native people was at risk. The responsibility for the future weighed heavily on his solid but aging shoulders. He sighed out the heavy and fragrant smoke, watching as the gray plumes rose into the air.

His mind wandered to events of the past. His beloved brother had died of a broken heart when the Longcoats killed his daughter, Pocahontas. His brother, his hero for so many years, had turned from one of the greatest warriors of all time to a shadow of a man. This had inflamed a fire in Opechancanough's belly that had burned for years. Revenge infiltrated his every pore, and the 1622 massacre of the English had been a consequence.

An image of John Rolfe as he lay dying flashed into his mind. The moment he witnessed the light of John's life fading, he received a vital message from the gods. The message was clear: Peace was the only way the Powhatans could survive. This divine intervention, a rare occurrence in his life, shook Opechancanough to his core and forced him to reconsider his lifelong beliefs and strategies.

Peace? How could this be? His whole life had been devoted to wiping the Longcoats from the face of the earth. In 1622, the massacre had been a success. He would have demolished enough of them to take control if he had continued on that path. But he could not ignore the divine message. It was a struggle against all his instincts, a battle within himself. He must do his duty and cultivate peace, as demanded by the gods. This internal conflict, the clash between his instincts and his duty, tormented Opechancanough, leaving him in constant turmoil.

He thought of the years he had spent since the fateful day of John's death trying to abide by the instructions from the gods. He had provided food for the Longcoats when their crops failed because of their greedy focus on gold instead of farming. He had disregarded many atrocities and mindless attacks from an out-of-control rabble of Longcoat cowards. He had tried time after time to negotiate with men who seemed intent on taking, not giving. But he was only a man, and his patience was running out after all the years of trying. This had to be the last attempt to get these bastards under control. But he had to try. The gods demanded it. Opechancanough's relentless efforts to negotiate with the Longcoats, despite their aggressive and selfish behavior, demonstrated his unwavering commitment to peace and the extent of his struggle.

John Rolfe's son Thomas was his last hope, but could he trust this boy from England? This boy who knew little of his Powhatan heritage, who had no emotional investment in the tribe? If Thomas had any loyalty to the Powhatans, it would inevitably be based on his slender connection with a mother he had known for only two years. Anything else would be idealistic, the motives based on a boy eager to make a name for himself. Nothing was wrong with that if, like his mother, the underlying motive was a genuine hope for peace. Opechancanough sighed. He had yet to meet the lad, but he was optimistic that with his parentage and age, he could be molded into the peacemaker they needed.

Opechancanough's mind searched for answers. What was the first step in ensuring loyalty from this boy from England? Kokee would have to play a large part. This would not be difficult, as Kokee had always wanted to meet with his brother. A meeting between the brothers would have to be engineered.

If that went well, Thomas would have to be integrated further into the ways of the Powhatan. How could this be achieved? he wondered.

A man's reason for existing was to carry on his genetic line. To do this, he must protect his wife and progeny. So a family would have to be found for Thomas . . . a wife . . . a child . . . yes, the next vital step to ensure the Longcoat's loyalty was if he fathered a Powhatan child. As a father, he would never betray his child. Thomas must father a Powhatan baby to ensure his loyalty to the Powhatan cause.

So, a bride would have to be found. She would have to be a girl of honor who was prepared to sacrifice her life for her tribe. If the lad was personable, Opechancanough knew just the right girl.

He smiled, nodded, and looked to the sky, thanking the gods for sending him the plan he needed to create the peace they required.

Twenty-One

Kidnapped

The start of 1636 came and went with little fanfare.

It was cold on the winter morning Thomas rode out to survey and plan where the next batch of tobacco plants should be sowed for spring.

He rode up and down the fields, calculating what was needed. He was lost in thought when he saw something moving in the trees. He reined in his horse, grabbing his rifle from the saddle bag and scanning all around. His horse snorted and backed up, rearing slightly. "Whoa . . . whoa." He patted its trembling flank.

"Who goes there?" he shouted, his eyes gleaming, his whole body on high alert.

A flash of red darted among the trees. Then the rustle of leaves and the sound of snapping twigs behind him, in front of him and to the sides of him. He froze. He knew he was outnumbered and he was powerless.

"Come and get me, you filthy dirty heathens," he yelled at the top of his lungs. Instinctively, his curiosity to meet his mother's family had died with the murder of Joan. He wanted nothing to do with a race of people so intent on aggression that they could kill such an innocent woman for no apparent reason. He pulled himself together, aimed the rifle and swiveled himself in the saddle, trying to locate the target. Lizzie, John, and Francis would be alone if anything happened to him. He had to survive.

They came all at once, surrounding him. He started to fire, but a warrior crept up behind him and pulled the rifle from his hands, the fired bullet soaring to the sky. Another pulled him off his horse in a simultaneous movement. He landed on the ground, winded.

He lay, not daring to look up. Brown legs surrounded him. They were shouting at one another in Algonquian, and he held his breath, waiting for the final blow that would end his life.

There was shouting, and he felt his arms being tied behind his back. They had not killed him. Perhaps they wanted a bit of fun before finally finishing him off. Thoughts went around his head about his father and Joan . . . he was next. He knew how ruthless these people could be. The brutalized body of Joan haunted him every day.

One of the warriors was clearly in charge. He shouted orders at the others as they raised him off the ground and pushed him staggering and stumbling through the trees. A warrior led his horse.

He had to think. He had to get away from these savages. He was concentrating so hard on escaping that he missed his foothold and tripped heavily onto his knees, unable to break his fall, as his hands were tied. He called out in pain; one of his knees gushed blood, sliced on a sharp stone. He tried to get up, but the pain seared through him, and he crashed back down on the hard earth, groaning. He would not be able to walk far with his injuries, and they would kill him for sure.

His heart sank.

The warrior in charge shouted what sounded like instructions, and he was raised up and placed down carefully on a bed of leaves. His captors were frowning and gesticulating, babbling to each other as they examined his bleeding knee. One of the warriors cut the ties that bound his hands, and tore his trousers, gently dabbing his wound with sods of grass to clear the blood. Another brought rags and wrapped them around his knee. As he did so, he looked up at Thomas and smiled.

Thomas was shocked. Why such kindness? Could it be that they were not going to kill him yet? Maybe they needed information from him about the resources of the British army. Previously, they had proved to be an indiscriminately violent tribe, but his treatment so far had not been harsh.

Having dressed his wounds, a warrior rippling with muscles walked over and picked him up, sitting him on his horse's back.

They walked for hours, leading Thomas sitting on his horse. Thomas did not know what to think. He held on to the saddle but could do nothing more as his knee was still throbbing. Maybe they knew who his mother was. Could that be the reason for his survival? Perhaps in these circumstances, his appearance was an advantage.

They came to a clearing, and Thomas smelled smoke and heard children playing and dogs barking. They had reached a Powhatan village. The rounded dwellings were strategically placed, surrounded by tall trees and guarded by warriors. He was confused and scared in equal measure, wondering what was happening. These people were his enemy; they had killed his father and stepmother. But he reminded himself that they were also his family and, apart from his initial capture, had not shown aggression.

One of the warriors helped him to dismount. His knee was throbbing, but he managed to stagger down, holding on to the horse, getting his bearings. He stood looking at the activities of the village's everyday life. It was ordinary. Men were chopping wood, tending to animals, and repairing the dwellings. Women were kneading bread, washing clothes, and hoeing the fields. Children played chase, laughing and pointing at the newcomer.

No chanting warriors or fearsome war paint. Just ordinary people going about the process of surviving and living in an inhospitable land. They did not look like the murderers he had imagined.

A small boy rushed up to him, smiling. He said something in Algonquian and held out his hand. Thomas stooped down and saw a childishly carved wooden animal of undecipherable species. The boy moved his hand toward Thomas and nodded towards his creation. Thomas took the animal and smiled. He bowed his head in thanks, and the boy ran behind a woman standing a little way off. He peeked at Thomas from behind her tunic, his eyes dancing. Thomas smiled and bowed again. The child's mother smiled and bowed in return.

He struggled to hold on to his anger and hatred in the face of such normality and welcoming gestures. He looked at the little boy again. The lad was different, but in many ways, so very like George Fitzgerald II. They were both cheeky, lovable children untouched by their respective peoples' hatred and prejudices. They were just two lovely children—who cared if one was dark and one was fair? The colour of their skin could not dictate their value. If only their parents could learn from them.

He glanced around at the warriors who had captured him. They were all looking at him without a trace of malice. At that moment, he realized they meant no harm to him. But he was confused. Why?

Thomas heard movement behind him, and when he turned, he saw an older warrior dressed in the magnificent headdress of the Werowance. He was flanked by at least ten warriors, all bearing swords and colored with the red puccoon[1] of ceremonial dress.

Opechancanough walked towards Thomas and put his hand out in greeting. "Welcome," he said in English.

Thomas stared in quiet astonishment. He had been transported to a different world. He could feel the spirit of Pocahontas in the sunlight as it twinkled through the trees. With this, he grew in confidence and stature as he shook his great-uncle's hand. They looked at one another, their faces stern but respectful. The significance of what was happening lay heavily in the air. Silence reigned in the village as all the villagers stopped their daily chores to watch, spellbound.

Opechancanough wanted to take things slowly. Was Thomas a friend or a foe? Would Thomas have a heart full of hatred for the murder of innocents at the hands of the Powhatans? Or would he understand the plight of his mother's people and that his Longcoat blood was tainted with the demise of a people clawing at the earth for their very survival against an aggressor? Whose side would he take? They had to know the answers to these questions before they welcomed him fully into the bosom of the tribe.

[1] Red pigment made from the puccoon plant.

Twenty-Two

A Different Family

After their brief meeting, Opechancanough had insisted that Thomas take refreshment. He had been taken to one of the Powhatan dwellings by the mother of the boy with the carved animal. She lit a fire and spread a soft bearskin rug over a bed of straw. She bowed and retreated.

Thomas was alone with a multitude of questions racing around his head. He sat on the bearskin-covered straw and closed his eyes as he breathed in the dusky smell of the roaring fire. The burning wood crackled, and he gradually felt the tension leaving his body. He lay down, staring at the flames, strangely at peace in this place that was so foreign to him. Once again, he was in the place he had been dreaming of for many years. He fell into a deep sleep.

His dream was vivid and frightening.

His father ran toward him, hand in hand with Joan. Out of nowhere, a band of Powhatans surrounded them. John Rolfe gazed at his son with despair in his eyes, his hands reaching for help. Lizzie, Jane, John, and Francis were in the background, screaming at him to do something. But his feet were bound, and he could not move. He watched as his father and stepmother were slaughtered by the marauding natives, who laughed as they saw him struggling, powerless to help.

Thomas woke, tormented by the dream that had seemed so real that he could feel the tears still running down his cheeks. The intense images had reflected and reawakened his anger at Powhatan aggression. He must not be fooled by the kindness they had so far shown him. The reality was that the Powhatans were heathens. He would never accept them or be accepted by them, no matter what his mother wanted.

He heard footsteps outside and readied himself for confrontation. Two warriors entered the yehakin, followed by his great-uncle Opechancanough. The warriors brought a seat of straw, indicating that Thomas should be seated. Opechancanough sat facing him, with the fire between them.

His uncle put his hands together and bowed his head. Thomas did not reciprocate; his dream had reignited the memory of the body of Joan lying mutilated. How could he, despite his familial connections, be forgiving and compliant?

One of the warriors held a pipe of tobacco. He passed it to Opechancanough, and the old warrior inhaled the scented smoke, closing his eyes. There was silence as Thomas watched his uncle's lined face. Thomas sensed that each line told a story of war and death. The old man may have looked benign and peaceful at that moment, but Thomas could not forget that he was the instigator of many crimes.

Opechancanough opened his eyes. He put his hand toward Thomas, offering him the pipe of peace. Thomas shook his head, knowing that to refuse such an honor was a great insult to the old man.

Thomas expected his actions to trigger aggression; instead, Opechancanough's eyes softened.

"My son, you have much anger," he said, looking at Thomas, his face grave. He continued, shaking his head, "There are many things that you do not understand. That is why we have brought you here."

Thomas was shaking. Fear combined with anger overwhelmed him. He took a breath as he looked at the old man. "Sir, for all my life, I have looked forward to becoming part of my mother's family." He paused, looking into the flames. "But arriving in Jamestown, I have seen that the Powhatan way cannot be my way. I witnessed the body of my beloved stepmother after your warriors had brutally murdered her, and the image of your cruelty will not leave my mind." He paused; there was no going back. "Powhatans murdered my father and many more innocent people. Therefore, I cannot share the pipe of peace with you." He looked up from the fire into his uncle's dark, sad eyes.

Opechancanough drew on the pipe, closing his eyes. Thomas's whole body was tense, waiting for a response to his outburst. The warriors stood still but alert.

When Opechancanough opened his eyes, he looked at Thomas and slowly nodded. "My son, the wind blows in many directions. Each wind brings with it a change to the universe. Each sentient being sees these changes from a different river bank. One looks at the rain that falls and is thankful for the nourishment it brings. Another sees the same rain and cries as it washes away his crops. Which one is the right one? Are blue skies the right skies? Are gray skies the right skies? There are no clear answers." He paused and drew on the pipe.

Thomas fidgeted. "But why did your warriors murder my stepmother? She was an innocent woman doing no harm. There is no other way to describe what happened. There is no other way to see it." His face was full of disdain.

Opechancanough clasped his hands together. "Wisdom lies with uncertainty, my son. Open your eyes to this. Indeed, your stepmother went to the gods in great pain . . . When we came upon her, the wolves had already feasted. Our arrows sent them off, but we could not save her for this life. We prayed for her soul and left her for her kin. We were too late, my son." He looked at Thomas, shaking his head. "Our only crime was tardiness."

Thomas was stunned into silence. The arrow they had found next to Joan was intended for the wolves that attacked her. He had been so wrong to accuse the Powhatans of such brutality. He had been so certain. "There is wisdom in uncertainty." He paused, his mind attempting to reorient itself.

"And what of my father? You knew my father fought for peace alongside my mother. How could you kill him?" It was the question that had been haunting him since that day in Heacham when he had been told of his father's death.

Thomas saw the old man's face crumble as he held his hand to his forehead and closed his eyes. "Your father was a good man. He loved and cared for Pocahontas, helping her in her quest for peace. When she died, he had to start his life again, and he did so, mindful of the difficulties between our two peoples."

Opechancanough opened his eyes and continued. "War is terrible and must be embarked upon only if the way to save lives is to take lives. When a leader of men, such as myself, opens that cauldron of war, men turn from loving fathers to fierce protectors. The primitive force of destruction and chaos envelops their every cell and sinew, turning men to savages. Unintended deaths of the innocent are the tragedy of the fallibility of men.

"That night, I ran to your father's house to warn him. I owed it to your mother to save him. It was an arrow from the unstoppable adrenaline of war that I could not contain: an accident, my son.

"It haunts me to this day that your father did not survive. The will of the gods does not always make sense to flawed creatures of the universe such as I.

"I have few regrets, but the biggest regret of my life is that I could not save your father that night. The irony never leaves my heart—war is waged so we may live in peace, and so many of the world's heroes are sacrificed on the bonfire of war. I am a flawed human being—let him who is perfect cast me down." He looked into the fire, lost in the memories of another time. "A tragic accident," he whispered. He lifted his arm to draw on the tobacco, then slowly exhaled the smoke and watched it swirling in the air. He looked at Thomas with rheumy eyes and paused. "Welcome, son of Pocahontas. Allow your eyes to see not only the bad in your mother's people but also the good. Many tragedies have pierced the hearts of both sides for the sake of survival," he said as he offered the pipe to Thomas, his arm shaking. "The peaceful make war for the sake of peace . . . We are all the same, humanity cannot change."

Thomas sat for many minutes mulling over what Opechancanough had said, his eyebrows drawn. It was true, in this war, no one had covered themselves with glory. These people were fighting for their lives, while the English were led by leaders who were fighting because of greed. He looked into the fire, nodded, and extended his hand to take the pipe.

Opechancanough closed his eyes, satisfied that things were going to plan.

***

Thomas sat staring into the fire's dying embers long after Opechancanough had disappeared into the night. It was as if his world had been shaken upside down once again, and his rage with the Powhatans had turned to dust, leaving him exhausted and confused.

He finally closed his eyes, only to be confronted with image after image of Joan's mangled body, but this time, she was being bathed and cared for by Powhatan warriors as British soldiers shot them dead. Who were the demons? They kept changing . . .

His cries of horror woke him, and he looked around, disoriented, his face damp with the emotions of his dreams. What should he think? What should he feel? He was torn in half.

A Powhatan squaw entered the tepee. She looked at him with gentle eyes, bowed her head, and placed bread and water before him. She began to rebuild the fire that was cold and black.

When she finished, she lit the fire, stood back and looked at him, pausing momentarily. "Opechancanough says you have his blessing and are free to go . . . but he hopes you will stay to meet with Kokee, who is your brother. I have made the fire so you will be warm, hoping that we have made you feel welcome enough to stay until the cock crows and Kokee comes." She bowed, turned, and walked away.

Thomas watched her leave, his heart beating. Her words echoed in his head: "Kokee . . . your brother."

His brother was here, in this village, and he had the chance to finally meet him. A close blood connection to his mother. He pulled her pearls out of his pocket, feeling their round, smooth shape. His head swam. What future could he have here with these people? Only hours ago, he had perceived them as his enemy.

He wanted more than anything to meet Kokee, but what of Lizzie and the boys, and dare he think-Jane? They would be worried sick. He had only been missing for one night, but in this conflict-ridden land, a person who did not appear after a few hours was presumed ambushed and murdered. He had to return to them, but he had to see Kokee. Would he be a traitor to Lizzie, the boys, and Jane if he stayed just a while longer?

Twenty-Three

A Proposition

He had once caught sight of his reflection in a pond in the grounds of Heacham Manor. Looking at the young man standing before him was like looking into that calm pond once again. His brother was older by four years, but there could be no mistaking that they shared the same genes.

Kokee smiled at him. "Welcome, my brother. For so many moons I have dreamed of meeting the other who called Pocahontas 'mother.' We share so much but have been separated by oceans and cultures." His dark eyes were dancing. His naked, painted chest glistened with the heat of the fire. He was a warrior through and through, but for now, his face was soft and his voice warm.

Thomas nodded and looked around him. It felt surreal. He paused. How could his being here—standing in a Powhatan yehakin—feel so normal? His uncle had dented his perspective on war, and sorrow for the universal pointlessness of it had superseded his rage. While the warriors outside with bows and arrows were aggressive in the scenario of war, in this situation they were his family, protecting him. And his brother—finally, he could say brother—was an ordinary man, similar to himself, who instilled a sense of calm in him. He had often visualized being with Kokee, but his hazy imaginings could only hint at the reality of the quiet connection he felt. He breathed in the smoky atmosphere, smiling and sighing.

"I shared your dreams, Kokee. Our mother's physical body left this earth many years ago, but her spirit remains. She shared her thoughts of you when her soul visited me in the night. Although we have led separate lives, I feel as if I know you well. She wanted us to be together, and she wanted peace."

Kokee bowed his head. "I would like you to know our family, Thomas. It is time that you knew your people, not as the enemy of your father's people, but as the roots of your mother.

"Pocahontas gave her life for her people and saw peace with the Longcoats as the only way we could survive. You are the link that she bequeathed to carry on that mission." His dark brown eyes were unblinking. "The gods have brought you to us. You are special." The seriousness of his sentiment hit Thomas like a blow.

He felt a lump in his throat. He looked at Kokee. There was an awkward silence. He was the chosen link? He had not appreciated that he might have a vital role to play in the lives of the Powhatan people; he had only ever needed a family to which he could belong. Pocahontas had whispered of peace. Was this what she had meant?

Before he could respond, the door of the yehakin opened. A young squaw entered, accompanied by two white greyhounds. She looked at Thomas, and he saw her beautiful eyes wide with anticipation. She bowed her head and put her hands together as her shiny dark hair fell like a curtain around her face. Thomas was mesmerized. Kokee's words were temporarily forgotten as she became his only focus.

Kokee put out his hand toward the young girl. "Thomas, this is Nikkiti. Her name means 'she who sweeps the dew from the flowers.' She is the daughter of Opechancanough," he said as he reached towards the two exquisite greyhounds, stroking their soft heads. One of the dogs put her paw up, scratching his arm, clearly wanting more. "Oh Manitou, you princess," Kokee laughed and continued stroking her. "These lovely ladies are Manitou and Waba, descendants of the gift given to our grandfather and our mother by the English king."

Nikkiti took one of the dogs by a rope tied around its neck and walked towards Thomas. Both dog and girl were slight and elegant, moving effortlessly.

Her voice was soft and musical, her eyes twinkling. "My father, Opechancanough, would like to offer you this dog as a token of our friendship. Our great princess Pocahontas, your mother, considered this greyhound's mother of four generations ago to be one of her greatest companions. Her dog became a mascot for her cause. Please accept Waba as a token of how much we wish the son of Pocahontas to become part of our lives and continue your mother's work." She bowed her head again and held the rope towards Thomas.

The dog looked up at him with large brown eyes as she walked towards him. She stood, quiet and calm by his side, instinctively knowing to whom she now belonged. Thomas stroked her smooth white fur and ruffled her soft velvet ears. He had never had a dog before, and this was one of the most beautiful creatures he had ever seen.

There was silence as they absorbed the symbolism, acknowledging the past while imagining the future.

Nikkiti gazed at Thomas, her eyes steady with confidence. Petite though she was, Thomas felt her charisma and strength.

Kokee broke the silence. "Thomas, will you stay with us a while?"

A Proposition

Thomas looked into the smoldering fire. He was overcome with emotion, his eyes welling up. How easy would it be to stay here and learn the ways of his mother? How easy was it to absorb the respect and status they offered him? Was it written that he should continue his mother's work?

But what of his duty to Lizzy, John, and Francis?

His head knew the answer as his heart bled. He took one last stolen glance at the beautiful squaw with the greyhound by her side, then turned to look at his brother.

"Kokee . . . I . . ."

His words faltered as he heard people shouting and dogs barking.

Kokee put his hand up to stop Thomas's words. "With respect, my brother, we must find out what is happening outside." His eyebrows were drawn as each person in the room became alert. Nikkiti flung her arms around Manitou, eyes fixed on the door, waiting to defend her loyal companion against enemies. The warriors tensed at the ready, as they must have done many times before. Thomas could see that this was the natural order of things. The door to the yehakin was flung open, the cold air crashing in on the previously cozy atmosphere.

All eyes were on the warrior painted in red puccoon as he launched himself into the room. Panic dissipated as they recognized him as one of their own.

"Kokee, where is Opechancanough?" the newcomer gasped, his eyes wild as he scanned the yehakin. He caught sight of Thomas. "This man is our enemy," he shouted, pointing at him, his eyes wide with hatred. "He may be your brother, but he is not our friend." He turned and spat on the ground in Thomas's direction. "The Longcoats have captured Nectowance, son of Opechancanough. They are threatening to kill him if we do not return this vile half-breed to them."

Kokee's eyes were staring as he absorbed the facts of the situation.

"Askook, Thomas is your cousin . . . Pocahontas's son. We must think carefully about who is an enemy and who can bring peace. Please calm down so that we can talk about what has happened. If the Longcoats have captured Nectowance, we must talk and plan, not shout and fight." His voice had a calming edge, cutting into the panic that was threatening common sense. "We must act quickly, but we must not act rashly."

Askook, a presence as significant as a mountain, would not be easily appeased. He stood his ground, eyes staring, nostrils flaring. "You cannot trust Longcoats, Kokee; you should know that by now. Think of how your father was cut down in cold blood as your mother was carted away to be beaten and raped by them. This man is the result of that rape, be assured of that. And when you stand up for him, you stand up for those who have blood on their hands."

Thomas started to tremble. The words were like a punch to his solar plexus: he was not born as a result of violence meted out to his mother. It was all lies. John Rolfe was his father and a loving husband to Pocahontas. He knew that this man was intent on demonizing him for his own ends, and that in the heat of the moment, words are cast like arrows to wound.

But it appeared that something had gone wrong if a Powhatan had been taken prisoner. He had been gone longer than expected, and Lizzie must have raised the alarm. He could lay no blame at her door. She was a child, alone and frightened. The colonists only had his best interests at heart. It was his own fault. He should have gone when he had the chance to prevent misunderstandings.

Thomas stood up and looked at Kokee; his face showed the emotions of the unfolding drama. "I must go back and right this wrong. I cannot let relations deteriorate because of me. I will see that Nectowance is set free."

He turned to address Askook with pleading eyes. "Please do not send warriors to fight. That would guarantee bloodshed. I understand

A Proposition

your hatred of me, but surely you must see that what I say makes sense. Trust me, and if you allow me to go now, and Nectowance does not return by sundown tomorrow, you can take matters into your own hands." His heart was beating. He could cause war or prolong peace, depending on what happened next.

Askook looked at Kokee, his nose in the air. "I do not trust this lying Longcoat. They are all the same," he hissed, scowling. "I will go and find Opechancanough; he must decide." He glared at Thomas, his body rigid with hate.

Kokee started to speak. "Askook—" But before he could get the words out, Nikkiti, the most petite person in the yehakin, rose, her face red with anger. All focus was on her as her energy filled the room. The two greyhounds stood, both on alert, their hackles raised, reflecting the angst of their mistress.

"I will not have it!" she screamed. "Askook! My brother is in danger, and you are squabbling. Kokee, do not listen to this cockerel crowing." She turned to look at Thomas, her large brown eyes flashing. "Nectowance is my beloved brother, Thomas. There is no time to be lost; you must go now."

She then looked back at Kokee and Askook. "I will speak for Opechancanough. We do not have time to consult with him; we must take immediate action. My brother's life is at stake. For the love of the gods, you are supposed to be warriors!

"Thomas, leave Waba here with me, and when you return to us, as I know you will, she and I will be waiting for you." She looked around the room, staring at the Powhatan warriors, daring them to challenge her authority.

They stood like statues; all eyes were trained on the small figure in the middle of the tepee who had taken control. The grown men trained to kill had been silenced like small children being rebuked for a misdemeanour.

Satisfied that her instructions were accepted, she bowed her head and raised her hands to her heart, looking at Thomas from under her long dark lashes, her gentleness returned. "May the gods be with you, Thomas. Bring yourself and my brother back to me," she whispered. Then she turned and walked towards the door with her head held high.

Thomas watched her small frame leave the tepee. Power and presence surrounded her like an invisible force. He stared in wide-eyed wonder as the two greyhounds pranced gracefully behind her.

Twenty-Four

Rescue

He had made a deal with Askook. He would return Nectowance by tomorrow, and there would be no more fighting. Was this possible? It had to be. The consequences of his failure were too catastrophic to contemplate. Why had he stayed with Kokee so long? It had been thoughtless, but he was seduced by the welcome the Powhatans had given him. Maybe someone had witnessed his capture and thought he was in danger.

His knee was still throbbing, but the pain was secondary to his need to act fast. Kokee helped him to mount his horse by forming a stirrup with his hands and then reached up to shake his hand, his face earnest with encouragement. "The gods are with you, Brother. I know you can do this."

Thomas nodded, with eyebrows drawn. "I will do my best not to disappoint you, Kokee. Maybe this can be the recommencement of the peace that our mother worked so hard to find."

"When this is over, we will talk again. But for now, I will accompany you through the forest to the outskirts of Jamestown. You will never find your way alone once it gets dark." He looked over his shoulder. "Can someone get my horse?"

Askook pushed himself forward. "No, Kokee, that will not work. They may kidnap you, and then where would we be? Besides, Rowtag is the best marksman we have, and he should accompany Thomas."

Kokee looked at Rowtag. "I would rather go myself, but Askook makes a good point. Can you do this, Rowtag? Take him only to within sight of the palisade. He can find his way from there on his own. We do not want to provoke another kidnapping."

Rowtag stood head and shoulders above the other warriors. He was strong and fierce. "I will do my duty, Kokee," he replied.

"Someone get Rowtag's horse," shouted Kokee.

Askook disappeared, returning a few minutes later with a black stallion that snorted and pawed the ground, ready for action.

Rowtag jumped on the horse and took control of the powerful beast, kicking him forward with his arm in the air and shouting a war cry.

Kokee slapped Thomas's horse on the rump to get him started. "To our next meeting, my brother!"

Thomas was propelled forward, following Rowtag. He looked back at the group of Powhatans watching him leave. He had come here believing his enemy had kidnapped him, and he was left feeling his Powhatan roots tugging at his heartstrings.

Meeting Nikkiti further complicated his newly found world, and he was sorry that she was nowhere to be seen as he left. Then suddenly, she appeared, her deceptively delicate frame flanked by the two dogs. She looked at him, her face solemn but her eyes twinkling. He stopped momentarily, imprinting her image on his mind, then nodded at her, turned, and spurred his horse on, following Rowtag.

Rescue

It was late afternoon and the sun was starting to dip in the sky. Jamestown was many miles away, and although Thomas could tell the direction he needed to go from the sun, the sun was going down, and he was unfamiliar with the terrain. He followed Rowtag for two hours in silence as it got darker and darker. The temperature dropped, and the horses' breath became like smoke from dragons. Thomas was frantic and frustrated that they were not covering more ground. Rowtag appeared unperturbed, as though he were on a pleasure jaunt instead of a mission of life and death.

Thomas could take no more. He spurred his horse on until he was neck and neck with Rowtag.

He shouted at him. "We need to move faster." Rowtag looked in the other direction as if he'd not heard. Thomas screeched at the top of his lungs. "Rowtag, we must make haste."

Rowtag smiled. "Do not worry, my friend. It is better that we do not tire the horses. I have carefully planned the route; you must leave it to me." He turned away, and his horse seemed to be going even slower than before.

It then dawned on Thomas. He recalled Askook's words: "This man is our enemy." The hatred on his face had been undeniable. It was a look he had experienced many times. This man must be one of Askook's allies. He had been chosen to accompany Thomas as he was a strong warrior, but it was becoming evident that there was another agenda. Thomas had thought nothing of it then, but now it was becoming apparent. They did not want him to release Nectowance; they wanted him to fail. Was Rowtag even leading him in the right direction? The sun had gone down, and clouds obscured the stars, and in this very foreign part of the world, Thomas did not have the knowledge to navigate with any degree of accuracy. They could have been going around in circles for all he knew. He could feel the panic rising from the pit of his stomach. If his gut feeling was correct, he was helpless.

At that moment, the silence of the wooded path was broken by the haunting cry of a wolf. The dangers these beautiful but deadly creatures posed to man in this part of the world were a constant fear to all communities. Thomas thought back to the mauled body of his poor, innocent stepmother. So frightened were the colonists of these beasts that killing one earned a week's wages.

All thoughts vanished when he heard Rowtag chuckle. "Ah, they have come at last. I have been waiting for them," his voice almost cheerful.

"What do you mean, Rowtag?" Thomas asked, his voice full of urgency.

No answer was given. Instead, Rowtag looked over his shoulder and dug his heels into the stallion's flanks. Throwing his fist in the air, he galloped away, his long hair streaming behind him as he disappeared into the night.

Thomas stared into the emptiness, his breath quickening as the reality of his situation started to take hold. He was alone. The dark silence was broken only by the sinister sounds of howling wolves. Shadows flickered on the ground as the silhouettes of the trees in the wind jumped to and fro like ghouls.

As he pondered, out of the darkness, . . . a gunshot. Rowtag must have stolen a gun.

Thomas threw himself flat on the saddle and spurred the horse towards the shelter of a group of trees. Then, too soon, *bang*—another shot. He felt the full force of the bullet as it thumped into his shoulder. Initially, he thought it was just a flesh wound. As he moved his hand toward the center of discomfort, he realized with surprise that the bullet was deeply embedded and close to his heart. Close, but thankfully not fatally so.

The pain started with a gradual crescendo. It seared through him

Rescue

like he had been stabbed with a red-hot poker. He cried out in agony, squeezing his eyes shut and biting his lip as he felt the blood run down his back. He eased himself down from the horse. As he slumped on the ground, his injured knee gave way, and he ended up lying helpless, face down, the bullet searing his bloodied flesh.

He pulled at the vegetation, crawling towards a large tree for protection, and closed his eyes for a second, trying to catch his breath.

He lay almost unconscious for what seemed like hours but was only minutes. When he opened his eyes, he saw the corner of Rowtag's feather headdress and red war paint.

He heard Rowtag riding towards him and stopping inches from his body. Thomas kept his eyes closed and held his breath, waiting for another shot to end the pain. He prayed that playing dead might fool his murderer.

"Ah, I see the bullet has made its mark. It is good that they sent their best marksman to 'protect' you." He laughed. "May the gods piss on your grave, Longcoat. Good riddance to your soul. The wolves will destroy any evidence, so I hope you are more tasty than you look!" Thomas felt large globules of warm spit landing on his face, dripping down his cheek. Rowtag chuckled again. *Job done.* He looked back over his shoulder. "Askook sends his regards," he hollered into the blackness of the night. The wolves howled. "Enjoy the feast!" he cried.

Rowtag rode into the trees and was met by his accomplice.

"Are you sure he is dead?" he asked.

"The bullet hit his heart, I saw the blood . . . and now he is a feast for the hungry ones."

Askook smiled. "Our job is done. We will never have a filthy Longcoat as our leader."

***

The bullet wound was like fire burning into his flesh. He gritted his teeth and took a large breath. The world swirled around him as pain engulfed him, blood oozing from the hole in his chest. He heard the howling of the wolf pack as it smelled his blood. Was this how it was all going to end? He blacked out.

Twenty-Five

Dark Mission

It had been hours since Rowtag had left with Thomas, and there had been no word.

As night descended, there was still no word. Nikkiti sat in the yehakin, listening for the sound of horses returning.

Then she heard them. Two horses arriving together. She jumped up, eager to be reunited with her brother. Her feelings were dashed when she turned the corner, full of joyful anticipation.

Askook and Rowtag. They were laughing and whispering. She could not make out what they were saying, but they were obviously pleased with themselves. Why were they skulking around like naughty children?

She ran over to them. "Askook, where is Nectowance? You are pleased with something"—she looked around—"but I do not see my brother..."

She turned to look up at Rowtag, who was still on his horse. "Rowtag, did Thomas get to Jamestown?" She looked up at him, eyes wide, grabbing the horse's head collar to slow him down.

Rowtag looked at her and smiled, saying nothing, pulling his horse away.

"What happened? Did Thomas get to Jamestown? Where is Nectowance?" She was breathless, brows drawn.

Askook looked into the distance as if distracted. "Thomas? Oh, you mean the filthy Longcoat," he muttered.

He stopped his horse and looked at her, his demeanor transforming as aggression crept behind his steely stare. "You stupid squaw. Rowtag did what he was told and set Thomas on the right path. What more do you expect?" He urged his pony on, looking away from her.

She called to him as she ran alongside him. "Why were you with Rowtag? He went alone . . . he did not need you to help him. It seems a bit strange . . ." Her voice began to waiver.

He turned the horse around and faced her, his eyebrows drawn. "I thought he was being a long time, and I went to make sure he did not need any assistance." He rolled his eyes and shrugged his shoulders. "For the love of the gods, why all the questions, Nikkiti?"

She put her hands on her hips. "How can you possibly ask a question like that? You know what is at stake here. My brother's life is in danger, and our relationship with the Longcoats is at risk of breaking down should anything happen to Thomas." Dainty though she was, her voice crescendoed with the force of her urgency.

Rowtag looked at the two of them. "I am going to get something to eat. You sort her out, Askook; I cannot be bothered with her whining." He jumped off his horse and walked over to the stables.

Askook dismounted, swaggering toward Nikkiti, his face darkened. "You must trust in the gods as you have been taught. They will do what is necessary." He looked her squarely in the eyes, his face too close for comfort. "Your brother will be back to you in due course."

She pulled back, a very bad feeling creeping into her stomach. "Askook, I know you, and I know from the way you are behaving that something is going on. Is Thomas safe? If you have harmed him, there will be dire consequences."

He looked at her defensively. "I did not do anything wrong." he kicked a stone into the bushes, looking to see where it had gone. "Thomas will be in Jamestown now, and Nectowance will be released as planned." There was guilt on his face, and Nikkiti could see it as plain as day.

"I do not believe you, Askook. Something is going on," she said.

Askook's demeanor changed to that of a defiant child. "I don't know what you're talking about. You swan around here, a whore to the son of Pocahontas, acting like you are better than the rest of us when we all know you're a Longcoat lover. But your plans for your Longcoat friend will never happen now, so stop moaning."

He stomped towards her, his face contorted in anger. She looked around for help, but no one was in sight.

He reached out to grab her. When she darted out of the way, his eyes became hard, his temples throbbed. She knew she had gone too far. She knew that his mood could change at the slightest provocation. The Askook that pulled wings off butterflies for fun was never far from the surface.

It took a will of iron for her not to give in to the rolling anxiety in her gut as she stood her ground.

She had to protect herself. It was no good running; he was almost on her.

"I have had enough of you talking down to me!" he shouted. He was insane. He was out of control.

"No Askook!" she cried, pulling a dagger from the belt of her tunic. "Keep away from me!"

The steel in his eyes dimmed for a split second before his anger was reignited, and he barred his teeth, pausing before he thrust forward and wrenched the knife from her. He rammed the blade against her throat.

The intense pain took her by surprise as the sharp edge of the knife started to cut into her flesh. Droplets of red trickled onto her tunic. His hand was shaking with rage. His demons were back.

"Askook," she whispered. "Askook, you are hurting me. Askook, we are friends . . . remember? You don't want to hurt your Nikkiti, do you?"

His hand gradually stopped shaking, and after a few seconds, he moved the knife, but only a hairsbreadth from her throat.

She could not trust that his sanity had wholly returned, and the knife was still very close to her neck. A wrong move and she would be dead.

She whispered, "It's alright; I won't ask any more about Thomas. I know you have not done anything. I was wrong." She forced her voice to be soft and soothing, at odds with the pulsing terror that inhabited every pore. She had to talk him down, say anything to break his madness. She had seen traces of his insanity before, but never to this extent.

He lowered his hand and looked at the knife as if he had never seen it before.

"Askook, give me the knife," she commanded, morphing from softness to authority as a loving mother to a wayward child. She held out her hand.

He paused and dutifully handed her the knife, looking at her with large, watery eyes. She threw the knife well out of reach and stood away from him. She put her fingers up to her neck, and when she looked at them, they were covered with blood. She shuddered to think of what would have happened if he had not responded to her words.

Something was very wrong.

***

The woods were familiar territory that held many dangers. Her instinct was to follow the route from the village to Jamestown—that was the obvious. It was not easy, though. Dusk made even the landmarks she had known since childhood difficult to decipher, and she had taken wrong turns several times.

"Thomas!" she shouted. "Thomas, are you there?"

Her heart was beating fast. Maybe this was a wild goose chase. Maybe Thomas was safely in Jamestown and Nectowance on his way home. She doubted it enough to continue her search. In her gut, she knew something was amiss.

The moon was high in the sky now, throwing eerie shadows in the inky blackness of her path. The rustle of wind in the trees and owls hooting and diving for rodents made her grimace. Even more disconcerting was the sound of howling wolves. She imagined them circling their prey, and she touched the knife that was secured to her belt. Of all the dangers for humans of any race, the wolves were the greatest.

On and on she traveled, her horse stumbling over protruding tree roots. Shapes of shy night creatures floated by, disappearing into the night, rustling through dry leaves.

"Thomas!" she shouted. "Thomas, where are you?" She shivered as the chill wind seeped through her warm fur mantle, her toes like icicles in her thin suede moccasins.

It was no good. It had been hours. The blackness of the night had hidden Thomas from her. Her heart was sore. She looked up at the moon, watching the clouds skidding past its glowing form like galloping horses. The forest was too vast, and the night had become too dense. He could be anywhere. Askook had revealed nothing, and to push him further could have reignited his demons.

Her heart sank as she turned her horse around, finally accepting that her mission was fruitless.

Then she saw the badger.

***

She knew Badger was from the spirit world. His small dark eyes shone in the moonlight, imploring her to follow him. He disappeared into the tunnel of dark trees, and she followed a tangled path that she would never have found without help from the spirit world.

Twenty-Six

Saviour

He had lain for several hours listening to the wolves on their nightly quest for food, knowing it was only a matter of time before they came for him. The blood oozing from his shoulder drained life and energy from his body as it fed the earth, and he accepted his fate.

Thomas was fading out of conscious reality into the spirit world of his ancestors as his eyes closed.

Two golden eyes appeared. They were a warm glow that stood out from the darkness of the swirling mists. Surrounding the face was a mantle of the softest gray fur flecked with white. Ears erect, affection was etched on his lupine visage as his agile body snaked towards Thomas.

Thomas could feel his heart melting and his body relaxing as he was compelled to put his hand out in welcome, stroking Naantam's coat, then wrapping his arms around his neck, resting his cheek in the dense coat. He felt the gentle lick from a soft pink tongue on his face. Like a tiny infant in his mother's arms, his eyes were closing, and for now, he needed nothing more from the universe.

Twenty-Seven

Back From A Dream

His senses were jolted from the warmth of Naantam's fur to the cold of the night air.

He knew he was not alone as someone touched his cheek. He opened his eyes, disoriented, clutching at a hand, eyes wild, looking from side to side, trying to focus, trying to remember where he was.

He saw the wolf in the distance bow his head and quietly slip away, his duty done, leaving his charge in the hands of another.

Thomas was transfixed by his noble stature. He instinctively knew that the creature had saved his life, keeping him warm and safe.

Nikkiti crouched down beside him. "Thomas, my dear Thomas, where are you hurt?"

Thomas rubbed his eyes, still trying to piece together his surroundings as context for what had happened to him. This time, the long dark hair and the beautiful face did not belong to his mother. She was not a vision; she was the girl with the greyhounds, Nikkiti. He closed his eyes, taking a moment to find words. Why was she here? Where was Rowtag?

He raised his head briefly to look at her. "Why are you here? It is dangerous . . . I don't know what has happened . . ." He felt the burning pain. "My shoulder is bleeding . . . someone shot at me . . ." He drifted in and out of consciousness.

As he came round, an image came to his mind. "Nikkiti, did you see the wolf? He saved me." He squeezed his eyes shut, remembering the terror. He let his head fall back, looking up at the trees. "I thought he was going to kill me . . . but instead, he befriended me." He smiled despite the searing pain in his shoulder. He looked at her. "How could that be?"

"That was no ordinary wolf. That was the spirit of Naantam. You are honored. Only those of Powhatan blood can see Naantam. He came to you as the beloved son of Pocahontas."

Thomas looked into the darkness. He started to shake.

"You are shivering. Let me look at your wound." She crouched down and gently pulled his clothing away. "Luckily, the bullet just missed your heart—it is near your shoulder, and the bullet has gone straight through. The bleeding has stopped. We must be careful you don't move too much, as it will start the bleeding again, and you have already lost a lot of blood." She packed the wound with a torn cloth she had on her horse and bound it with rags.

"Here, wrap this blanket around you; we do not want the cold night air to undo the good work that Naantam has begun."

Thomas huddled under the blanket for a moment. Then he shook it off and tried to stand. He got as far as his knees, wobbled, and fell, cursing as he hit the ground. He held his shoulder as he gasped with pain. "We must get to Jamestown, Nikkiti," he spluttered. "You have to help me get your brother released before Askook convinces

Opechancanough to attack Jamestown." He was breathless and closed his eyes momentarily, trying to regain his strength.

She knelt in front of him, gently holding his shoulders and looking straight into his eyes. "Thomas, we will not make it if we try to go now. We must rest for a bit and make sure your bleeding has stopped. The way to Jamestown from here is very hazardous—Rowtag brought you through difficult terrain. I can navigate it, but it will not be easy. It is better to wait until the morning comes. I will make a fire to keep us warm, and in the morning, we will try and get you onto my horse."

Thomas watched her as she gathered a few twigs and windfall logs to make a fire. She rubbed sticks to create a spark, and the flames started to appear from the smoldering pile in no time.

She sat beside him, her flawless face illuminated with the fire's golden light that danced in their surroundings' cold darkness. He looked at her, his face stricken. "Rowtag tried to kill me, Nikkiti."

She shook her head. "I am so sorry, Thomas. I think Askook is the one behind it. Rowtag, although a very good and strong warrior, is a weak man. He is easily led. I think he was taking instructions from Askook. Askook is angry and very jealous of your good relationship with Opechancanough and Kokee. He believes the Longcoats have come to destroy our people, and he sees you as one of them. He must have convinced Rowtag to make sure you did not reach Jamestown."

"But I would never do anything to hurt my own mother's people."

"Our people have been at war for so many years, Thomas. Powhatans killed your father and have done some treacherous things in this war. Some might think it would be difficult for you to forgive such acts."

He looked at the ground, shaking his head. "My heart is torn in two. When I saw Joan mauled and broken, and I assumed it was your people, my heart was filled with hate. Then I met your father, and he told me the truth. I was ashamed of my thoughts. When I met my brother, I felt elated to be with another son of my mother. And when I met you . . ." he faltered, looking at her, willing her to connect with him, ". . . I felt that I belonged."

She lowered her eyes.

"You do belong. Opechancanough has seen you in his visions. He sees you as our leader, Thomas. He wanted you to stay with us and to take your rightful place amongst us. He was going to talk to you after you had spoken to Kokee, but events overtook us."

Thomas stared at her. He had never been important. He had never been respected. He had no words. He shut his eyes. Visions of his mother mingled with Naantam, and floated in front of his eyes. He was Powhatan, of that there was no doubt.

"Thomas, the Gods will guide you." She smiled at him.

He took her hand. "We must get to Jamestown, Nikkiti. Your words humble me, but my first duty to my Powhatan family must be to achieve the release of your brother. I cannot think of anything else until that is done."

"You must sleep now, my Powhatan cousin. There is no point in trying to make the journey now. It is better to wait and make sure you have the strength," she said. "I will lie next to you for warmth." She pulled a blanket around herself and laid her back against him.

He felt her body solid and warm, her heat radiating through him. His tension started to melt away. Despite the circumstances, he could not stop smiling as he imagined being with her forever. A friend... a good friend, and maybe more?

Then he remembered the words he had spoken to Joan and Lizzie not so long ago. He remembered their kindness. He remembered Joan's father sponsoring his passage to Jamestown, the acceptance and love he had been given, and the promises he had made.

He remembered Jane.

He once again felt cold.

Twenty-Eight

Back On The Road

The milky sun peeped through the early morning mist as Thomas woke. He looked around, blurry-eyed and uncomfortable from lying on the hard ground. The sun was starting to rise, but it was still cold. The fire had long since gone out, leaving only charred remains. He pulled the blanket tighter around him. Nikkiti was nowhere to be seen, but the pony was tethered nearby, snorting and pawing the ground in frustration. He knew she could not be far away, but her absence unsettled him. They were miles from the Jamestown settlement in a place fraught with danger and uncertainty.

His shoulder throbbed, and his knee ached, and the fitful sleep had given him scant energy to focus on the task ahead. He scanned the trees, trying to see where Nikkiti had gone. Within a few moments, he saw her with a folded blanket full of berries, dodging the undergrowth as she walked towards him, and he sighed with undisguised relief.

She smiled. "There is not much left at this time of year, but something is better than nothing, and we must have fuel in our stomachs before we face Jamestown." She put the blanket in front of him and sat down on a protruding root opposite, taking a berry and pointing at him to do the same.

He took a berry and nibbled it. Then he looked at her, his head on one side. "It was dangerous coming to find me in the dark. Why did you take such a risk? You hardly know me."

She looked at the ground. "I know you are a good man. When I saw Askook and Rowtag coming back laughing, my instincts told me things were not right. I could not waste time thinking about what to do. You, Nectowance, and potentially the future of the tribe were at stake. At the same time, I could not be sure things had gone wrong, so I did not want to alert Kokee, as he would have lost his mind with worry and gathered a whole army to find you. War would have been a certainty."

"You are brave, Nikkiti."

She shook her head. "Not brave. I live with fear as my bedfellow, so if I avoid it, I avoid life itself." Her eyes were soft as she looked at a berry before putting it in her mouth.

Thomas paused, uncertain. "I have been waiting for so long to come here, and the reality is so different from my dreams."

She looked at him as if her life depended on him. "We have waited so long for the legacy of Pocahontas to continue . . . and it is my calling to ensure her son takes his rightful place among us."

His face reflected the churning panic in his stomach. "I had not realized the expectations of me." He looked at his feet. "What if I am not the man you have dreamt of? What if I fail?" His eyes met hers.

"You and I are only instruments of the gods. Wise men know this. The universe determines our destiny. Allow yourself to be yourself;

all will be as it should be."

He looked down again. "Perhaps. But that suggests we have no free will . . . no choices, no responsibility for what we do. The gods take the responsibility. If that were the case, Askook could claim the gods told him to kill me and would remain innocent of a crime."

She smiled. "Maybe it is the gods that determine our free will. Maybe the gods wanted Askook to try to kill you because it was part of a greater plan. Maybe the gods decided that we were meant to be here, together at this moment, because what we do now determines what happens next in their greater plan." Her eyebrows were drawn.

Thomas sighed. "You and I could talk for hours, Nikkiti, and never find the answers. Whoever is guiding us has given us an immense responsibility. We must go as soon as possible."

She nodded. "Yes, you are right. Hopefully, we will have a lifetime to debate the way of the world." She frowned. "We will go, but you must ride on the horse because of your injuries."

It was against all his principles, but he knew she was right. He would never make it otherwise.

She walked towards him, putting her hand out. "Let me help you get on the horse. It will be too difficult for you to do it alone."

He shook his head. "No, thank you. I can manage it. I feel much better," he said with an air of confidence.

He limped towards the horse and paused, catching his breath. Then, bracing himself, he stood on his good leg and jumped, trying to throw his bad leg across the horse's back. He couldn't get high enough, and he fell in a heap, red-faced, cursing his disability. He got up from the ground, holding his shoulder, and tried again. Again he fell, calling out in agony as he did so.

She walked over, concern on her face. "Are you alright?" she asked.

"No, but I'll live," he admitted.

She sighed. "You do not have to prove anything, Thomas. We will be here all day if you insist on doing it yourself," she said, raising her eyebrows, trying to hide the smile that lay behind her eyes.

He nodded, looking at the ground. He knew she was right, but his pride was the part of him that had suffered the most. He visualized the scene, and it dawned on him how ridiculous he must look. A smile crept onto his face. She rolled her eyes and reached for his hand, giving it a comforting squeeze.

He tried again. This time, he allowed her to give him the shove he needed to finally land on the horse's back.

He looked down at her. "Thank you," he whispered under his breath.

She laughed. "One day, you will realize that not all girls are delicate flowers that must be impressed like your fancy Longcoat women!" She walked before the horse, leading the way as if she were a tiny commander in chief.

He was lost for words as his admiration grew.

Twenty-Nine

Friends Or Foe

The palisade was in the distance and Thomas could see the soldiers patrolling back and forth with their rifles at the ready. His suspected kidnapping must have put Jamestown on high alert, as there were many more guarding the town than usual.

He stopped the pony and signaled to Nikkiti to retreat. "They might think we are a Powhatan war patrol," he whispered. He pointed to a dense area of the forest. "Let us hide in the trees while I think this through."

She turned and followed him, glancing back at the palisade.

They sheltered behind the trees for a few moments. "You must take the horse and escape while you can; it looks dangerous. I can manage from here," he whispered.

Before she could respond, they heard a commotion behind them.

Turning, they saw a unit of British soldiers standing with their guns pointing straight at them, menace on their faces. "Do not move, you filthy heathens!" shouted the commander.

"Sir!" Thomas shouted. "I am English. My name is Thomas Rolfe."

"English? You don't look English. You have an Indian pony, your skin is dark, and you are traveling with a squaw. All of that adds up to only one thing in my eyes."

Thomas's heart sank, but he insisted, "Look at my clothes. I speak perfect English. My father was John Rolfe, one of the founding fathers of Jamestown."

"I have no knowledge of the son of John Rolfe. All I know is you filthy heathens have to be kept off our land," the commander shouted. "Get off your horse and lie flat on the ground." He looked at Nikkiti. "You too, you heathen whore," he spat.

Thomas looked at the man. A career soldier, red in the face from last night's ale and a one-track mind with no room for intelligent thought. He had been told to arrest Powhatans, and arrest Powhatans was what he would do.

Thomas gingerly threw his leg over the horse, edging himself gently to the ground, gritting his teeth as his injured leg made contact with the hard rubble, and his chest wound throbbed.

He looked over at Nikkiti, who was a stone's throw away. She was watching, eyes wide, uncertainty on her lovely face. He was powerless to protect her. He signaled for her to lie on the ground. This zealot was not going to deviate from the instructions he had been given, and his ruthless insensitivity was plain to see, so for now, the safest way was to be compliant.

The commander turned his attention to Nikkiti. "Tie the bitch's hands, Private Green; we don't want our prize escaping," he barked. A scrawny lad blinked and jumped to attention, wandering over to Nikkiti with a length of rope.

Thomas saw her face change. Rage emanated from her every pore.

He tensed with apprehension. What would she do? He had seen her in action and knew injustice was her catalyst for revolt.

As the unsuspecting lad reached to grab, what he thought, was a weak and compliant squaw, she launched herself at him, slapping him on the face and kicking him between the legs. He screamed out in agony and fell to the ground, clutching his groin. "You heathen whore!" he cried.

Nikkiti took her chance and started running, dodging the soldiers as she went. She was young, lithe and spritely, and her limbs moved like a gazelle, but there were too many soldiers. They formed a large circle around her, blocking her escape route in every direction. She halted as she realized her fate, falling on her knees, her face red with emotion and her teeth gritted like a rabid dog. She looked at them one by one, her eyes boring into them, daring them to approach her. They shuffled their feet, looking away, hoping someone else would take the initiative.

"For God's sake," cried the commander, stunned in disbelief. "She is a tiny little squaw. Will one of you lily-livered cowards please put a rope around her hands?"

They glanced at Private Green, who was still holding his groin, his eyes squeezed tight with the throbbing pain inflicted by this little fireball of a squaw. Who would be next to put himself in the sights of this small girl with a large sting?

At last, one of the soldiers decided to make a name for himself and tentatively sidled up to Nikkiti as if he were approaching a mad dog.

She faced him head-on with a thunderous expression. He tensed, gritted his teeth and grabbed for her arms. She kicked and punched like a prize fighter. Another soldier came to the aid of the first, and they could not get her still long enough to tie her arms. It took another two soldiers to finally hold her arms and legs and pin her down, binding her arms behind her back. She screamed and wriggled, spitting at them like a wild beast.

When she was securely bound hand and foot and could not be a danger, the commander ventured forward to look at her.

"For the love of God, be quiet, you filthy little animal!" he shouted.

She stopped for a moment, looking at him with contempt. When he leaned down to look at her, she spat in his face with full force. He paused, wiping the spit from his chin, and glared with his face contorted with hatred.

He pulled back his arm and punched her in the face with such force that she was propelled backwards, knocking her head to the ground. "How dare you! You heathen bitch," he snarled through gritted teeth.

She lay motionless.

Thomas's hands were tied, but he lurched forward, straining against the two soldiers who held him in a viselike grip. Terror crept onto their faces as the consequences of Thomas's escape became a possibility, and they held him tighter.

"Nikkiti, Nikkiti!" Thomas screamed in distress. She was so small and delicate, lying like a rag doll on the ground. He used his elbows to try to ram his way forward. Still, despite winding a few of the soldiers, there were replacements aplenty, and he accepted defeat, never taking his eyes off the unconscious Nikkiti.

Gradually, her eyes opened, and Thomas breathed a sigh of relief. She struggled to sit up and looked around bleary-eyed at the circle of soldiers. They were watching, grinning and smirking, happy that this violent little squaw who had revealed them as cowards had been shown a well-deserved lesson.

Thirty

Whose Side Are You On?

He had felt the humiliation of racism many times, but never to this extent. The ignorant soldiers believed him to be a Powhatan warrior, and no amount of protestations would alter their perception. He was treated like an animal.

Despite his lack of understanding of the situation, the commander did recognise that Thomas could not walk to Jamestown. A live Powhatan warrior would garner more recognition than a dead one, so Thomas was thrown unceremoniously back onto a horse. No care was taken as he cried out in agony; even a dog would have received more gentle handling. Nikkiti followed behind, hands tied, surrounded by smirking soldiers making uncouth suggestions about what they would like to do to her. Her nose was covered in dried blood, a nasty bruise covered half of her face, and her hair was matted with mud.

The palisade gates were opened, and after walking for a while, they eventually entered the gates of the town itself. Rumors were rife about the capture of Powhatans, and the streets were lined with hecklers. Thomas saw the look of hate on the faces of people he had only seen a few days before as fellow colonists. No one recognized him. Out of context, they did not realize who he was. They believed that these bastards had captured Thomas Rolfe, and they wanted blood.

This was what it was like to be Powhatan.

Thomas had to be half carried into the military headquarters and dumped in a small room with Nikkiti. His body was wracked with the pain of the gunshot wound and his throbbing knee. He had to receive medical attention soon, or he would start to deteriorate.

Nikkiti was silent. Her tiny body was bruised with the punches and kicks she had received, but her eyes still held the defiance and spirit of the daughter of Opechancanough. She sat next to Thomas, resting her head on his arm.

The door was flung open. Standing before them was Sir George Fitzgerald, accompanied by two shuffling companions. He looked at the disheveled figures huddling before him, and Thomas could see his face blanching as recognition filtered into his consciousness.

"Good Lord, Sergeant Cartwright—this is Thomas Rolfe! What the blazes is he doing incarcerated? It looks like *we* have kidnapped him, not the blasted Powhatans . . . What a bloody fiasco!"

Cartwright's face fell, the expectation of a pat on the back snuffed out. "Sir," he said, his face turning bright red, "we captured him sneaking up to the palisade with a squaw . . . a filthy heathen spy," he said.

"You imbecile! Get Rolfe out of here and get him some medical attention now!"

Sgt. Cartwright jumped forward, and Thomas found himself clumsily pulled up, only to fall heavily down again as Cartwright was too weak to hold him on his own.

Eventually, aided by several soldiers, Thomas was taken for medical attention. He had a hot meal and some ale and found himself seated in a chair in front of Sir George Fitzgerald.

Since his previous disastrous meeting with Fitzgerald, Thomas had had nothing to do with the pompous wife beater. There was no love lost between the two of them, and now Thomas was at his mercy. He gritted his teeth waiting for confrontation.

Sir George looked down his nose at Thomas without a hint of warmth. "What the bloody hell is going on, Rolfe? Captain Pierce assured me there was no foundation to rumors that you are a Powhatan sympathizer. We even retaliated on your behalf when your sister reported you kidnapped." He sat back in his chair, taking a deep breath. "Quite honestly, when you show up with a Powhatan whore, sneaking around the gates, it is no wonder you were arrested as a spy. Considering your background, I am considering banging you up with the other two and hanging you all as an example."

Thomas sat stunned into silence. There was little chance that Fitzgerald would let him off the hook. He was not frightened of this bully, but he had to play his cards well to do minimal damage to the cause.

"Speak to me, Rolfe!" Fitzgerald yelled. "If you were kidnapped, then the two heathens we have in custody will be put to death. We cannot have Powhatans kidnapping our people willy-nilly and getting away with it. But if you went to their village of your own accord, we would have to think very carefully about your future in this colony. Your allegiances become even more questionable than they already are. We all know you are related to these damned people, Rolfe."

Thomas bit his lip. He had to outsmart this imbecile. If he told the truth, Nikkiti and Nectowance would be killed. He had to sacrifice himself for them. They kidnapped him to bestow on him the greatest of honors, but to reveal the real situation would make it even worse for him and them.

"You must release the two captive Powhatans at once. They are the daughter and son of the great Opechancanough himself. If you do not, you are in danger of starting hostilities like you have never seen before."

Fitzgerald leaned towards Thomas. "Do not tell me what I must do. Just answer my question . . . Were you or were you not kidnapped?" His face was red with hatred.

Thomas remained silent, both buying himself time, and deliberately taunting his adversary. Fitzgerald pulled back, glaring. "In the name of the king, whose side are you on, Rolfe?" he bellowed.

This was the question at the heart of Thomas's personal dilemma. Images of his sister Lizzie's look of trust and Jane's beautiful smile mixed with the respect and honor shown to him by Nikkiti and Kokee. He knew there was no simple answer to this question. He had the disadvantage of knowing the extraordinary richness of both cultures. He thought of the little lad with the carved animal, and he thought of Fitzgerald's own son.

The glaring and ignorant man staring at him demanded a straight answer, when there wasn't one, so he had to make something up. He could stall no longer.

"I went to the Powhatan camp of my own accord to meet with my uncle to try and forge peace. I saw a chance to end the constant random hostilities that plague us. My motives were honorable and were in the interests of the people of Jamestown. The Powhatans were not at fault in any way and should be released immediately."

Fitzgerald squeezed his eyes into little slits and looked at Thomas as if throwing daggers. "A likely story," he growled. "I don't believe you are the saint that Pierce thinks you are. There has been a shadow surrounding you from even before you set foot in Jamestown. My wife stood up for you, but she is a brainless woman and easily manipulated.

A dark cloud follows you. Wherever there are clouds, there is usually rain . . . and you, my friend, are soaking wet!"

Thomas was quiet for a few seconds, formulating his response and trying to put Fitzgerald's condescending reference to Sarah out of the equation. "Sir, I have done nothing other than attempt to make peace with the Powhatans. I had thought that my unique heritage could be an asset to this colony, and if used well, would progress our relationship with them to good advantage."

Fitzgerald put the tips of his fingers together and looked directly at Thomas. "Pah . . ." He spat. "Time will tell whose side you are actually on, Rolfe. Pierce's faith in you does not convince me. But because of his rank in this community, I must again bow to his opinion of you. However, keep in mind that I do not like you; I do not believe you are loyal to the colony, and I will be watching your every move."

He got up, and as he marched out of the room, he looked back. "If I have any more cause to doubt your loyalty to this colony, I will not hesitate to have you arrested and, if necessary, put to death—with or without the blessing of Lieutenant Governor Pierce."

Thomas stared after him, shaking his head.

Thirty-One

Release

Kokee saw them from a distance, riding into the Powhatan village: two people on one horse. He could not make out who they were. He ran towards them, and his face drained of color as he recognized them.

"Nikkiti! Nectowance!" he shouted. He was exhausted after a night of worrying about the safe return of Nectowance and the potential escalation of further hostilities with the Longcoats. But now he could see Nikkiti was with Nectowance, and she was in a terrible state. His heart stopped.

He rushed to the side of her pony. "Nikkiti . . . oh, Nikkiti . . . what has happened?" His brows were drawn, and his eyes stared with concern.

"Kokee, I had to go," she said.

He shook his head, concern still etched on his face. "What have you done? You are hurt. Nothing is worth that!" His words were like bullets as he tried to control his distress at seeing her this way. "Where is Rowtag? . . . And is Thomas safe?"

"You should ask Rowtag what happened; he could tell you the whole story," said Nectowance, his face grim.

"But I asked him last night, and he said Thomas had been delivered to Jamestown safely, and we should await your safe arrival in the morning."

Nectowance shook his head. "Rowtag was lying, Kokee," he said, jumping down from the pony and putting his hand out to help Nikkiti. "There has been treachery. Rowtag never intended to get Thomas to Jamestown. He is a traitor."

Kokee's face fell. "Where is that lying cur? What has happened to Thomas? Where is he?" He felt his stomach turn.

Nikkiti walked over and put her hand on his shoulder. "It worked out in the end, Kokee; Thomas is injured but safe . . . He is with his people, and maybe that is where he needs to stay, at least for a while, until he fully recovers." She looked up at Kokee and lifted her hand to his cheek with a gentle smile. "Nothing has changed," she said.

He looked deeply into her eyes and shook his head. "Nikkiti, I am glad he is safe, but I cannot bear that you have been hurt."

She turned to face him, taking both of his hands in hers. "Kokee, you cannot wrap me up like a child. There are things that must be done. I am fine. Just a few bruises."

Kokee leaned down and kissed her on the cheek. "Never do something like that again," he whispered.

She sighed. "I cannot promise that."

She turned away, looking for someone. "Where is Askook? I am sure he had something to do with Thomas's shooting as I saw him with Rowtag earlier . . . but we will never be able to prove it." Her face altered, stern disapproval in her eyes. "As for Rowtag, I expect he will be miles away by now."

"Shooting . . . you never said anything about shooting. Are you sure he is alright? There was panic on Kokee's face as he took both of her hands and looked into her eyes.

Nikkiti gave him a watery smile. "As I said, Kokee, it turned out alright in the end. Our plan will still go ahead, I am sure."

Kokee shook his head. "It is getting too dangerous, Nikkiti."

***

When Askook saw Nikkiti returning with Nectowance, he knew something must have gone wrong. Why would they release Nectowance if Thomas never got to Jamestown? He crouched down, listening to the conversation, and heard Nikkiti say, "It worked out alright in the end, Kokee; Thomas is injured but safe. He is with his people, and maybe that is where he needs to stay, at least for a while, until he fully recovers."

Askook swore under his breath. He had heard enough. He slinked away, panic in his gut, trying to think what he should do to rid himself of any blame. He ran to find Rowtag, who was grooming and feeding his pony.

"Rowtag, Nikkiti and Nectowance have returned, and Thomas is still alive. You must leave now!" he said in a loud whisper.

Rowtag's eyes opened wide. "What has Nikkiti to do with anything? And besides, Thomas is dead—I checked, I shot him, he was bleeding . . . He cannot be alive," he stuttered with disbelief in his eyes.

Askook grabbed him by the shoulders. "Well, you didn't check very well, did you? She knows that you tried to kill Thomas. She saved Thomas, and he will be able to tell everyone that you tried to kill him, so you're in big trouble."

Rowtag shook his head, shock on his face. "But I was sure Thomas was dead," he whispered. "The wolf pack was there . . . how could things go wrong?"

Askook sighed. "Thomas wasn't dead, believe me. The wolf pack didn't get him either. You stupid idiot, you should have made sure he was dead before leaving him!"

Rowtag stood tall and towered over Askook. He paused for a moment, assimilating the situation. "Askook, if I am in trouble, so are you. It was your idea." His mouth was agape with panic.

Askook drew back. "Well, I would not be so sure about that, Rowtag. No one saw me do anything. Nikkiti thinks I might have something to do with it, but she has no proof, and neither does Thomas."

Rowtag's face turned red with rage, finally seeing the overall picture. "You coward! You planned this all along. But you're forgetting one thing: I can tell them it was your idea. They would have no trouble believing me, as everyone knows how you feel about Thomas and the Longcoats. You've made that very clear."

Askook looked at Rowtag for a few seconds, nodding his head, his eyes full of innocence. "Yes, I hadn't thought of that. I suppose you're right. You could tell them, but what would be the point of that?"

He sauntered towards Rowtag, his face thoughtful as if giving due consideration to Rowtag's point.

He was as quick as lightning. Before Rowtag saw Askook's dagger, it had sunk up to the hilt into his heart. Rowtag's eyes opened wide with surprise as the blood spurted from his chest, pulsing out with the last dying beats of his heart. Blood trickled out of his mouth, and his eyes turned glassy and staring. One of the strongest warriors in the tribe fell to the ground like a giant tree cut down in the prime of life. A groan of pain left his lips as his life ebbed away.

Askook stood back, covered in splattered blood, and looked at his handiwork with a smile. "Well, you wanted to give the wolves a good feast . . . They will not be disappointed." He laughed.

He stopped for a moment, looking up at the sky as if addressing the stars. "I still have to finish off that half-breed Thomas Rolfe. We are warriors; we must fight for our land, not sleep in bed with an enemy! A Longcoat will never rule the Powhatan tribe!"

Thirty-Two

Best Friends

They were best friends. It didn't matter that he was only six years old and his companion was twenty-six. They'd had a bond since Chogun was a baby. Kokee had witnessed his tiny cousin turn from squalling infant to mischievous little friend, and his love for the lad had grown. Kokee had a natural affinity with children, which had blossomed into a wish to have his own children one day. His dearest hope was for a family to replace the one that had been torn from him.

He looked at his little friend.

Chogun smiled at him. "Who was that Longcoat that looked like you?" Chogun asked, his eyes twinkling as they collected wood for the fires.

Kokee smiled and kicked a stone through the trees. "Well, Chogun, that was my brother, Thomas." He looked down at his young nephew.

Chogun's eyes opened wide. "I did not know you had a brother, Kokee. So, if he is your brother, that means he must be my cousin?" His smile went from ear to ear.

"Well, he is a half brother . . . but yes, you could say he is your cousin."

"Did he like my carving? I thought he had kind eyes and I wanted to give him a present."

"Kokee ruffled Chogun's hair. "You are a kind person, Chogun."

Chogun looked at the ground, smiling with pride at having pleased his hero cousin. "What happened to your brother? He disappeared with Rowtag and never came back again. What was going on? You grown-ups were making noises yesterday. You were shouting at Nikkiti but hugging her, too. I don't understand."

"So full of questions today, my little friend! Well, I am not too sure what went on. Everyone is safe, though, and my brother is with his people. I hope he will come back soon."

He looked wistfully through the trees. He knew Thomas had survived after the ordeal with Rowtag, but Rowtag was still missing and had probably fled forever, knowing his wicked plan to kill Thomas was now well known. It could have ended very differently. The main thing was that Nikkiti was safe, and he trusted that his brother would return when the time was right for him. He shook himself back to the present. "Come on, my tiny warrior, we have to make sure we get enough wood for the fires, or your mother will be cross with us."

"Chogun noticed his thoughtful mood. "Will Thomas come and live with us?" he said as he picked up a large stick.

Kokee smiled. "We all hope he will . . . but it is very complicated."

"I don't think it is complicated. I think he should come and live with us. He could marry Nikkiti, and I could play with their babies, like you play with me."

"Oh, Chogun," he laughed, shaking his head. "I am glad you have

Best Friends

it all worked out." He picked up another large stick and put it in the sack. Chogun did not realize how close to the truth he was. Kokee sighed. He was pleased for his brother; he had to be . . .

The two of them continued stooping and picking up twigs, both lost in thought.

Time ticked on, and the silence between them was easy as they both ruminated on possibilities and dreams. Two dark shiny heads, one large and one small, bobbing up and down as the sacks of twigs got heavier.

Gradually, without noticing, their paths separated. Kokee was engulfed in a mirage of swirling thoughts: Thomas . . . Nikkiti . . . Longcoats . . . peace . . . war . . . twig into the bag . . . twig into the bag . . . He took no notice of where he was going.

Then suddenly, "No, no . . . help!" Chogun's piercing cries ricocheted through the trees.

Kokee froze, his heart racing as he realized the lad was out of sight and obviously in danger.

He ran toward the child's cries, stumbling over roots and branches, blindly pushing his way through the trees, desperate to reach his charge.

"Help, please, Kokee!"

Kokee could hardly see for the sweat running down his face.

He finally saw Chogun and stopped in his tracks.

Chogun was crouched on the ground in the fetal position, trying to make himself small. Around him was a pack of wolves, staring at their prey, salivating and growling.

Kokee held his breath, knowing he did not have time to ponder; he had to act, regardless of the danger to himself.

He threw a rock at one of the wolves to distract attention from Chogun. The rock hit the wolf full force, and it screeched. It turned and stared at Kokee, snarling, white fangs bared, lips quivering. The rest of the pack turned to look at the new, larger prey. Hackles raised, they slinked towards Kokee, away from Chogun. Their large teeth glistened with the saliva of anticipation.

"Chogun, run and climb that tree behind you," Kokee screamed as he edged backwards, staring into the alpha wolf's red eyes.

In the corner of his eye, he could see the rest of the pack, silent as cats, circling, their menacing growls mixing with the beating of his heart. He stood petrified. He had only one chance.

He dashed.

They sprang like lightning.

He reached the tree, and they were snarling and snapping at his heels. Their survival depended on food, and his on well-practiced climbing skills.

The tree was not his friend. It did not have branches to aid his assent, and he struggled up the trunk, grappling and scratching at the bark, pulling his legs up, clinging with his knees, and reaching up to find the lowest branch. He inched up, his fingers slipping, his muscles burning. He heard the wolf using all his might to jump at his hanging foot. He felt teeth like a vice on his foot, the sharp pain of ripping flesh.

One last life-or-death push, and he managed to grasp the first branch, wrenching his foot from the jaws of the aggressor. Despite the searing pain, he pulled himself to safety with all his strength.

He looked down at the disappointed wolves who were jumping with frustration, eyes glowing with excitement, tongues lolling and dripping.

They circled round and round, eyeing their prey, salivating with anticipation. After a while, dejected, they sloped into the trees.

He waited and waited. The pain in his foot throbbed with each heartbeat, and when he looked down, he was horrified to see part of his moccasin missing. On further inspection, two of his toes had also been torn off. The blood was pumping out of his foot. Trying to balance gingerly on the tree branch, he managed to tear a strip off his tunic and, with great difficulty, bind his bleeding foot.

He shouted through the trees. "Chogun, stay where you are. I will come and get you when I know it is safe."

The seconds ticked by . . . the minutes ticked by . . . the pain becoming intense, the cloth bandage saturating with his blood. He looked down, his eyes scanning his surroundings.

Had the wolves gone, or were they waiting in the trees for two morsels of human food to drop into their grumbling stomachs?

"Chogun?" he screamed. "Chogun? Are you still alright?"

"I am still up the tree, Kokee. I am very scared and very cold." His childlike voice was timid and whimpering. Kokee could not see him, but he could feel the child's terror.

"Do not worry, my little friend. It will be fine. Stay where you are, and I will come and get you very soon."

Kokee waited and waited. He saw no movement and decided the wolves must have gone to find easier prey by now. He jumped down, crying out in pain when he hit the ground. His foot, bloody and bandaged, was agony. He squeezed his eyes tight and took a deep breath as he limped toward Chogun.

He saw the lad and reached his hand up to him. "Jump down, Chogun, and I will catch you."

The small boy leapt from the tree into Kokee's arms and clung to him like lichen. Kokee struggled to maintain his balance but put his arms around the lad, squeezing him tight. Chogun burst into tears.

"Don't worry, Chogun, we will soon be home."

No sooner had the words left his mouth than he caught a glimpse of red eyes through the trees.

The alpha slinked into sight, poised to spring. Kokee clung to Chogun, defenseless.

Chogun buried his head in Kokee's shoulder, screaming. Kokee prayed to the gods that it would be over swiftly.

Thirty-Three

Mission Of Mercy

Kokee lay on his cot sweating, eyes closed.

His voice was hoarse and rasping. "Thomas . . . Thomas . . ." he said, his arms flailing in all directions. "Nikkiti . . . where are you?Find Thomas! You must find my brother!"

Chogun had not left his friend's side since they had been rescued two days previously when Nikkiti had noticed them missing. A search party had scoured the woods. They had found them within seconds of being attacked as the wolves closed in. The alpha male was pierced through the heart as he sprang towards Chogun. Several well-aimed arrows later, the remaining wolves slinked away, and Kokee and Chogun staggered to safety.

Kokee's wounds were dressed, and he was placed on a soft bed, worried brows watching over him. At first, he slept heavily, and then, after a few hours, he drifted into a state of otherworldly agony. He was conscious, but he was raving—screaming from his half-sleep in a dream world that Chogun was not a part of.

Chogun's mother, Unity, and his aunt Cleopatra periodically cleaned and tended Kokee's foot, making him drink water and trying unsuccessfully to feed him gruel. Their faces were drawn, and they talked in whispered voices, looking at each other and glancing at him, shaking their heads but never giving up.

They pleaded with Chogun to leave, but he refused. How could he leave his friend like this when they had shared so much? Kokee had saved Chogun's life, and they were bonded forever.

Hour after hour of hearing his friend's tortuous pleas, watching him deteriorate by the hour, he decided on a plan of action.

He crept away from Kokee's bedside early in the morning and made his way through the forest.

His young heart was beating with fear, but he needed to do this for his friend. After many hours winding through the trees, the tobacco farm came into sight. He watched from afar as two young boys sauntered around the farmyard, kicking stones, grooming horses, and chopping wood. Now and again, they would stop and playfully punch each other, laughing and joking, and sometimes push each other in anger.

A young girl with curly hair and a kind face shouted something to them from the shelter of the wooden porch surrounding the house. They shrugged their shoulders, smiling, and hid in a huge barn. She put her hands on her hips and raised her voice, but they paid no attention. Eventually, she walked over to the barn and returned with them following her, faces glum but looking at one another and grinning when she was not looking.

Chogun thought they looked as mischievous and nonthreatening as the teenagers he had seen in his village, not at all what he had prepared himself for. Longcoats had massacred his brave father, and he had an image of scary people in funny clothes who wanted to kill Powhatans. When he met Thomas, he did not know he was a Longcoat. He was just a stranger with kind eyes. He was surprised to learn the truth. Looking at Thomas's siblings (he assumed that was who they were), he could see that perhaps this family was different from other Longcoats. Maybe because Thomas was related to Kokee he was different from the evil Longcoats who killed his father.

Chogun had never seen a Longcoat's house before, and he stared at the wooden structure in awe as the three Longcoats walked up the steps. He watched them disappear inside. He wondered when he would catch sight of Thomas. Would Thomas recognize him? How would he communicate what he wanted when he did not know their language? Maybe he should have thought his plan through a little more thoroughly.

Eventually, he heard the noise of horses' hooves as Thomas rode into the yard. Chogun hesitated, trying to make himself invisible behind a hay bale. Thomas jumped off his horse and led it into the barn. When he came out of the barn, he ran up the wooden steps, the dust flying as he went.

Chogun waited several moments, and when he thought no one was around, he stood up. He gingerly started to climb the steps to the front door. He felt as small as a mouse as he looked up at the door handle. Suddenly, the door swung open.

Chogun jumped backwards, his eyes wide with terror.

"Chogun! What are you doing here?" Thomas cried. He smiled and held out his hand, welcoming him.

Chogun looked up at him, mouth trembling, wishing he had not come.

"It is alright . . . it is Thomas."

Chogun looked at Thomas's hand and inched backwards.

Thomas smiled, raised his hands to his heart and nodded.

Chogun recognized the gesture and replicated the greeting, a wave of relief washing over him.

Thomas put his hand out again, smiling, and Chogun looked up at him with sparkling eyes. He clasped his hand and followed Thomas inside the house. He looked around at the roaring fire and smelled the venison roasting. The girl with the kind eyes and curly hair walked towards him.

"So, who do we have here, then?" She asked as she stooped down to his level.

Chogun knew she was being kind, but he did not understand what she was saying. He put his head on one side and pursed his lips, shrugging his shoulders.

Lizzie smiled at him. She pointed to her chest. "Lizzie," she said. Then she pointed to him with eyebrows raised.

"Chogun," he said.

Lizzie clapped her hands and said, "Welcome, Chogun." He nodded his head in appreciation and then looked around to find Thomas. When their eyes met, the seriousness of the situation struck him again, and his face changed, showing the distress of his mission.

"Kokee, Kokee . . . ahkij . . ." he said. He put his hand to one side of his face and closed his eyes. He pointed at Thomas, then himself and then at the door.

Thomas stared at the little lad. He had come so far on his own and was distressed. Chogun wanted him to go to Kokee. He was not sure why, but that did not matter. He nodded his head.

***

Chogun clung to him; his tiny arms straddled Thomas's waist as the horse wove through the trees towards the village. Thomas dug his heels firmly into his horse's flanks, allowing her full rein to fly like the wind towards Werowocomoco. The urgency on the little boy's face had communicated more of the story than mere words ever could.

He did not know what he would find when they reached their destination, but he was preparing himself for the worst.

When they arrived, Chogun jumped off the horse and ran shouting, "Kokee, he is here! He is here! I have brought your brother!"

Thomas followed him.

When they got to the yehakin, Chogun lifted the flap, and they entered the darkened room. He walked towards the bed in the corner. "Kokee, he has come. I have brought Thomas to you," he whispered.

As they drew nearer, they could see no one in the bed.

Chogun looked at Thomas with terror in his eyes. "Where is he?"

Thirty-Four

Plans

Chogun ran out of the yehakin, tears streaming down his face. "Where is Kokee" he screamed, his eyes darting around trying to understand where his friend had gone, hoping that the worst had not happened.

His mother hearing his desperate cries, ran to him, crouching down with her hands on his shoulders, looking into his eyes. "Chogun, be calm. Kokee is fine. He was tired of lying down and moved to where he could move around more freely. He is over there" she said pointing towards a nearby larger Yehakin.

Chogun pulled away from her and ran as fast as he could, disappearing through the flap.

He rushed over to Kokee, who was sitting on a seat of rammed hay in the dimly lit yehakin.

He threw his arms around his hero. "I thought you were dead!" he sobbed.

Kokee kissed the top of his young friend's head. "You cannot get rid of me that easily." He hugged Chogun in a brotherly embrace, wincing as his foot moved. "When I woke up, and you had disappeared, I wondered where you had gone. I asked, but everyone thought you were playing in the woods."

Chogun shook his head and looked behind at the figure standing in the shadows who had followed him. "I went to find Thomas for you," he said, pride written on his face.

Kokee looked up. "What? Thomas . . .?" He peered into the shadows. "Is that you?"

Thomas stepped forward. "Yes, Kokee. Chogun traveled to Varina to let me know that you had been badly injured. He is going to make a powerful warrior one day."

"Yes, he is a good lad," said Kokee, grinning at the boy.

Thomas walked closer and sat down opposite Kokee on a hay seat. "So, how bad are your injuries? What happened? I could not understand exactly what Chogun was trying to say."

Kokee pointed to his bandaged foot. "The wolves had a very small meal, thank the gods...only three toes are gone, because of Nectowance's timely rescue. I was very sick, though. The wolf's mouth made my foot go bad, and a fever set in. They were not sure I was going to make it."

Thomas stared at the bandaged foot. He had no words. What if Kokee had died? His mother, his father . . . and now Kokee. He realized how much he cared for his brother, and his heart sank.

Kokee felt his sadness and reached towards him, touching his arm. "We have a good future together, brother. I can learn to walk again without my toes, and we will do many things, just you and I. I can teach you to be a Powhatan warrior. You will be the first Longcoat Powhatan warrior."

Thomas looked at Kokee. Feeling this close to someone was new to him. All his dreams were coming true. All he had to do was reach out and grab them. But it was as if he were swimming against a strong tide . . . wanting to move forward but being pulled back.

"To find and be with you is one of the greatest things that has ever happened to me and gives me great joy. But as for being a Longcoat Powhatan warrior . . ." He shook his head and looked at the ground.

Kokee paused. "We will make this work. We have to . . . for Pocahontas."

Thomas looked up. "But I cannot be in two places at once, no matter how much I want to be—for me . . . for you . . . or for Pocahontas." His face was long, reflecting his internal conflict.

Chogun sensed the atmosphere. He jumped off the straw seat, not totally understanding but guessing what had been said, eager to contribute. "I think you need to stay with us, Thomas. You and Kokee can become werowance[1] together. Then we will have peace with the English, and you can have both of your families." he stared at the two brothers, grinning from ear to ear. "And another thing . . . Thomas will have to marry Nikkiti."

Thomas knew only one of Chogun's words: Nikkiti. He looked at Kokee to see his reaction.

Kokee frowned. "You have no understanding of these things, Chogun." His voice was stern, and Chogun's face fell.

"But I thought that is what you wanted, Kokee," he whispered, looking at the ground.

Kokee smiled weakly at Chogun and put his arm around his shoulder. "It is not what *I* want; it is what the gods want that matters." He looked down, his face solemn.

Thomas knew from Kokee's expression that there was something amiss.

"What did Chogun say, Kokee?" He glanced at Chogun, eyebrows drawn.

"It was nothing, Thomas. He is full of childhood dreams . . . like us all," he hugged Chogun. "He just wants you to come and live with us . . . as do I." He smiled.

Thomas looked at his two new friends with his head tilted on one side and eyebrows raised. There was something Kokee did not want to share with him, something about Nikkiti, but he did not want to push him. Maybe in time . . .

"I can see the first thing I will have to do is learn Algonquin; I can't have you two conspiring and making plans for me without knowing what they are." He smiled, hoping to lighten the mood.

Kokee nodded. "I agree." He patted Thomas on the back playfully.

"So, who will teach me?" Thomas asked.

Kokee turned and looked at Chogun, his face softening, guilty that he had snapped at him. "So, will you teach Thomas how to speak Algonquin, Chogun?"

Chogun's face lit up. "I think Nikkiti should teach him," he said, his confidence returning after his previous rejection.

Thomas looked at the two of them. "Even though I do not understand Algonquin, I can guess what you were saying. Do you think Nikkiti would be prepared to do that, Kokee?"

"I think it is what the gods would want," he said, looking at the ground, his face showing no emotion.

For the first time, he felt a distance between himself and Kokee. What had happened?

[1] "Leader" or "chief."

Thirty-Five

Peace Or Blame

Thomas was pleased to be back at Varina, but his mind constantly wandered to the village of Werowocomoco, recalling the events of the past couple of days.

He sat with the family, but his mind was elsewhere. Lizzie cleared her throat, trying to break his trance. "What happened to the little Powhatan boy, Thomas? Was your brother well?" she asked as they ate breakfast.

John and Francis were bickering with each other as usual, but they stopped for a moment to hear what Thomas's answer might be. He had arrived late the night before and had gone straight to bed after a brief greeting. "Yes, Thomas, what the hell happened? You disappeared last night before we could ask," said John, looking up from his bowl of oats.

Thomas sighed. It was true he had avoided them, and he felt elated but confused. "Yes, I am sorry. I was exhausted, and to be honest, it was a bit of an anticlimax in many ways. A wolf had attacked Kokee; he was badly injured, and the wound had festered. Chogun saw him at his worst and thought he should let me know. But by the time I arrived, Kokee had recovered—although he had lost three toes."

Francis looked up from his breakfast bowl. "I do not see why you are so involved with those people. *We* are your family; you needn't be going over there to see those heathens." He stared at Thomas.

The atmosphere in the room turned cold. Lizzie got up to get some more milk, talking at them as she went. "I'm sure if one of you had an accident, Thomas would want to know about it, the same way he wanted to know about Kokee. Is that not right, Thomas?"

Thomas looked at the two young brothers, both of whom were bristling.

"Lizzie's right. I care about my family. Unfortunately, my family are in different places, so I will have to do my best." He started eating his breakfast again but could feel the heaviness in the room.

John, the feistiest of the twins, banged his spoon down with a clatter. "Well, I think it is disloyal going to see those heathens. It's outlawed to visit them without permission, and you will get us all in deep trouble if anyone discovers that you are visiting them. There are already mutterings in Jamestown about you being a traitor . . . People are starting to talk."

Thomas put his spoon down, looking at them with hurt in his eyes. "I meant no harm by visiting Kokee. I am hoping to visit them more often to learn their language. That way, there is more chance I can help with negotiations, and maybe we could work towards peace."

John's chair scraped across the floor as he stood up. "So now you are the big peacekeeper. Well, I, for one, do not buy your excuses. I think you want to desert us and go to live with them. You look like one of them, so why not go and take over—why not be their leader? That's what 'the great' Pocahontas would have wanted, isn't it?" His green eyes flashed as he looked at Thomas across the table. "You do not care about us. Why should you? You've only been here five minutes. Well, if you want to go, go . . . we don't need you." He turned his back and walked out of the door, slamming it shut.

The silence that was left in John's absence hung in the air. Francis and Lizzie stared at their food, faces grim.

Thomas sat, trying to arrange his thoughts. He did care about Lizzie, John, and Francis, but he also needed to get to know his Powhatan family. Why were his English brothers being so difficult? They were young. In time, they would understand. The age difference might have something to do with it. He had not built a rapport with John and Francis. They were immature, constantly bickering, always together, seemingly self-sufficient. Kokee, on the other hand, was older . . . he was Thomas's childhood fantasy hero who could do no wrong.

With a stab to his heart, he realized that he had failed John and Francis. It had been easy to build a relationship with Lizzie; she was so down-to-earth and full of life that he immediately warmed to her. Kokee was the best brother in the world. But he had found the boys more difficult, and they were sure to have felt his unease.

He reminded himself that they were only teenagers. Francis, the taller of the two, was shy and quiet, while John was bold and extroverted. They were innocents caught up in a war that had left them orphans. He was the adult; he would have to do more for them.

He looked at Francis and Lizzie, who were silently eating their breakfast.

"I'm sorry," he said. "I've been thoughtless. You have been kind and accepting of me, and I've taken that for granted in my naive excitement to know my mother's people."

Francis looked up. "If we're being honest, John and I feel that we don't matter. We get on with our chores, we keep out of the way when we're not wanted, but no one talks to us. We've lost our mother and father, and apart from Lizzie, we have no blood relatives left except Grandpa and Grandma Pierce, and they don't take any interest in us.

"Lizzie has done her best, but we were excited to think we had a new brother when you arrived. You're not a blood relative, but we hoped that did not matter. Our mother had loved your father and regarded you as her son, and we hoped that would be enough. But you've barely looked at us, and that has been hard. When you were kidnapped, we were so worried you would not return to us . . . and when you went with Chogun, we were sure you would never come home. We've been living on a knife edge."

Thomas's heart sank. He had been blind and selfish. "What can I say? You are right, and I regret the way that I have behaved. I hope that you can forgive me and we can start again. It is no excuse, but having family is very new to me, since I was raised an only child."

Lizzie got up from the table and started to clear away the plates. "Please don't let there be bad blood between us—we need one another," she said, looking at them with a frown.

Thomas nodded. "I'll go and find John. We're on the same side, even though I've done a bad job of communicating that to everyone. Will you come with me, Francis?" He looked at the boy, his eyes imploring him.

Francis hesitated. He looked at Lizzie, who nodded her head, her eyes stern.

"Alright," he muttered, gazing at the floor, shoulders hunched.

The two of them walked into the sunshine, looking around to see where John had gone.

"Where would he have gone, Francis?"

"He might be in the barn, or . . ." he hesitated, ". . . we have a secret place we go sometimes."

"Can I come to your secret place, or do you want to go there by yourself?"

"I think, for now, I had better go on my own."

Thomas shrugged. "I understand. I will wait here, and you can ask John if he will come and talk this out."

Francis wandered off around the corner of the barn, kicking a stone into the undergrowth as he went.

After about twenty minutes, he came back. "I have spoken to John and convinced him to hear you. He wants you to come to our den."

Thomas nodded. He was invited into their world, which was a huge step forward. Francis must have convinced John to give him a chance. He followed Francis for several minutes through undergrowth at a corner of the plantation. As they came away from the clearing and into the woods, Thomas felt the coolness of the shade as they walked along a dappled path.

Eventually, they approached a small thatched hut. It was built with childish skill, slightly at an angle, made of sawn wood with two windows and a ragged front door. Francis creaked open the door, and Thomas walked forward into the coziest little dwelling he had ever seen. Inside, there were blankets thrown over hay bales. There were cups on a little table, ale, bread, and cheese ready for a feast. The boys had created their own little haven.

Thomas smiled weakly at John. "Maybe we can start again? I have not been fair to you and would like to make it up to you."

John stared at the floor, silent.

Francis moved forward. "Why don't we all sit down and have a mug of ale?"

John indicated for Thomas to sit down without looking at him.

They all sat in silence.

Thomas looked at the twins with sincerity in his brown eyes. "I understand what you feel like," he said.

John looked up. "You have no idea. We've lost both of our parents to these heathens. We're alone in the world, apart from one another."

Thomas nodded. "I lost both of my parents, too. The English poisoned my mother, and the Powhatans killed my father. I do understand. That's why I have wanted peace for all of my life. Peace would mean that no children would grow up like us."

The twins looked downcast.

Thomas continued, "It's easy to blame one side in a war, but war is complex. You lost both of your parents to the Powhatans, and I lost my mother to the English. The English came and took the livelihoods and land of the Powhatans, and they retaliated. There is no easy answer. For us, as children of the warring nations, maybe it is best to hope for peace rather than to look for blame as our parents have done." The boys watched his every move and listened to every word he said.

"If I visit the Powhatans, it's because they are my family, but also because I care about you and want your future to be a future of peace. I need you to understand and support me. We have to fight for peace and live alongside the Powhatans . . . if not, there will be more bloodshed. I want it all. Maybe it is aiming too high, but I have to try."

The boys nodded, looking at one another.

They sat in silence—the bigger picture of war emerging through the tangle of their individual needs.

Thomas felt the heaviness and wanted to lighten the mood. "Come on then, let's eat this bread, cheese, and ale. If Lizzie notices it has gone missing, we'll never hear the end of it . . . so we might as well enjoy it!"

At last, a faint smile appeared on John's face. He looked at Thomas, fidgeting with his hands. "I . . . I . . ." he stuttered. Thomas put his arm around John's shoulders. "You don't have to say anything. Shall we drink to 'us'"?

As they raised their glasses, their eyes connected with a new understanding of each other.

Thirty-Six

Lost Love

Varina was home. Lizzie, John, and Francis took Thomas to their hearts, and life was easy. Thomas had seen John and Francis through different eyes since the day at their lodge, and the boys understood his need to see Kokee. The bickering continued, and the constant need to nag them into doing tedious tasks was an everyday occurrence, but Thomas held a respect for them that he never had before. They were teenagers who had suffered because of politics and war, as he had done.

They sat at the dinner table together, like any other family, after a hard day working on the plantation. Lizzie looked at the twins. "Boys, would you clear the table?"

Francis pulled a face. "Do we have to?"

Thomas started to get up. "I will do it then."

John pushed back his chair. "Come on, Francis. We are being bullied again." He smiled as he got up and put one plate on top of the other.

Lizzie looked at Thomas. "So . . . Production seems good at the moment."

"Yes, everything is running smoothly. I hope the weather is kind to us for planting," he said.

"So, what are your plans for tomorrow, Thomas?"

"Well, much the same as today and the day before that," he answered, looking quizzical.

The weather's not too bad at the moment," she said.

"Indeed," he answered. Thomas blinked. Why was she making small talk?

"Ahhh . . . So . . ." she fidgeted with a strand of her curly hair.

"Is there something you want to say, Lizzie?"

"Well, I met with Jane in town today . . ." The words came out like rapid gunshots. The boys stopped clearing the plates and stood still, waiting to hear what she would say.

"She said she would like to come and have lunch with us. She has some exciting news." Everyone looked at Thomas.

Thomas could feel his heart in his mouth. If only he could never see her again, he would manage. He cleared his throat. "It would be lovely to see Jane again." His face was flushed. He looked at the three expectant faces. "Please do not look at me like that. Jane and I are friends, and it would be a pleasure to see her again."

Lizzie put her hand on Thomas's shoulder and stooped to make eye contact. "We know how you feel. I would not have asked her, but she invited herself as she was so excited about whatever news she has and wants to share it with us."

"I look forward to it," he muttered. "Now, it's my turn to wash, isn't it?" He got up from the table, avoiding eye contact with any of them, and immersed himself in the washing up, clinking the plates a little louder than usual.

***

He watched her as she walked up through the trees, as he had done before. He did not want to, but it was a compulsion. No one was watching and he could drink in every line of her face, strand of her hair, and curve of her body without judgement. She wore a blue dress and her hair was tied into a bun at the base of her neck. She was beautiful as she un-self-consciously looked around her, singing to herself and now and then twirling as if she were in a ballroom, her skirt flaring out and her arms around an imaginary partner. If only that partner were him . . .

He hid behind the barn as she approached and walked up the steps to the front door. He watched her go inside and then sat down on a fallen tree trunk. He needed time to put on his mask and appear as though he did not care before he met her face to face. He closed his eyes, took a deep breath, and rose from the tree trunk, walking up the stairs with leaden legs.

He opened the door, and there she was, sitting at the kitchen table, just like she used to before there was awkwardness between them. She looked up, and when she saw him, her face flushed. "Thomas . . . I thought you were still visiting your sick brother. How . . . lovely to see you."

He took her small hand and raised it to his lips, looking into her eyes. "Likewise, Jane. It has been a while."

Lizzie rushed over like a whirlwind. "Thomas, could you carve the venison for me . . . I think we need some more logs for the fire. John . . . Francis . . . can you set the table while I get the vegetables ready?"

Jane looked around. "Can I do anything, Lizzie? I was always one of the family, so you can still use me as slave labor too, you know," she said, smiling.

Thomas was grateful. He knew what Lizzie was doing, and it gave him time to regain his composure.

"Oh, Jane, if you insist . . . can you stir that gravy for me?"

Jane got up and did as she was asked. The kitchen was a hive of activity, and John and Francis pranced around the table, banging down the knives and forks, looking at Thomas, then Jane, then one another, and smirking. Lizzie shook her head at them with a frown on her face.

When the meal was finally ready, they sat down and bowed their heads to say grace. They sat in silence.

Jane looked up. "So Thomas, how is your brother? Lizzie told me he had had an accident."

"It was a bit of a storm in a teacup. He is fine but had a bit of a run-in with some wolves. He was rescued in time, though."

Jane cleared her throat. "Oh, that is good. So . . ." She paused. "So . . . are you going to visit the Powhatans again?"

It was small talk, but Thomas knew all eyes were on him. "Well, I hope to visit and maybe start learning their language." It was so formal, so factual. He could not think of anything clever to say. He wanted to be anywhere but here.

Jane nodded. "I see. That sounds interesting." She was looking at her food, not at Thomas.

Lizzie broke in. "We've not seen you in ages, Jane. You must have been very busy."

Jane looked up from twiddling with her food. She had not eaten a bite. "Yes, as a matter of fact, I have been quite busy. I've made some new friends.

"Do you remember Governor George Yeardley, who sadly died two years ago?"

Lizzie nodded. "Yes, he was a great friend of my father, in the Bermuda days. His wife died too, last year, did she not?"

"Yes, that is right. It was devastating. Our families have known each other since I was a child. They had two sons—Argall and Ambrose. Growing up, we saw a lot of their family, and Ambrose and I played for hours together. I have been spending more time with him since the death of his parents and we have become even closer. The news I wanted to share is that he asked me to marry him."

She looked down at her food, biting her bottom lip.

John, Francis, and Lizzie stared open-mouthed.

She looked at Thomas with a tear in her eye. "I have to announce that, in the absence of alternatives for my future, I consented to be his wife."

Thomas felt her statement like a punch in the gut.

The silence of lost possibilities descended on them all.

Thirty-Seven

Permission

They rumbled into Jamestown in the horse and cart. Lizzie needed more provisions from the store; John and Francis came to help her. Thomas had an appointment to see the General Assembly to apply for permission to meet with the Powhatans.

Jane's sudden announcement had thrown him into a spin. But after days of moping and berating himself for what he had done to allow her to meet someone else, he finally had to accept she had a right to move on, and there was nothing he could do.

To take his mind off his heartbreak, he decided to put all his resources into addressing Anglo/Powhatan relations, and he needed to do this within the bounds of the law, even if it meant coming face to face with Sarah's husband again.

As the inner gates were opened, the now-familiar small triangular village lay before them. They drove past the church and drew the cart into the parking bays next to the pier, walking across the square to the general store, which was the only shop within the inner barricade, having been there since almost the beginning of the foundation of the settlement. Apart from the church and blacksmith, all other buildings were governmental—either housing or administrative.

Granny Joan and Angelo stood behind the dusty counter as usual, chatting with the customers who came in most days to get provisions, socialize, and gossip.

As Lizzie and the family entered, the middle-aged women stopped babbling and turned to look.

"Ah, Lizzie, did you hear about Jane?" said one. Another smiled.

Lizzie glanced behind her to see where Thomas was.

"Such good news for that young man. He has had a lot of bad luck. Money and status do not mean everything, you know." One more joined in. "I wonder when the wedding will be? Soon, I hope; we could do with some joy around here." She nodded her bonneted head.

"Well, the wedding will not be for a while," said Angelo, her face beaming. "Mr. Yeardley has insisted on importing the best silks for his bride's dress, and that will take some time to arrive."

"What color is it to be, Angelo? Do tell us!"

"It should be a secret, but I will tell only you ladies, as I know you will keep the confidence." She winked. "It is to be of the softest sky blue," she whispered, "to match the bride's eyes."

Angelo was rearranging the scarf around her curly dark curls. She laughed. "Have you ladies got nothing better to do than stand around gossiping? I have work to do. And our Mr. Rolfe is here too. I am sure he is not interested in all your tittle-tattle."

Thomas came out of the shadows. The finality of Jane's arrangements bore into his heart, but he needed to keep his mask of indifference in place. "I came in to say hello to you and Granny Joan,

Angelo . . . and to make sure they bought enough fig jam." He smiled. "Looks like I am not needed. I think John and Francis had better go around the back for the potatoes too . . . sounds like women's talk in here." They both nodded and bolted out of the shop.

Granny Joan walked towards Thomas and put her arms around his shoulders. "Well, maybe one day we will talk about *your* wedding, Thomas. Haven't you found a nice young lady in Jamestown yet?"

Thomas's face drained of color. "There are many lovely ladies in Jamestown, 'tis true, Granny Joan . . . but I fear they are above my station." He tried to laugh, but awkwardness reigned in the room. Joan gave him a grandmotherly hug.

Angelo appeared from the back of the shop with a plate of hot scones and butter, with a large dollop of her famous fig jam. "Here you are, Thomas. Why don't you sit down here"—she pointed to a soft armchair in the corner—"and help me use up these scones?" She had a broad smile and a twinkle in her eye.

"Thank you, Angelo. I have a meeting with the general council about visiting the Powhatans, but I have some time before the meeting starts, and those scones look too good to go to waste," he laughed.

Granny Joan nodded. She had grown fond of Thomas and admired how he had stepped up to his responsibilities at such a young age since the tragic death of her daughter. While her hatred of the Powhatans was deep, she felt that any attempts at peace should be encouraged. "Keep your strength up, young man," she patted him on the back. You have quite a challenge ahead of you. I wish you the best of luck. Now if you will excuse me, I must see all these gossiping customers." She walked to the back of the shop, smiling at the many eager ladies willing to support the store. It had become a hub for not only buying provisions but socializing. "So . . . what else has been going on in the town, ladies?" She looked at the assembled gaggle of gossiping wives of Jamestown, her grandaughter, Lizzie, among them.

Thomas melted into the comfortable chair, savoring the warm scone, the melted butter oozing out, and the sweet jam lingering on his tastebuds. For a moment, he could forget the impending meeting, which could decide his future direction. What was he going to say? Would Fitzgerald give him a fair hearing, or would their past altercations completely ruin his chances of an open relationship with his Powhatan family?

The ladies of the town continued their melee of conversation, the gentle sound filtering through Thomas's unconscious. Their words mingled with his thoughts until one name caught his attention: "Sarah Fitzgerald."

Thomas immediately tuned in to what was being said.

One voice could be heard above the others. Mrs. White was a well-known gossip, but her information was carefully collected, and her ears were always open for a juicy story. ". . . yes, that poor woman . . . and that little mite."

Another piped in. "I remember her when she arrived. What a pretty and dynamic little woman she was with that beautiful auburn hair. That lad was as cheeky as they come. What a transformation!" She shook her head, and all the ladies looked at each other with tragedy on their faces. "Now she talks in a whisper and keeps looking around to see who is watching her. The shame."

Lizzie looked pained. "What has happened to her?" she asked.

Thomas was on the edge of his seat. He had an inkling of what was happening to Sarah and little George. He could not calm his imagination. But what could he do? He was virtually powerless.

Mrs White bit her lip. "Ladies, we must not talk about what goes on between a man and a woman. It is not seemly." She stopped talking but then gestured for the ladies to come closer. "Suffice to say she will survive as so many women in her place survive. No doubt he will get tired of that Powhatan slut in time."

Thomas was in a dilemma. In under an hour, he had to meet the council headed up by Sarah's husband. He tried to put the gossip to the back of his mind. How was he going to maintain his composure?

Thirty-Eight

Caught

Thomas walked out of the store, his mind in a whirl. What was going on with Sarah? How could he keep a level head when negotiating with her husband? The meeting with the General Assembly was in a few hours, and he had time to kill. Thinking fresh air and distraction would do him good, he wandered from the store, out of the gates of the inner town, and down the street, watching as people carried out their daily chores.

A mix of Powhatan and English laborers shouted instructions as ships were loaded and unloaded, bread was baked, ale was brewed, and glass was blown. He looked at them all—on the face of it, carefree souls who were minding their own business, helping with the running of the town. He himself felt anything but carefree. Thoughts of Jane's marriage plagued him, and he not only had Lizzie and the boys to worry about, but it seemed he also now had Sarah and George. And what of the expectations of the Powhatans that he would be the catalyst for peace?

He continued down the track, aimlessly looking at the rows of houses, some primitive and made of wood, and others, the substantial homes of the well-to-do, made of brick. He took a small turning between the houses, deciding to explore the town he, as yet, knew little of. Alleyways of ramshackle buildings, hastily erected as temporary accommodation for arriving colonists, were situated behind the main dwellings. There was no one around at the moment, as everyone was working in the main part of the town.

As he continued on, taking in the sights of the settlement, he was halted by an unfolding scene. He hid behind the corner of one of the houses.

In the distance, coming out of a side door of one of the huts, was a familiar figure. He was followed by a young Powhatan girl in her late teens. The man gestured for her to return inside, but she was crying, her face red with anguish. The man pointed at the door again, and he looked around furtively. Assured that no one was watching, he hit the girl full force with the back of his hand. She stumbled and fell, clutching her swollen belly protectively. She lay looking up at him, clawing at the air for him to come to her. He turned his back and marched away, leaving her struggling on the dusty earth.

It was then that George Fitzgerald I saw Thomas. There was no hiding place. Fitzgerald's face blanched. He paused, then stood tall, striding toward Thomas as if nothing had happened. Thomas stood in his path, glaring.

"What's the matter, heathen? These girls have to be shown their place. I am sure many a squaw has seen the back of your hand after they have succumbed to your dubious charms." He laughed with a menacing tone, standing directly before Thomas, his face too close for comfort.

"I am due to meet with you in half an hour, heathen. You had better let me pass. I wouldn't want this chance encounter to influence any decisions that might be taken."

Fitzgerald was so close that Thomas could smell his rotten ale breath of the night before. Thomas was younger and fitter than the older man, but they both knew where the power lay. Thomas turned away and spat on the ground, imagining it was in the face of this aggressor. Punching him now would burn the bridges of many people, so he had to restrain his impulse to see Fitzgerald scrabbling on the ground like the young girl he had just left.

Thomas stood aside, glaring. "You are filth . . . and you'll get your comeuppance in a timely manner. You're not fit for the office you hold."

Fitzgerald laughed. "You have no understanding of the culture here, boy. Having a whore is the sign of a strong man."

"And beating your wife too?" Thomas growled.

Fitzgerald rolled his eyes. "Don't be obtuse. You know nothing of women. And as a half-breed yourself, you have no grounds to be judgmental about the heathen bitch. Your mother was a whore, like all of them. And as for my wife, that is none of your business." He started to saunter away. "I'm looking forward to seeing you at my mercy later. You'll have to be very nice to me, will you not?" He winked. "If it were up to me, I would wipe out your heathen relatives—saving a few women, of course." He laughed.

Thomas could take no more. His rage at this pompous, cruel man overtook his good judgment. He drew back his arm and punched Fitzgerald to the ground. "Have a taste of your own medicine, you coward!"

Fitzgerald, stunned, lay on the ground, nursing his bruised chin. "You have definitely burned your boats now, you filthy heathen." he croaked. Thomas looked at him with contempt before turning and walking away. He had eradicated any chance of getting what he needed from Fitzgerald, but he knew deep down that Fitzgerald would have refused anyway.

Thomas walked back to the little girl, who had struggled to stand. Her head hung low as she turned and disappeared into the tiny, shabby hut.

He knocked at the door. Nothing happened. He gingerly turned the rusted handle and pushed on the roughly hewn door. It creaked open. He went inside. One window shed scant light on a dwelling with an unmade bed and little else. The teenage girl huddled on the floor in the corner, shaking. She was tiny, like a small child, and the bump of her pregnancy was incongruous as she made herself as small as possible.

Thomas put his hand out to her, and she shrank from him, whimpering.

He crouched down and touched her arm gently. "It's alright. I will not hurt you."

She turned to look at him, her huge, doe-like eyes wide with fear.

He put his hand on his chest. "Thomas," he whispered. Then he pointed to her with his head on one side. "You are…?"

"Odina," she whispered.

"Do you speak English, Odina?" he asked.

She nodded her head.

"Odina." He smiled. "Do you live here?"

"Only for a while," she said, "till the baby comes." She put her hand on her belly and then started to get up.

He put his hand out to help her to stand. "It looks like your baby might be here very soon. Maybe we could find some ladies to help you if you came with me?"

She shook her head. "I cannot. Sir George wants me to stay here. I am not allowed to talk to anyone."

"Where is your mother?"

She looked at the floor. "My family do not know."

He looked at the pathetic child before him.

She cried out as the floor below her became wet with water.

Thomas was ignorant of such things; confusion clouded his face.

Odina clutched her belly again. "The baby is coming, Thomas. You must leave."

He put his hand to his head, pausing. "I will get help, Odina. You cannot be alone for the birth of your baby; that much I do know." He helped her to lie on the bed and left her. As he ran from the hut, he heard her cry out. He rushed back, concern on his face. When he went inside, she was calm and smiled at him.

"It is normal, Thomas. Pain is normal; do not worry. The baby will be here soon, I think." She flinched and squeezed her eyes shut.

He shook his head, still conflicted about the best way to help her, knowing he could not do anything alone. He turned and started towards the main triangle of the town.

As he dashed through the gates, he saw that Lizzie's horse and trap were gone, and his heart fell. He sped up as he ran to the general store. Angelo was behind the counter, and the shop was deserted. She saw his disheveled demeanor. "Thomas, whatever is the matter? I thought you would be at your meeting by now?"

"I have more pressing matters now, Angelo," he spluttered breathlessly.

"More pressing than seeing your Powhatan family?" Her eyebrows raised.

"Indeed, far more pressing. I need your help urgently, Angelo. A young Powhatan girl is about to give birth in one of the immigrant houses in the outer town. She is completely alone and in need of feminine assistance."

Her eyes opened wide, and she hurried from behind the shop

counter. "Goodness, me. We must make haste. Show me where to go."

"You had better bring rags, water, and whatever you need for such things, as there's nothing at the hut."

Thomas and Angelo ran through the town, dashing and weaving through the townspeople towards Odina's hut. Angelo disappeared inside, signaling Thomas to wait.

Screams could be heard as Thomas marched up and down outside, concern etched on his face. He had no idea what was happening, but it sounded as if Odina were going to die. As her screams subsided, he knew she must be dead, and he gingerly opened the creaking door. In the half-light, he saw her lying on the bed, holding a tiny bundle in her arms. She was looking down with love at the little blanket-covered shape. Then he heard it cry, and he knew all was well.

Angelo walked towards him, looking down her nose at him. "You have a son, Thomas."

Thirty-Nine

Broken Hearts

Jamestown had been rife with rumours of the child being Thomas's, but these were soon dashed. Sir George did not care enough to deny his part in the birth of the little mite, and much to Thomas's disgust, no one seemed very surprised or outraged. Thomas was concerned about Sarah. While Sir George was unscathed by his behaviour, the gossip centered on his wife; some sympathising, but many blaming her for her husband's need to stray outside the marital bed.

There had been no mention of Thomas's altercation with Sir George. The humiliation of anyone knowing he had been brought down by the likes of Thomas would have been too great. However, the rearrangement of Thomas's meeting was pointedly ignored by both parties.

Odina was very weak, both physically and psychologically. Her tears of shame and humiliation touched Lizzie deeply, and she suggested that the young girl and her baby stay at Varina until they were strong enough to go back to the tribe. Odina was frightened. Would she be accepted back into the tribe?

Thomas had many feelings, mainly a deepening hatred of Sir George Fitzgerald. How could anyone do such a thing to a young and innocent girl and then abandon his own baby?

The little one had not asked to be brought into the world, and Thomas's heart melted when he saw him. Every time he looked into the baby's dark brown eyes, he saw a helplessness that stirred his protective instincts. The little mewing sounds of his cry and his sighs of contentment were enough to blur thoughts of the abusive way that he had been created.

Thomas held his finger out and felt the little hand grasp with all his might. "What will you call this little rascal?" Thomas smiled at Odina, who was holding her son with the ease of a natural mother.

"His name is Chepi," she whispered. "Yes, Chepi is a nice name…" Her voice was like that of a little bird.

Thomas noticed that her face was flushed, and beads of sweat were starting to form on her forehead. "Are you alright, Odina?"

She looked at him with sorrow in her eyes and shook her head. Icy fear crept into his chest. She must have been too timid to alert them.

He ran out of the room. "Lizzie! Lizzie!" he screamed.

She came running. "What is the matter, Thomas?"

"It is Odina. She is unwell…" He grabbed Lizzie's arm and pulled her into the room.

Lizzie's eyes opened wide when she saw Odina. She paused, biting her lip in concentration. "You must go to Jamestown and bring Angelo and Granny Pierce. They will know what is to be done." Her voice was uncharacteristically low and measured, churning Thomas's stomach with recognition of the seriousness of the situation.

Thomas took one last look at the tiny mother and thought of how like his own mother she must be—so alone in a culture that she did not understand, with people she did not know, at the mercy of those whom she thought were her enemies.

He touched her arm and smiled encouragement, before striding out of the room.

***

When Thomas returned with Granny Pierce and Angelo, they ran up the stairs, shedding their outer garments as they went, entering the room with their hearts beating. Odina had deteriorated significantly, and she lay, beads of sweat covering her face, trying to keep her eyes open. Lizzie, panic-stricken, held the screaming baby, who wriggled as she attempted to drip goat's milk into his little mouth. The two women at once took command.

"Thomas - take the baby from Lizzie. Lizzie go and get some cool water and some rags. We must try and get this fever down," commanded Granny Pierce.

Odina opened her eyes as if they had lead linings. "Please get help from my tribe. They have powerful medicine." Her voice was a whisper as she squeezed her eyes shut again, consumed by a spasm of pain.

Angelo and Granny Pierce looked at one another, and Granny Pierce raised her eyebrows.

"Thomas, go to your brother and ask for his help. Odina is right. If someone cannot come, let them give you the herbs to save Odina. Go quickly; we have no time to spare for this little girl."

Thomas put the baby in the softly lined box that had been made for him, kissing his forehead as he left, and ran to his horse. As he approached his horse, he realised the poor animal was exhausted from his recent trip to Jamestown. She would never make the journey - or at least it would be a very slow journey. His heart sank.

"Thomas" a voice behind him startled him out of his despair.

A lightning bolt shot through his body when he saw who it was.

"Jane. I did not hear you coming."

"You were going somewhere in a hurry… do not let me stop you." She lowered her eyes.

"We have an emergency, Jane," he said breathlessly. "The little Powhatan girl we took in is very ill. I need to get to the tribe to see if they can help. I am not sure my horse will make it. We have just raced from Jamestown with Granny Pierce, and she is exhausted. No matter… I have got to try… Odina is suffering." He turned to mount the horse.

"Wait, Thomas!" she cried. "Take my horse. I have not come far, and she is a good little worker. She will do what is necessary."

Thomas looked at her. He did not have time to think about his feelings or savour this unexpected encounter. He nodded his head. "My Lady, you have my gratitude."

He took the pony from her, mounted and turned toward the Powhatan village. He stopped himself from looking back and kicked the pony forward, crowding out thoughts of what might have been and concentrating on getting the job done.

When he approached the village, the warriors welcomed him in. He had become well known as the brother of Kokee and would have felt a certain degree of satisfaction at how comfortable it felt to be back if it had not been for the seriousness of his mission.

"Where can I find Kokee?" he shouted as he slid off the pony.

"He is in the Yehakin with Opechancanough - over there," said one, pointing toward a large yehakin.

Thomas ran to the yehakin and opened the flap. Inside, it was dim and peaceful, an antithesis of what he was feeling. Kokee and Opechancanough sat in the warm, smokey atmosphere, eyes closed, deep in meditation. At the sound of his entrance, they both opened their eyes. A hurricane had entered the calm waters of their meditation and propelled them into alertness.

Thomas stood still, trying to get his breath to speak.

Opechancanough stared in his direction, his face blank of emotion. "Son of Pocahontas, you must have urgent business to approach your Wahunsenecka this way."

"Indeed, Sir. I apologise for this rude interruption. It is a matter of life or death for one of the children of your tribe." Thomas's eyes were wide, and beads of sweat sparkled on his forehead.

"Our tribe," said Opechancanough. "Tell me, my son…"

***

Nikkiti gathered her herbs together carefully. A life was at stake, and she knew exactly what needed to be done.

"Take me to her, Thomas. This young woman can be saved if we get to her before the fever gets too strong." Her large brown eyes bore into him, propelling him into action.

Thomas dug his heels into the flanks of Jane's pony, and the two of them sped towards Varina.

Arriving at the house, Thomas ushered Nikkiti upstairs to the bedroom. Odina lay as he had left her, eyes closed, face flushed with beads of sweat on her forehead. The life force seemed to be seeping out of her.

Jane sat by her side, bathing her forehead with cool water. The windows were open, and a cool breeze filled the air. Angelo was sitting with baby Chepi, who was wailing and then spluttering as Granny Pierce dripped droplets of goat's milk into his tiny mouth.

Nikkiti rushed forwards. She glanced at Jane, nodding approval for her efforts, then turned towards the fever-struck figure lying in the bed. "Odina, you will be fine. I have herbs that will give you the strength to fight. You must try swallowing this medicine I have prepared for you."

Odina attempted to open her eyes, straining to see who was talking to her. She tried to move but flinched with pain and sank back down into the darkness of her fever once again.

Nikkiti looked at Jane. "What is your name?"

"I am Jane Poythress."

"Jane, I need you to help me get Odina to a sitting position so I can give her the medicine."

Jane smiled and nodded. "Whatever you need."

Thomas watched in awe as the two women worked as a team to tend to the child who had prematurely become a mother. They moved with efficiency and synchronicity—two young girls as different as the sun and moon pulled together with feminine compassion for one of their own, symbolic of what was possible. How could he not love them both?

When Odina took the medicine, they asked Thomas to leave while they bathed her body, changed her clothes, and tucked her in bed to rest.

Granny Pierce and Angelo had been giving baby Chepi their full attention, and his cries had turned from red-faced shrieks of utter distress to whimpers of exhaustion. A tense calmness descended on the room.

Nikkiti and Jane's job was done for now. As they left the room, they looked at one another with respect.

"It is a matter of waiting and praying now", whispered Nikkiti.

Jane nodded, looking at the floor. "Shall we go and find Thomas and Lizzie? We have all had quite an anxious time."

They went downstairs, where Thomas had been pacing up and down with worry. When he heard them coming, he rushed towards the door, eager for news.

Jane entered first. In his heightened state of emotion, Thomas ran over and took her hands in a familiar gesture of intimacy, looking into her eyes. "Jane, how is Odina? Will she make it?" Jane stood back apace, retrieving her hands, her sad eyes lingering on Thomas. Abruptly, she pulled her gaze away as if seeing something forbidden.

"Nikkiti knows more about her medicine; perhaps you should ask her." She distanced herself, allowing Nikitti to come forward.

Nikkiti had sensed Thomas's response to Jane. Something unspoken had transpired between the two of them. She looked at Thomas and then back to Jane. There was concern for Odina, but there was so much more. Her heart sank. She looked at Thomas, whose brown eyes were still gazing past her at Jane.

"Thomas," Nikkiti said as she waited for him to look at her.

He started and looked around trying to reorientate himself away from Jane.

Nikitti waited.

"What do you think Nikkiti?" he gushed.

Nikitti had the look of tragedy on her face. "The life of this little girl is in the hands of the Gods", she said, her heart breaking as she turned away from him.

Lizzie bustled over. "Come and sit down. I have prepared some broth for you all, as you must be tired and hungry."

They sat around the table; the only sound was the clanking of spoon on bowl as unspoken emotion hovered over each of them.

Lizzie looked at the three of them and cleared her throat. "So Jane… we weren't expecting you today. It was fortuitous that you were with us… I could never have helped as well as you did. How did you happen to be in the neighbourhood?"

"Oh… it doesn't seem important now. I was just coming to tell you the material for my wedding dress had arrived, but that seems so trivial when that poor little girl is lying upstairs fighting for her life…"

Nikkiti looked at Thomas. From the look on his face, she knew that he, like herself, was going to make many sacrifices in the name of peace. For her, it was worth the pain, she just hoped he had the same determination.

Forty

Back Into The Fold

Odina made slow but steady progress. Lizzie took over from Nikkiti and Jane, and fed and bathed the young girl back to health. Thomas observed the process with wonder.

The baby suckled greedily as soon as Odina was able to take him in her arms again. His little cheeks began to fill out, and a healthy pink hue adorned his face, which was framed by a mop of dark hair. Thomas was smitten. Never having had baby brothers or sisters, his fascination knew no bounds.

Lizzie laughed as she watched Thomas gazing at the sleeping Chepi. "Can you leave that baby alone, Thomas? You do have work to do on the plantation. We must return Odina and Chepi to their tribe soon, so don't get too used to them being around."

And that day finally came. The baby was bundled in blankets, and Odina cradled him in her arms as Thomas accompanied her on the journey through the woods to her village.

Odina was apprehensive about her return. "I am worried that my family will not want Chepi and me. I left them to make my living with the English, and then I had a relationship with a Longcoat. Chepi is half English; he might be an outcast."

Thomas could see the angst on her face. "He and I share that honor, Odina. The world is changing, and people will have to recognize that in our shared world, judging a person by the blood that flows through their veins or the color of their skin is wrong. You may have some people raising their eyebrows to start with, but they are your family, and once they start to know him for who he is, his parentage will be forgotten. You and he must be the first ones to forget it."

As he spoke the words, he looked at the tiny innocent wrapped in his blankets, and he realized with a pang of regret that they were words of hope rather than reality, justified solely because Odina needed reassurance more than truth. They were a sentiment he should, rather than could, abide by. Maybe it would be different for Chepi. As time passed and more mixed-race babies were born, such babies may become treasured as the uniting force for the New World. One could only pray.

The buggy rumbled on down the path between the high trees, and Chepi slept, unaware of the new life he was about to commence. Thomas glanced at him and his mother from time to time, a sense of responsibility in the forefront of his mind, hoping his charges would be accepted back into the fold of their Powhatan family.

At last, they turned the corner and saw the village of Werowocomoco which was guarded by two warriors. Thomas stopped the buggy and put his hands together at his heart, indicating the peaceful nature of his business.

The warriors nodded in recognition. Thomas jumped down from the buggy. He took the baby from Odina while she climbed down, glancing towards the village. Thomas handed Chepi back to her as she stood, looking, eyes wide with apprehension, towards her old home.

Suddenly, from nowhere, there was a commotion.

"They are here! They are here!" A crowd was approaching, all cheering and shouting, headed by Chogun, who led Nikkiti's two greyhounds bounding, legs flying as they sensed the excitement of the arrival of newcomers.

In the rear, Thomas caught sight of Kokee, who smiled and raised his hand in welcome when their eyes met. It seemed that all would be well.

Opechancanough made his way through the crowd of well-wishers. When he reached Odina, she bowed her head. He put his arm around her shoulder. "My child, you left us for a while, but now you are back. Let us welcome this little one as a symbol of the peace between the Powhatans and the English."

He smiled at her and ushered her towards the village, surrounded by her welcoming crowd.

Thomas sighed as he watched her move away from him. He was happy that Odina was back in the fold of her tribe. He could not help thinking that the symbol little Chepi made was not so much of peace but of an invading people taking advantage of a more compliant opponent.

He was forced out of his train of thought and almost knocked over by Waba, the large white greyhound that instinctively knew Thomas was her new master. Her paws reached Thomas's shoulders, and she nuzzled his chin. Thomas laughed. "So you do remember me, Waba!"

Nikkiti emerged from nowhere, her face soft with a sadness he had not noticed before. "Of course, she remembers you, Thomas," she whispered.

Thomas looked at Nikkiti. He had almost forgotten how beautiful she was and how he felt in her presence. But he sensed a new reticence in the way she greeted him.

"Nikkiti," he stuttered, ". . . Odina was worried about coming home, but I can see all her fears were unfounded."

There was a pause and a silence.

She looked at the ground. "Thomas . . .?" Her voice was hesitant.

He looked at her, giving her his full attention. Her brows were drawn, and her brown eyes looked at him with something approaching pity. "What is it, Nikkiti?"

Kokee walked towards them, closely followed by Chogun and Manitou, who bounded towards Waba, eager to see her greyhound friend. "Welcome again, my brother," Kokee bowed, looking from Thomas to Nikkiti. Aware of tension in the air, he raised his eyebrows.

Nikkiti pulled her gaze from Thomas and smiled furtively. "You caught me just in time, Kokee. Who knows what Powhatan secrets I could have divulged to our new cousin." She walked over to Kokee, grabbed his hand and squeezed it affectionately.

Kokee looked at Nikkiti without smiling. "We have no secrets, do we Nikkiti?"

Nikkiti stared at him. "Of course not," she said, a little too abruptly.

Thomas waited to see if more was revealed. Something was going on, but Kokee was not ready to tell him.

Waba bashed Thomas with her nose and stood back from him, waiting for her usual adoration. Thomas ignored the confused dog and continued to stare at Nikkiti. What was going on?

Nikkiti looked at him. "Do not worry, Thomas. I am just a little mischievous today." She reached out to fondle Waba's velvety ears. But her eyes held no mischief, only sadness. "Everything will be as the gods wish," she said as she turned and walked away.

Forty-One

A Brother's Plan

After Nikkiti walked away, the two brothers were left alone. Kokee looked at Thomas. "Now you are here, my brother, perhaps we could continue the conversation we were having when we were so abruptly interrupted by kidnappings, rescues, and other minor events." He smiled.

"Let us adjourn to the quioccosan. Having more time to get to know one another is something I have been looking forward to for many years."

Thomas was still pondering Nikkiti's strange behavior, aware of Kokee's avoidance of an explanation. He would discover what was happening at some point, but it seemed now was not the time.

Waba pranced at Thomas's side, and he followed Kokee into the quioccosan. The enormous structure was where he had previously met with Opechancanough. It was dark and smoky, the fire surrounded by makeshift seating. At one end was a platform with what looked like a throne, where Opechancanough and his wives sat during tribal meetings.

Kokee led Thomas to the fire and invited him to sit down, handing him a pipe. Waba stretched out on the ground beside him.

Thomas stared at his surroundings, putting the pipe to his lips and slowly inhaling the fragrant tobacco smoke. It all felt like a dream.

"Kokee, I am so proud to be here."

"We are honored that you are here, Thomas. I look forward to building a relationship that goes from strength to strength. We have missed many years together, so we must compensate for this lost time." Thomas passed the pipe to Kokee.

"Kokee," Thomas's voice was tentative, "all my life, I have imagined our mother. She comes to me in my dreams, and her image is with me guiding me, but . . ." He cleared his throat and looked at the ground. "I was only two years old when she was killed, so I only have sketchy memories of her. I have had no one to talk to about her, as my father left me. I gleaned what I know of her from overhearing conversations and talking to servants." He looked up at Kokee. "What was she like?"

Kokee smiled. "I am surrounded by people who knew our mother, but her name is rarely mentioned. I was young, too, when my father was killed, and Pocahontas was kidnapped. My early memories are sketchy, like yours.

"I remember when she visited us with your father just before you were born. I will never forget her words to me: 'Do not hate them . . . Find your brother . . . Make peace together. You are my legacy.'" His eyes softened and he paused. "I have pondered those words every day of my life, praying that I could fulfill her expectations." He sighed.

Kokee's face crumpled as memories resumed. "She cried hysterically when I was torn from her arms . . . and that was the last time I saw her." He looked up at the roof, his dark eyes searching for something.

"I never knew when she died or how she died, and no one spoke of her again until one day, not long ago, our aunt Cleopatra told me of the past." He looked at Thomas. "She told me about my mother and father's love for one another, and she described the day he was killed and she was kidnapped." He gazed into the fire. "Although my memories are sketchy, her words brought it all back to me. It is carved into my brain with blood." His eyes filled with tears. "So much so that now the scene is played out daily in my head."

He looked at Thomas again. "Cleopatra also told me about our mother's quest for peace and the baby she bore John Rolfe. Pocahontas's hope was invested in the first Powhatan English baby . . . a hope that, finally, peace could reign through the union of the two races."

Thomas leaned down and patted Waba's head. His eyes were sad. "You must hate the English, Kokee," he said.

Kokee shook his head. "For many years, the image of the English killing my father instilled a burning hatred; I cannot deny it. But learning of Pocahontas's selfless sacrifice for peace, remembering her words, and knowing of your existence has given me a different perspective. I feel I must turn her death into something positive. Too many have died senselessly."

Thomas smiled at him. "There are so many similarities between us, Kokee. But since I arrived in Jamestown, my allegiances have bounced backwards and forwards in my head. I was angry at the English for killing my mother; I was angry at the Powhatans for killing my father. I did not know where to turn. I am still confused."

Kokee smiled and nodded. "It is a complex situation, Thomas. There are no easy solutions. Your heart and my heart are in the same place. We want the same thing, and maybe if we work together, we can achieve at least a will for everyone to work towards peace.

"Opechancanough is trying very hard to keep relations with the English peaceful. However, I fear that if they push him too far, there will be another massacre like the one that killed your father in 1622. I was only young then, but I remember the devastation of that time. War does not achieve anything. If it had, we would live alongside one another now."

Thomas took the pipe from Kokee and drew long and hard. He coughed, unused to the intense strength of the Powhatan tobacco. He looked at Kokee. "I am so naive. It is not only the tobacco that is unexpected. As I grew up, my head was filled with the fantasies of my native family laughing and socializing with my English family. My dreams were filled with childhood fantasies of a fun-filled life in a carefree paradise riding a painted pony. How wrong I was." He shook his head and looked at the ground.

Kokee looked thoughtful and inhaled the pipe as if it were second nature.

There was an easy silence.

As Kokee looked up to pass the pipe to Thomas, his eyes were steady, and his mouth was set. "You know the gods have told Opechancanough that you and I are to be his successors?"

Thomas looked into the fire, digesting Kokee's momentous statement. The disappointment of knowing he could never be a Powhatan leader drowned his joy at the honor his brother bestowed on him. "You were the one born to lead this tribe after Opechancanough. While I, too, am the son of Pocahontas, I was not raised as a Powhatan. I am not a Powhatan warrior. I am not familiar with your culture or your values. It would be arrogant to think I could come in and take such a hallowed position." He shook his head. "After the attempt on my life, I got that message loud and clear." Thomas's face was drawn. "Deranged though he is, Rowtag has a point of view that is probably shared with many in the tribe." It was painful to finally acknowledge that his dreams of becoming a Powhatan were unrealistic. He inhaled the pipe a little too vigorously and went into a paroxysm of coughing.

When he had calmed down, he looked at Kokee. "See . . . I cannot even smoke the pipe with you." His eyes were sad.

"Do not rush to such a conclusion, my brother. The wishes of the gods are more powerful than rebel warriors and strong tobacco. Rowtag knows he has done wrong, and he has disappeared. If he comes back, he will receive harsh punishment. It is unlikely he will return."

Thomas searched within himself for a flicker of hope. Maybe he could still embrace his Powhatan heritage, but there were other obstacles. "What of Askook? What of the views of the rest of the people?"

Kokee passed the pipe back to Thomas. "I believe that Askook conspired with Rowtag to attack you. Everyone knows that there is something wrong with Askook. It is not just his hatred of Longcoats . . . he has a cruel and illogical side to him that many regard as madness."

Thomas grimaced. "He is smart enough not to get caught, though."

Kokee sighed. "He is a coward. He will always find someone else to do his dirty work."

"How has he gotten away with his behavior for so long? Opechancanough seems fond of him," Thomas said.

Kokee sighed. "When Askook was a baby, his father died in battle while saving Opechancanough's life. Since that day, Opechancanough has treated Askook like his own son. Askook can do no wrong in Opechancanough's eyes . . . but neither can you."

Thomas took another puff on the pipe and gazed into the fire, pausing to reflect. "But Kokee, *you* are the son of Pocahontas, and *you* have been preparing to take over from Opechancanough since you were a child. Why am I in the picture at all?"

Kokee locked eyes with him. "Because not only are you the son of Pocahontas, you are a Longcoat. The gods believe that you are the answer to peace because the blood that flows through your veins is mixed. Do you not see how special that makes you? You symbolize a peaceful fusion of different races. Ultimately, the English will become another tribe, working and living alongside the Powhatans. There need be no hostilities. You and I can make this happen."

Thomas pursed his lips and shook his head. He thought of the prejudice against him in Jamestown and how he had destroyed his relationship with Fitzgerald. Maybe it could be overcome if he worked on it.

Kokee took the pipe. "There would be no need for you to forsake your English family. There would be integration, not separation."

Thomas nodded. "It would take a long time for two such different cultures to live side by side though, Kokee."

"Yes, I accept that. But once we cultivate friendships and maybe even, in time, marriages between English and Powhatan, families will be drawn together naturally . . . as *we* have been." Kokee looked at his feet, taking a breath, and then raised his eyes gradually to look at Thomas. "Nikkiti told me of your heartbreak, Thomas. I am sorry."

Thomas shook his head. "It was not meant to be."

Kokee sighed. "We are alike in that respect, too, my brother. The love of my life is promised to another."

Thomas raised his eyebrows. He had never confided in or been confided in by anyone about such matters. He was unsure how to respond.

Kokee bit his lip. "I keep telling myself that I must move on, but when I see her every day, my heart is broken over and over again."

Thomas shook his head. "I rarely see Jane, and knowing she is betrothed to be married has forced me to accept that I must move on. I cannot imagine what it must be like for you when you see her every day. If you don't mind my asking, why can you not be together?"

"It has been decreed that we are not to be together. She is destined to marry another. Our feelings are secondary to the will of the gods."

The two brothers sat together in silence, each grieving for the love that they had been denied.

Forty-Two

A Team

As Thomas returned to the plantation, his head was bursting. He felt at one with his brother. He had never met someone he could relate to in the same way. This was what it was like to have a brother: someone who shared not only the blood in his veins but also similar views and experiences.

He had not realized the trauma that Kokee had been through. The tears Kokee shed when describing the loss of his father activated feelings about his own father. But there was a difference. Kokee's father had been murdered; he had not chosen to leave his son.

He sighed as the buggy rumbled on, with Waba lying in the back. He and his brother had so many regrets . . . so many losses. And Kokee's description of his thwarted romantic relationship was uncannily similar to his own.

As for Kokee's plan for peace, it was like a door to his dreams had been unlocked. It was up to him to push it open. Kokee was right. He had to continue what Pocahontas had started despite the ill will of rogue warriors and Jamestown politics, no matter how difficult it seemed. Namontack had spared him for a reason. He was the son of Pocahontas, and he should never forget that.

The plantation came into view. He rumbled up to the house and stopped beneath the steps.

He turned around and looked in the back of the buggy, seeing Waba ready to jump out. She was a symbol of his connection to his Powhatan family.

"This is your new home, Waba," he said as she jumped with greyhound ease from the buggy, bounded up the steps, legs flailing, and stood waiting, looking expectantly at him.

Thomas laughed. He walked up the stairs and opened the door. Waba careered in and stood by the roaring fire as if she owned the place. Lizzie was making the supper, and John and Francis sat on either side of the fireplace. They all stared at the large greyhound that had crashed into their lives with such enthusiasm.

"Thomas!" said Francis, glancing over at the prancing greyhound. "It looks like a productive day."

Lizzie came over and looked at Waba. "So what have we here, Thomas? Is this a new family member?" she patted Waba's head and fondled her ears. Waba looked adoringly at her with huge brown eyes.

Thomas smiled. "Yes, she is a new member of the family. Nikkiti gave her to me."

"Why did Nikkiti give you such a gift?" asked John.

Thomas walked over to the dog and patted her. "Waba and her sister Manitu are descendants of the greyhound that the King of England gave to my mother. Nikkiti wanted to welcome me to Virginia by giving her to me."

Francis smiled. "Nikkiti is quite pretty, isn't she?" He winked.

Thomas shook his head. "There is no denying that. But she is too good for me."

John laughed. "That's a yes, then." His green eyes sparkled.

Thomas shook his head again, his voice abrupt. "There are too many more important things I have to think about," he said, a rosy hue creeping onto his face as he realized his increasingly romantic feelings for Nikkiti.

Lizzie felt his discomfort and looked at John and Francis, raising her eyebrows. "Why don't we sit down and eat, and you can tell us what these 'more important' things are, Thomas. Before you do that, you'd better give Waba something to eat and drink." The greyhound heard her name and jumped up from where she had been lying by the fire, looking at Thomas, drooling.

Thomas put a bowl of food down for Waba and sat with his sister and two brothers at the table. There was silence as they all started to eat the warm stew that Lizzie had put in front of them. It was calm, friendly, and peaceful, and Thomas savored being part of such a family, but his mind was restless. Feelings for Nikkiti faded into the background as he ruminated on the expectations placed on his shoulders. It was as though he had gone from being an outcast to a hero of peace—neither of which felt authentic.

Lizzie cleared her throat, sensing his heavy mood. "So, did Odina and Chepi settle in at the Powhatan village?" she asked.

Thomas looked up. "They had a very warm welcome," he said, looking down at what he was eating again.

Everyone waited for him to elaborate. He said nothing more.

Lizzie looked at Thomas, her eyebrows raised. "Well, what are the 'important' things you're thinking about?"

Thomas felt the blood rising to his face. "Lizzie, I don't know how to explain, and I don't want to talk about it." He could feel his emotions rising and hoped she did not press him further.

He felt her hand on his arm, giving a friendly squeeze. "Thomas, I know you've not had much of a family up until now, but we are your family, and we are here to help and support you. That's what families are for." She gave him another friendly squeeze.

He looked up at them all and saw they were gazing at him fondly. With a twinge of guilt, he said, "I'm sorry. I don't want to burden you with my problems."

"You never know; we might be able to help. Why don't you give it a try?" said Lizzie.

"Very well," he said, sighing at the uncomfortable but welcome intrusion.

"Kokee thinks that my mixed heritage could give me an advantage in progressing peace talks. This might have been so, but for the fact that I have already had several run-ins with Sir George. In fact, in the last one, I lost control and he ended up on the ground. How can I negotiate to lead a peace process when there is mutual hatred between myself and the one person I need on my side?"

The four of them sat around the table, deep in thought.

John looked up. "I have an idea. Why don't you bypass Sir George and go to the governor instead?"

"Yes," said Lizzie. "He or his brother will have known your father. At least there will be some common ground."

Thomas pursed his lips and nodded. "Mmmm . . . yes, but Sir George has always taken command of the day-to-day running of the colony, so I believed him to be the best one to deal with." He paused, mulling over what had been said. "Maybe you're right; I probably need a different perspective on this issue. But Sir George would be furious with me for going over his head."

Francis nodded. "Yes, but that doesn't matter if you get what you want. He's hardly on your side now; it can't get much worse."

"You're right. He could not hate me more than he does at the moment." Thomas stifled a laugh.

Lizzie touched Thomas's arm again. "See . . . we are a team."

"Yes, we are." Thomas smiled, looking at them in turn. It had been difficult to share his problem, but now he felt relieved that he had a way forward, plus a renewed sense of belonging and friendship.

They all started eating again in silence. Thomas could feel the tension leaving his body with each spoonful of the warm stew. He was home; he had a plan.

Francis put his spoon down. "On another note, something peculiar is happening with the chickens," he said.

They all stopped eating and looked at him.

"I found one chicken dead yesterday and another today."

"What did they die of?" asked Lizzie.

Francis shook his head. "That's the strange thing. There was no obvious cause. I shrugged the first off as having caught an illness or something, but when I found the second, it felt very odd."

John pursed his lips. "Chickens don't die without a good reason. We'll have to keep an eye on them. It might be a new strain of illness that has no symptoms. I hope it's not contagious, or we might lose them all." Everyone nodded in agreement.

John looked at the fire. "Oh no, the fire is fading." His chair scraped along the floor as he got up from the table. "I'll go get some more logs," he said.

The other three finished their stew and sat back as John disappeared out of the door.

"Would anyone like some more?" asked Lizzie.

Suddenly, they heard heavy, rapid footsteps running up the outside stairs. John crashed through the door, breathless, his face scrunched up with panic. "The barn is on fire!" he screamed.

Forty-Three

The Fire

It was the smell that hit them first, choking them and burning their noses, throats, and lungs. The concept of fire, so warm and comforting when sitting in the kitchen, was now transformed into a frenzy of crackling, out-of-control danger. The orange forks scrambled up the sides of the barn, devouring the newly painted wood while spitting out a suffocating black smoke that obscured visibility. The barn was alive with movement as the fire ate into it.

Thomas stood for a few seconds, stunned. How long had the fire been going? It looked like it had been quite a while. How had it started? He could not think of that now.

"Quick—lower the bucket into the well; we must try to save it," he shouted over the roaring inferno.

John ran over to the well and did as he was told. When the bucket came up, he threw it to Francis and sent another bucket down the

The Fire

well. Francis threw the first bucket to Lizzie, and she to Thomas, who threw it with all his might onto the fire.

Bucket after bucket was filled and emptied. Down and up, the bucket went as it was passed along the line of coughing firefighters. Droplets of water sizzled and spat as they collided with the heat of the burning wood. In response to the watery attack, the angry fire sent black smoke spiraling into the atmosphere and continued with relish, devouring the defenseless barn.

It was relentless. The more they fought, the stronger the fire became.

The whole season's hay was going up in smoke. The rats nesting in the nooks and crannies scampered in every direction, squeaking and blind with terror.

They fought on, exhaustion setting in with no visible signs of progress. They gasped for air as the thick smoke filled their lungs. Tears rolled down their cheeks from swollen, bloodshot eyes.

After what seemed like hours, Thomas stopped, put his hands on his hips, and stared at the defiant flames. "The structure is getting weaker. It will start falling soon. We must stand back. We've done all we can, and it's starting to get dangerous to be this close." He looked up at the blackened roof. "We just have to be thankful it's too far from the house for the fire to spread." As he stood back, part of the side of the barn fell, and the roof it supported crashed to the ground, as if announcing nature's victory over feeble humanity.

Waba lurked in the background fearfully, observing the noisy spectacle and instinctively keeping her distance. Suddenly, from inside the barn, a rabbit broke cover. The instinct for chase overriding that of safety, Waba sped towards the fire.

Thomas and his siblings saw a flash of white in the side of their vision and turned to watch with horror. They were rooted to the spot, powerless, as the greyhound, as if in slow motion, collided with a piece of burning wood as it fell from the crumbling structure.

Waba howled in agony as the red-hot beam pinned her to the ground. Thomas ran towards her, followed by John and Francis. The massive smoldering beam could not be moved easily. They strained and heaved, hands burning, to no avail. Waba lay, her cries becoming weaker as consciousness started to dwindle.

Lizzie rushed up, hands either side of her face in panic. "Try and use something as a lever, and I can pull her out," she shouted.

Thomas looked around and spied a nearby shovel. He placed it under the beam and, heaving with superhuman strength, created a small gap between the dog and the beam. With lightning speed, Lizzie grabbed the dog and, with the help of Francis, pulled her to safety.

Thomas's muscles spasmed, and the beam slipped from his grasp, crashing down, ash and dust flying, missing the injured Waba by a whisper.

"Is she still alive, Lizzie?" John shouted the question they all wanted to ask.

Lizzie crouched down next to the unconscious dog. She put her fingers on her neck and looked up. "Yes . . . her heart is strong. Let's take her into the house."

Using an old blanket and each taking a side, they lifted her up the steps to the kitchen and laid her down gently.

Thomas knelt beside her to look at her injuries. The burning beam had landed on one of her delicate back legs, which now looked red, blistered, and swollen. It was jutting out at an angle, with a sharp piece of bone protruding through the oozing flesh. He stroked her silky white head, his large hands gentle as a feather.

Her oval brown eyes started to open as a tear ran down Thomas's face. How could this happen to such an innocent and graceful animal?

She looked at him, eyes wide, brow furrowed. As he stroked her, he whispered her name over and over, his words washing over her like a warm blanket.

Lizzie crouched down beside them. "Thomas, we'll have to do something with that leg. It's broken. She may lose it. The injury looks very complicated."

Thomas remembered the last time he saw Waba running up the steps. Such ease, such grace and speed. How could God be so cruel?

"I'll take her back to Nikkiti. She'll know what to do, and Waba will feel more comfortable with her sister Manitu by her side."

Lizzie nodded. "I can see how much you love her, but taking her back to the Powhatans is the right thing to do for now. Hopefully, she can return and live with us when she has recovered."

Thomas stood up. "I'm still confused about how the fire started so randomly."

Francis frowned. "It's strange that so many unexpected things are happening around here . . . the chickens dying was random, and now this. Do you think they could be connected?"

Thomas's mind drifted back to the last time he had seen Askook.

***

Nikkiti worked through the night, trying to save Waba's leg. The injuries were severe on a limb that was slim and extremely delicate. Thomas sat by Wabas's head and stroked her, his face gray with worry. The bloody and knarled leg disfigured her slender white body. Why had he taken this exquisite creature out of her environment? This was all his fault. This was about his ongoing feud with Askook. There was no proof, but it added up.

Nikkiti gave Waba an herbal tincture to ease her into an oblivious sleep while she maneuvered the splintered leg back into position. Her small hands worked deftly but gently as she aligned the leg. She dressed it with herbs and wrapped it tightly with woven cloth. Thomas watched her with admiration. Her talents and kindness knew no bounds.

Nikkiti looked up, and for a split second, their eyes met. She looked down again and stroked Wabas's flank. "I have done what I can. Hopefully, she will not lose the leg, but she will never be the same," she sighed. "How cruel for this to happen to such an innocent and carefree soul. Life is so unfair."

"It's my fault," said Thomas.

Nikkiti looked up again. "How can it be your fault, Thomas? The fire was an accident, and Waba's instinct for the chase overtook everything. You cannot blame yourself for this." She looked at him, her eyebrows drawn.

"I'm pretty sure it was Askook who started the fire. This would never have happened if it were not for the feud between us."

"Even if it was Askook . . . you cannot take the blame." She put her hand out to touch him.

He looked down at her hand and picked it up, raising it to his lips and gently kissing it. "Thank you," he said. He searched her eyes for acceptance of his gesture and saw softness before she eased her hand away, looking at the ground.

He felt she was on his side. "I am grateful for your support, but I cannot absolve myself from the part I played in this."

She shook her head. "You know it is not as simple as that. Askook is deranged."

Thomas leaned down and stroked Waba. "I must put an end to this. There's no telling what he will do next. He killed some of our chickens, and there have been other strange things going on that I did not connect to him until now. Last week, one of the cows had a large gash on her leg. We thought she had cut it on something in the field, but now that I think of it, nothing is sharp in that area. Then the horse was untied, when I was positive I tethered her. It took hours to find her, as she had wandered into the woods. Each thing could have an alternative explanation . . . but a picture is building up."

Nikkiti touched his arm again. While her gesture was as light as a feather, it felt like a thunderbolt through Thomas's heart, a feeling that took him by surprise. She appeared unaware of her impact on him as she continued, "It will be difficult to get justice for any of the things that have happened. Even if we could prove it, Askook is untouchable because of Opechancanough's promise to his father."

Waba opened her eyes and lifted her paw towards Thomas, whimpering.

Thomas was jolted back to the moment and leaned down, gently caressing Wabas's ears. "It's alright, beautiful," he said. Nikkiti knows what she's doing." He stroked Waba until she relaxed.

"We must make sure she does not try to lick the wound, because it will stop it from healing," Nikkiti whispered, her voice hoarse with emotion as she stroked the dog. "Wounds heal, but there are always scars."

"Yes, of course," said Thomas.

The more he was with her, the less thoughts of Jane plagued his mind. Perhaps his wound was starting to heal. But would he always bear the scar?

Forty-Four

The Governor

The man before him had a presence. He was the forty-five year-old governor, in immaculate uniform and wearing a rehearsed smile. Leadership was in his blood, as he had followed in the footsteps of two of his elder brothers. Before Governor West had opened his mouth to speak, Thomas felt the atmosphere of calm authority that surrounded him.

"Well, at last, I am meeting the son of John Rolfe properly," the governor said, holding his large hand out to Thomas. "Do take a seat." He pointed to the chair opposite his desk. "Our families have been friends for many years, Thomas."

Thomas nodded and sat down. "Yes, sir," he said smiling. Your brother shared many of the trials and tribulations of the founding of this colony with my father. Sadly, I have few memories of my father, as he felt it safer for me to grow up in England." A shadow crossed

Thomas's face.

"Your father was a good man, Thomas. I had many a glass of ale with him when I first arrived in the colony. Your mother, too . . . what a brave woman to have crossed the cultural divide. I often wonder what would have happened if she had not had such an untimely death. You never know; we might have been living shoulder to shoulder rather than living with these horrible skirmishes and disagreements."

Thomas nodded. "Yes, who knows what might have happened. Now, I have a legacy to try and carry on what she started." He looked at Governor West with a penetrating gaze.

"I see," said the governor, leaning back in his chair and making a cathedral of his fingers. The atmosphere in the room changed from frivolous to serious. "And to do this, you must visit the Powhatan settlement."

"Yes, that is correct, sir."

Governor West leaned forward and looked over his desk at Thomas. "I understand you have already visited, though, Thomas."

Thomas's heart sank. What had started so well was taking a turn for the worse.

The governor looked deeper into Thomas's eyes. "Sir George has told me about the debacle of your supposed kidnapping by the Powhatans. What the blazes was going on, Thomas?" His voice was raised, his immaculate composure fraying at the edges. "As governor of this colony, I need to be thoroughly versed in the truth of your motives before I agree to any contact with the Powhatans." Generations of authority and leadership resonated through his words. He was not a man to trifle with.

Thomas would not be bowed despite his tender years and inexperience. He would have to put his case coherently. His whole purpose was at stake.

"Sir, my motives are set in stone. I am uniquely positioned to heal the rift between my mother's and my father's people."

The governor nodded, his face softening. "Yes, I agree with that." He paused, suddenly pinning Thomas with his stare. "But I must be convinced you will use this position wisely. Fitzgerald tells me you broke the law and visited the Powhatans of your own free will—you were not kidnapped. What is the truth, Thomas Rolfe?"

It was too much to hope that Fitzgerald had not already prejudiced his cause. Internally, Thomas's heart sank. Externally, determination shone in his eyes.

"Sir, I believed that the lives of two innocent Powhatans were at stake. If I had accused them of kidnapping me, Fitzgerald was going to put them to death. The two Powhatans in question were the son and daughter of Opechancanough. If I had allowed Fitzgerald to kill them, the consequences would have been unthinkable."

The governor sat back in his chair and looked at Thomas long and hard.

"There was never any question that we would kill Nikkiti and Nectowance. We are not complete idiots," he said.

Thomas felt trapped. To accuse the governor's right-hand man of lying would not endear him. "I am sure Sir George had his reasons for leading me to believe their lives were at risk," he said. "The truth is that the Powhatans kidnapped me as it was the only way they could contact me. My uncle wanted to meet the son of Pocahontas. It was not a malicious act, and if my sister had not reported me missing, I would have been returned unharmed with no one knowing.

"At the time, when faced with the option of discrediting myself or causing the death of two innocents, I had to do what I felt best. While lying is not in my nature, I felt removing the blame from the Powhatans would prevent bloodshed."

The governor shook his head. "So if you lied then, how can I trust you in the future, Thomas?"

This was the crux of the matter. In the governor's position, Thomas would have asked the same question. How could he win his trust?

"Sir, I must lay myself at your mercy. Preventing war is something my mother gave her life for. I intend, with the help of my brother, Kokee, to continue this quest. I admit to lying, but I lied to prevent not only the death of Nikkiti and Nectowance but the deaths of many. My mistake was naivete. I have enemies, such as Fitzgerald, who do not want me to succeed, and I walked into his trap. I hope that you will be able to see through the political tangle and appreciate the sincerity of my goal."

The governor crossed his arms and looked at Thomas. "Young man, I am impressed by your passion, and I can see the dilemma in which you have been placed. My concern has been that your understandable loyalty to the Powhatans could result in your becoming a spy for them and putting the colony at risk." His face softened.

"If we are to carry your ideas forward, it needs to be done slowly and carefully. We must have a partnership. You cannot take matters into your own hands. I need to know your plans and when and how they will be executed. My trust in you can only be partial, as I am realistic enough to know that your loyalties must be divided. You will be the facilitator, but ultimately, I will make any decisions that are to be made. It is the only way."

"I agree, sir. I promise I will not let you down. I can arrange to meet with Opechancanough and Kokee again to continue what we have already started. They kidnapped me to try to instigate talks; they are as desperate to end hostilities as we are."

"Do your homework, young man. Get to know these people. Get to understand their motives and how they think. We need to know how to live alongside them peacefully."

The governor put his hand out for a handshake. "If I see or hear anything that causes me to doubt you, I will cancel this agreement."

His face was stern.

"I understand," said Thomas as he stood to walk out.

The governor pushed his chair back. "Oh, I meant to say, we have another acquaintance in common."

"Who is that, sir?"

"My late brother's wife, Temperance, has a son called Ambrose, one of my nephews. He is one of my most prized officers. I will be his best man when he marries a very good family friend of yours . . . a Miss Jane Poythress? Perhaps I will see you at the wedding?"

***

"Fitzgerald? Can you come in, please?" shouted Governor West.

Fitzgerald entered the room and stood to attention. "Yes, sir!"

"At ease. Please take a seat," he said. He waited until Fitzgerald was settled and looking expectantly at him. "What are your feelings about Thomas Rolfe?" he asked.

Fitzgerald paused and twirled his handlebar mustache. His political mind was searching for an answer that would align favorably with the views of his superior. The truth was irrelevant.

"Recent events do not cast Mr. Rolfe in a particularly good light." He waited to see the governor's reaction and saw a blank face. "However, if our goal is to forge peace with the Powhatans, in theory, Mr. Rolfe may be a way in." There was still no clue from the governor's face as to whether he was on a favorable tack. "He broke the law and visited the Powhatans—he is a loose cannon," he blurted.

The governor looked Fitzgerald squarely in the face. "You lied to him when you told him we would execute the two Powhatans," he said quietly.

Fitzgerald looked at the floor, arranging his thoughts. "He is a bloody Powhatan, sir. He cannot be trusted."

"It would seem that neither can you, Fitzgerald!" his face was like thunder. "From now on, I want you to cooperate with Mr. Rolfe. I am using his connections to try to move forward with these bloody people. We need their land, and getting it peacefully will be preferable. The king is watching, and if we can make progress, it will be a feather in my cap. I do not want you messing things up." His eyes were staring. "Do I make myself clear, Fitzgerald?"

Sir George shuffled and mumbled, "Yes, sir, of course, sir."

"Now get out of my sight!" screamed the governor.

Fitzgerald shuffled out of the room, looking at the floor.

How dare that half-breed upstart put him in this position with the governor. He, Sir George Fitzgerald I, as an upstanding loyal servant of the king, would have to rectify this injustice and expose the bastard.

The gauntlet was down, and it was only a matter of time before Rolfe would be squirming and begging for his life. Fitzgerald smiled at the image as he stomped out of the building.

Forty-Five

Peace Summit

It was the culmination of years of preparation. Many people had lost their lives in pursuit of the negotiations that were about to take place, and the significance of the occasion hung in the air.

Thomas sat opposite Opechancanough and Kokee in the quioccosan. The fire smoldered between them, and the aroma of burning hickory wood was sweet as it filled the room. Opechancanough wore the full ceremonial dress. His feathered headdress surrounded his face and reached the floor, creating a centerpiece for the tableaux of players.

"Thomas, we welcome you as not only the ambassador for your English kin but also as part of our tribe," he said.

Thomas smiled. "Uncle, it is with great pride that I come today to talk with you about the way forward for our people. There is a will on both sides of the divide to forge a working relationship that will benefit us all."

"Indeed, Thomas." Opechancanough paused and looked at each of the Englishmen opposite. "We must put aside past grievances and look to the future. What we decide today will benefit present and future generations." His rheumy eyes were sad. "I begin by apologizing for any perceived wrongdoing on the part of the Powhatan Nation and honor those on both sides whose lives have been taken in senseless conflict." He closed his eyes as though absorbing the seriousness of his own words. He passed the pipe to Thomas.

Thomas looked at the pipe and drew on the pungent tobacco, forcing down the cough in his throat. As his breathing returned to normal, he looked at his uncle.

"On behalf of the English settlers, I accept your gracious apology with the understanding that we also take responsibility for and repent of any misplaced aggression towards the Powhatans."

Opechancanough nodded. "Thank you, Thomas." He bowed his head. "I will instruct my warriors to behave towards our English brethren with respect. From our side, there will be no more random acts of violence, and we will regard your kin as our kin."

Thomas drew on the pipe and passed it to Opechancanough. "Uncle, the winds have blown me to you. My wish has always been for the roots of my mother and father to intertwine in peace. To ensure this, I will instruct Governor West of your magnanimous intentions so that he, likewise, can order the soldiers of King James to put down their arms and regard the Powhatan as friends, not enemies."

There was silence in the room as everyone contemplated his momentous words.

The wind whistled outside as the rain pelted down on the roof. The smell of damp earth mingled with the smoke of the fire. The silence was charged with anticipation for what was to come.

Opechancanough looked up.

"For many moons, the gods give us meager rain in summer to grow the corn. In winter, they sent us daggers of ice and earth as hard as stone. Our crops have failed many times, and our rations have been small. We have little, but what little we have, we share. I hope that in our new world of brotherhood, food will not be the focus of conflict."

Thomas put his hands together and bowed his head. "This is a wish that I share, Uncle." He looked up. "Perhaps your experienced warriors could teach us the ways of cultivation, as this is a land of which we are unfamiliar. Our attempts at growing crops have yielded pitiful amounts of food, and your knowledge would greatly benefit us." His eyes were sparkling, and adrenaline-fueled anticipation was written on his face.

Opechancanough nodded. "My nephew, your heart and my heart are in harmony. However, such things must be done slowly and with forethought of the difficulties that two cultures will have as they integrate. The closeness of instruction may feel invasive to those whose hearts yearn for the ways of the past. We will help you, but we must first allow positive feelings for one another to grow. In time, our cultures will blend organically. As the winds blow warmer between us, the English Colony will become a part of the Powhatan Nation, and we will live in harmony, cultivating the land hand in hand."

Thomas could feel fidgeting behind him. He turned and saw Sir George red in the face, angry and rising to his feet. "Sir, I must contribute to these negotiations. I am Sir George Fitzgerald the First. I alone speak for the governor of the English Colony." He glared at Thomas. "We are a proud and superior nation. The Powhatan will never rule us, and we will never become part of the Powhatan Nation. I wish to clarify that before any further pacts are made." He stood erect, staring at Opechancanough, aggression seeping from every pore.

The audience held their breath as tension hung over them.

Opechancanough, unaffected, nodded and held up the pipe of peace, handing it to one of his warriors. "Please give this pipe to Sir George."

The pipe was duly passed. "I welcome you to our first meeting, Sir George. To show my respect, I invite you to sit and smoke this pipe of peace with me." He smiled calmly.

Sir George was unsure what to do. His anger had been met with a wall of composure that was as unexpected as it was destabilizing. He paused. If it got back to the governor that he had refused the peace pipe, he would be out of favor again. Reluctantly, he took the pipe and sucked longer and harder than most to demonstrate his strength and dignity: he would show them how true leaders behave. This heathen would get away with nothing!

As the pungent smoke hit his virgin English lungs, he collapsed into a spasm of uncontrollable coughing. A warrior rushed up and handed him a flagon of water, which he took, glaring at those around him who were stifling instinctive laughter. Sir George threw the pipe on the ground, stamping on the embers that jumped around his feet. After a few minutes, he tried to speak, but the smoke had left its mark on his throat, and every time he tried, he started to cough again.

Opechancanough looked on, sagely pondering the measure of this man who had the power to erect a barrier to peace.

"Good friend, my apologies for the harshness of our tobacco. Those unused to it are often taken by surprise." His ceremonial headdress shook as he swallowed his laughter. "The next time we meet, we will ensure you have the lighter blend that we save for the squaws."

Fitzgerald was overcome with rage but still unable to speak. He rose from his seat and walked out of the quioccosan without a glance backwards.

Opechancanough watched him go with a smile on his gnarled face and turned to Thomas. "My son, despite interruptions, we have come far in our discussions today. I hope that we may continue at our next meeting."

Thomas nodded. "I have been dreaming of this moment for many years. I will do anything to ensure that the blood of Powhatan and English that flows through me will be the blueprint of our peaceful integration."

Opechancanough put his hands together and closed his eyes, starting a chant that filled the room. The mystical chant, in minor discord, continued for several minutes. When he finished, he opened his eyes, stood up, and looked at Thomas. "Thomas Rolfe, we officially welcome you into our family." He signaled for one of the warriors to come forward. The warrior carried some moccasins and a deerskin tunic. Opechancanough continued, "Please take these as our way of recognizing you as part of our Powhatan family."

Thomas took the items and got to his knees. "Sir, this is a great honor." He bowed his head.

Opechancanough smiled. "We have one more thing for you that demonstrates our trust in you and will unite our people." He clapped his hands.

Thomas looked around him, uncertainty on his face. At the back of the room, he caught sight of Nikkiti.

She was dressed in a beautiful suede tunic and adorned with jewelry around her neck, arms, and ankles. Her black hair was braided with small white flowers. She was a vision of beauty.

Nikkiti walked towards him and held her hand out, glancing from Thomas to Kokee. Thomas was overwhelmed and unsure but took her hand, smiling weakly, uncertain of what was happening.

Opechancanough smiled. "Thomas . . . Nikkiti will be your Powhatan bride. Your ceremony will be in six moons, and Powhatan and English are invited to come together to show their solidarity and support for the union, paving the way for all of our futures."

***

Askook would bide his time. Thomas Rolfe's precious peace summit had provided him with a gift—an ally in the English camp. Fitzgerald was as against Thomas Rolfe as he was; he saw it in the Longcoat's eyes as he marched out of the quioccosan, coughing his guts out.

He chuckled, thinking about how ridiculous Fitzgerald had looked. Ridiculous or not, he had power within the Longcoat hierarchy and would be an invaluable asset. There would be no friendly integration between Powhatan and English if he and Fitzgerald colluded to destroy Thomas Rolfe.

When Rolfe was out of the way, Askook would have a clear pathway to manipulate the old bastard, Opechancanough, who had as good as killed his father. He smiled. Thomas Rolfe did not know what was coming, and neither did Opechancanough. No one would ever laugh at Askook again. They had all underestimated him, including that bitch Nikkiti who had always spurned his advances.

His "voices" had assured him he would be the next leader, and nothing would stand in his way.

***

Thomas lay awake, his mind racing. What a shock! He was trapped. Perhaps this was a test of his loyalty and commitment to peace. Refusing marriage would not only be disrespectful to Opechancanough and Nikkiti, but it would also be rejecting a significant opportunity for peace. It was a clever but radical move from Opechancanough, but it showed his commitment.

Nikkiti had smiled in approval, but he detected something in her eyes that he could not decipher. Was she pleased to be his wife or resigned? Perhaps she was feeling the overwhelming anxiety that was also plaguing him.

The whole process of peace was reliant on their relationship succeeding when they hardly knew one another. Opechancanough was already decreeing their children as the holders of the destiny of all the inhabitants of Virginia. Although he had spent time with Nikkiti, there was no intimacy between them.

The plan was for him to spend as much time as possible with Nikkiti and get to know her better over the next six months. She was visiting Varina tomorrow.

He thought of the times they had already spent together: Lying next to him in the woods when she had rescued him . . . standing up to the English soldiers . . . tending to the tiny mother and her baby . . . Yes, she was an extraordinary girl. He was fond of her and thought her beautiful and courageous, but did he love her? Before Opechancanough had intervened, they were friends. With time, they may have grown closer. He was attracted to her, admired and liked her, but would not have been ready to marry her. Love could have grown, but it was not the burning need he felt with Jane. With Jane, he had known immediately that he wanted to be with her for the rest of his life.o

His mind darted around and around. He had always wondered why Nikkiti had come alone to rescue him. She had given a plausible explanation at the time, but now he could see that it had all been a part of Opechancanough's plan. Opechancanough must have sent her.

When he first arrived, Nikkiti had joined his meeting with Kokee, and she had always been at the forefront of every meeting he had had with the Powhatans.

Even before he arrived in Virginia, Opechancanough must have chosen Nikkiti as his wife, knowing her loyalty to her people. Thomas could see the logic of an arranged marriage between himself and a Powhatan girl, but how did Nikkiti feel? And could he marry a girl who might not want to be his wife, even if it was for the good of everyone else?

He thought of his mother and father. Had they been in this same situation? Was their union forced upon them? What about his conception? What was it that Askook had said? . . . "This man is the result of rape, be assured of that."

His heart skipped a beat. No . . . that could not be. Mr. Jenkins had told him of the love between his parents. But why did his father leave him in England and never bring him to Virginia? Joan had assured him of his father's love, but she was a kind person; conceivably, she had, at the very least, embellished the truth. How would she know what actually happened when his parents were together? He forced himself to stop speculating on the past. There were no answers, and he would go mad trying to find them.

Now, it was up to him and Nikkiti to take responsibility for creating a peaceful future. Could they develop an enduring love, or would they live as friends?

He had thought the pursuit of peace was his life's only goal. But now he felt doubt working its way through his resolve.

Forty-Six

Family Meeting

N ikkiti had been at Varina before when she tended to Odina and Chepi. This time, she was arriving as the future mistress of the house.

Thomas heard the drums and chanting of the procession as they approached the plantation. When he went outside, the spectacle before him stopped him in his tracks. His face drained of color as the significance of his impending marriage played out before him. He knew she was coming, but he had imagined an informal visit; this was anything but. Not-so-subtle messages were coming thick and fast that he was to be the next werowance.

Six warriors accompanied her. The extravaganza of magnificent headdresses, glowing naked chests, and red puccoon–painted bodies was a sight to behold. Nikkiti wore a magnificent headdress of white feathers encrusted with jewels. She was carried on a litter as befitted

Family Meeting

the future bride of the next leader. Lying beside her was Waba, whose leg showed the scars of the fire. The chanting and drums continued until the litter stopped at the bottom of the stairs.

With heart racing, he rushed down to greet her, taking her hand and helping her from the litter. The litter was laid on the ground for Waba to disembark, and when she had done so, she stood, her large brown eyes gazing at Thomas. The warriors moved aside and bowed, their hands together, their precious cargo delivered.

Thomas turned towards them and bowed his appreciation. Then, holding Nikkiti's hand, he turned towards the dog, who stood obediently waiting. Thomas stooped to fondle her white velvet ears. She pushed her head into his hand, increasing the pressure of his touch.

"Nikkiti, it looks like you have performed a miracle," he said, running his hands down the injured leg.

She shook her head. "Not quite a miracle. She still limps, and at times, it causes her some pain, but she will survive. The poor girl has suffered, though. My heart aches for her."

"Askook has a lot to answer for, and I will make sure he pays for what happened," Thomas said, his face like granite.

Nikkiti took his hand. "We have to prove that he had something to do with the fire, and then we will have to convince Opechancanough of Askooks's guilt. For today at least, let us try and put that behind us." She looked up towards the veranda and waved at Lizzie and the boys waiting to take her into the house.

Thomas braced himself, took Nikkiti's hand and Waba's rope and walked sedately up the steps to be with his family. He opened the door, and they all went inside.

Inside, the silence, the familiar smell of roasting venison, .and the flickering firelight made for the usual homely scene that vastly contrasted with Nikkiti's colorful and noisy arrival. Lizzy and the boys crowded around her, eager to welcome her into the family. Waba lay by the fire as if she had never been away.

"Welcome, Nikkiti," said Lizzie. Congratulations on your betrothal. We are all delighted to welcome you into our family and to have this beautiful girl back," she said as she glanced at Waba luxuriating in the warmth of the flickering fire.

Nikkiti smiled. "Thank you, Lizzie."

"You make quite an entrance nowadays," said Lizzie, laughing.

"Opechancanough wanted you all to know how important our marriage is. If Thomas were to become the next werowance, he would be treated with the respect that the role demands and all the splendor he deserves."

There was silence as her words hung in the air.

Thomas stared. "It's not definite that I will become werowance. This has not formally been discussed . . . has it, Nikkiti?"

"No. But Opechancanough sees our marriage as the first step," she said.

John had been listening intently, and his face turned red. "I knew it. I knew all along that you would leave us and go to them. You have been lying to us from the beginning. I don't know how I fell for it." His freckled face was screwed up, and his eyes were moist. The vulnerability of his tender years was laid bare.

Thomas's heart sank. "No, please, John, believe me . . . nothing has been agreed apart from my marriage to Nikkiti."

John ran his hands through his sandy hair. "I think the circus we have just witnessed would say otherwise, Thomas," he spat.

Thomas stood directly in front of John. "I promise you, no matter what, I am here for you, Francis, and Lizzie. Nikkiti can live with us, and if I have to carry on with peace negotiations, I will do that without leaving you. I have not agreed to become werowance, as I do not think it is my place."

John shook his head, turning away from Thomas. "You will say anything to get what you want, Thomas." He marched out of the room.

Thomas looked after him, his face crestfallen. "There's little point in my going after him; he's too emotional. Francis, you're the only one who can talk sense into him; perhaps you could try?"

Francis looked at Thomas and sighed. "I'll go to him, but I'm going because I agree with him this time. You're letting us down again, Thomas. It was one thing marrying a Powhatan . . . and we are happy for you and Nikkiti," he smiled and nodded at her, "but it's another thing to become the Powhatan leader," he said as he turned and walked away.

Thomas watched him go and stood in silence. "I can see things are not going to be easy. If I cannot get my family onboard, what chance do I have with the British Army?"

Lizzy came towards him and put her arm around him. "It will take time," she whispered. "Those boys have had a lot of pain in the past, and they just need space to get it through their heads that you are not leaving them." She hugged him. "You will just have to be patient," she said, turning to look at Nikkiti.

"And Nikkiti, this time is really for you and Thomas. I'll go and see where those boys have got to. Don't worry about them. You need time for yourselves; you must have much to discuss." Before she walked out, she went over to Nikkiti. "I'm sorry about the boys, Nikkiti. They're young. They will come around in time, I know they will," she said as she gave her a peck on the cheek and walked outside.

When they were finally alone, Nikkiti and Thomas looked at one another with solemn faces.

Nikkiti was the first to speak. "I am sorry I have upset your family, Thomas." She looked at her hands resting in her lap.

Thomas shook his head. "You have nothing to apologize for.

Marrying you will be the greatest of honors." He walked over to where she was sitting and knelt before her. "Dear Nikkiti, I cannot lie . . . it was a huge shock when Opechancanough made his announcement, but it will be a privilege to be your husband. My feelings for you have grown over the months we've known one another." He took her hand and looked into her eyes. "If Opechancanough had not arranged our marriage, it would only have been a matter of time before I asked you without any prompting from him."

She smiled. "You are such a good man, Thomas Rolfe. But I know your heart belongs to Jane."

He looked deeper into her eyes, pulled her hand up to his mouth and planted a gentle kiss. "Yes, Jane was special to me. But I've had to close that door to my heart. It's time I opened another one. Jane was my past, you are my future."

She smiled weakly. "Thomas, the Powhatan Nation deserves a man like you as their werowance . . . and I will happily marry you." She clutched his hand.

He pursed his lips. "Opechancanough has not discussed my becoming werowance, Nikkiti," he said, frowning. "I cannot take that role. It should belong to Kokee alone."

"It is what the gods have decreed, Thomas. When the time is right, you and Kokee will become werowance. Opechancanough wants to invite you into our world slowly. The first step will be our marriage."

Thomas looked at the ground. His every dream was coming true, but his heart had no joy. His gut was telling him that something was not right. "I know you are very loyal to your Powhatan family, Nikkiti," he looked up at her, still frowning, "but how do you feel about becoming my wife?"

She smiled. "Thomas, you are a good man, and I will marry you with gladness. Sometimes, there are things in life that are bigger than us. I trust the gods, and I trust Opechancanough to know what is best."

Thomas looked at her, eyes wide. "That is exactly what I mean! It may be for the best for everyone else, but is it what is best for you?"

"Yes, it is best for me, Thomas," she said. Her voice was strong and determined. "You and I are to follow in the footsteps of Pocahontas and John Rolfe. For me, this is the greatest honor that I could be awarded. If we are fortunate enough to have many babies, they will start a new integrated society. There is nothing more important than that." The earnestness written on her face told Thomas all he needed to know. She did want to marry him, but not for the reasons he would have liked.

Perhaps she was right. This was a calling. He loved her in his own way but did not think she felt the same way. Maybe her affection would grow.

He took both of her hands in his and gazed into her eyes. "I will be the best husband I can be for you, Nikkiti," he said, his eyes soft. "Jane is marrying another, and you need have no fear that I would ever betray you or that my thoughts will be of her. You will be the center of the world for me. I only hope that you truly have no regrets."

She shook her head. "Have no fear, Thomas. We will make a formidable team. I have no regrets whatsoever," she said.

There was a loud banging on the door. "We must take you back to the tribe now, Nikkiti," shouted one of the warriors.

Thomas started walking towards the door, then stopped suddenly, turning towards Nikkiti and gently wrapping his arms around her. He breathed in her sweet herbal scent. It felt nice. Instinctively, he stooped to give her a gentle kiss. "Our first kiss," he said, smiling.

Nikkiti put her hands gently on either side of his face, looking into his brown eyes. "You and I will make a difference," she said, her eyes sparkling.

He looked at the floor. He had hoped his kiss would spark affection rather than a confirmation of their duty. But perhaps that would take more time. For now, at least, she seemed content to comply with Opechancanough's manipulative plan.

Forty-Seven

Uncertainty

Thomas received a formal invitation to meet with Opechancanough out of the blue. The purpose of the meeting was not made clear. Perhaps it was about the wedding? Maybe it was about his status within the tribe? It made sense; bringing it out into the open would be welcome. Thomas also wanted to discuss Askook's behavior. Although Opechancanough favored Askook, he could not be allowed to continue his vendetta unchecked.

These topics were controversial, so Thomas was preparing for a challenging meeting.

He also wanted to meet with Nikkiti. She was a challenge of a different kind. He wanted to get to know her better and charm her into loving him—perhaps an unachievable goal, but one he had to pursue.

For his first visit to the Powhatan village since being presented with his Powhatan apparel, he decided to don his native clothing, to show Opechancanough his enthusiasm for his new family and to impress Nikkiti.

Thomas unfolded the fringed deerskin tunic and ran his fingers over the material, which was as soft as butter. It was a deep chestnut brown and smelled of sweet, musky leather. The moccasins matched, and as he slipped them onto his feet, they felt like they were a part of him.

He stood breathing in the aroma of the deerskin, imagining himself as a Powhatan warrior, the way he had done so many years ago in Heacham. It felt good.

He reached for his mother's pearls, placing them in the pocket of his tunic. Her image appeared, and he smiled. "Be safe, my Powhatan baby," she whispered. Thomas's heart soared as he watched her image slowly disappear.

He walked down the stairs and began feeling unease burning through his body as his previous elation disappeared. On moving towards the gaze of others, he felt as if he were playing the part of someone else. The beautiful fringed tunic was only fancy dress; instead of feeling authentic, he felt ridiculous. He took a deep breath. If others were to treat him seriously, he had to believe in himself. So, instead of fleeing back to his room and tearing the tunic off as he was compelled to do, he steeled himself and walked into the kitchen.

Lizzie looked up from washing the dishes. Her eyebrows raised, and her mouth dropped open. John and Francis took one look and walked out of the front door.

"Thomas, you look wonderful," Lizzie gasped.

He sat down and put his head in his hands. "That is not what your face told me when I walked in. I'm not sure this will work . . . and the boys are upset again, too."

She walked over and crouched in front of him, looking at him with a soft expression. "I'm sorry, Thomas, I'm not used to seeing you dressed like this. Neither are John and Francis. I was just surprised, that's all. I think you look at home in those clothes, and I have to say, you look very handsome. Nikkiti will love it."

He looked at her. "I'm not so sure about that, Lizzie, but if I am going to get to know the Powhatans, I have to respect them by wearing the clothes they gave me."

She stood up. "I know you do, Thomas. We all have to get used to it—even the boys. They will come around. It will just take time. They have to grow up and accept reality instead of fighting it and running away all the time. You're half Powhatan, and you should not have to apologize to anyone for that."

Thomas smiled. "You're the feistiest and loveliest sister anyone could ever want," he said, hugging her.

***

As Thomas approached Werowocomoco, he saw Kokee chopping wood in the distance. He waved at him, and Kokee stopped his work, looking up and peering toward him. As it dawned on him who was waving, he ran forward to greet his brother.

"Thomas, I did not recognize you at first; it is good to see you again." He smiled and patted him on the back. "You look like one of us now, which is as it should be. Rumor has it you are meeting with Opechancanough. I hope he can persuade you that you and I will be formidable werowances," he said.

Thomas shook his head. "You never give up, do you, brother," he said.

"I am not giving up until I see you with the full headdress and mantle of the werowance and with me standing next to you," said Kokee with a twinkle in his eyes.

Thomas shrugged his shoulders. "I can see there's no point in discussion, is there?"

Kokee shook his head and walked closer, putting his arm around him and giving a brotherly hug.

Out of nowhere came a child's voice in Powhatan. "Thomas! Thomas!" shouted Chogun, running up and throwing his arms around him.

Thomas picked him up and threw him playfully in the air. He turned to Kokee. "Tell Chogun I am pleased to see him and that he has grown since I last saw him."

Kokee spoke to Chogun, relating the message, and the lad beamed from ear to ear.

Chogun grasped hold of Thomas's hand and started pulling him. He pointed to one of the teepees. "Chepi . . . Odina," he shouted.

Thomas laughed, looking at Kokee. "I think he wants me to see Chepi."

As they approached one of the outlying yehakins, Thomas could see a tiny little person taking cautious steps, falling, getting up, and taking more steps. Chogun ran to the baby and sat on the ground before him, clapping his hands. Chepi laughed, fell, copied Chogun, and looked around to see who was watching. Odina then appeared and swept Chepi into her arms, kissing him and burying her face in his neck, focusing solely on her baby son. "My clever, wonderful Chepi," she said.

Looking up, she saw that Thomas was watching her. "Ah, Thomas, it is so nice to see you again. I am pleased to see you wear the clothes of your mother's people . . . I mean your people." She smiled. "I hardly recognized you, but that is only because you fit in so well with us."

Thomas was surprised at the strength of his emotions. The closeness he felt for Odina and Chepi was akin to that of family. He remembered the first time he had seen her; her vulnerability and innocence cut him to the core. Now, she was a happy young mother. He had a flash of tiny Chepi on the day he was born, a child whose heritage bore so much similarity to his own. These were intimate moments shared between family, and a flash of belonging swept over him.

Odina beamed. "You have come on the day that Chepi took his first steps. Thanks to you, we are both well and happy."

"He is a credit to you, Odina. I am glad I could witness such a milestone," said Thomas.

Odina looked beyond Thomas. "Ahh, I can see Nikkiti coming. By the way, congratulations on your betrothal, Thomas," she said as Nikkiti joined the group.

"So, what is happening here?" Nikkiti said, eyebrows raised, going over to Chepi, who was wriggling in his mother's arms. She put her hand out to the baby and he grabbed it, putting her finger in his mouth and biting it.

"Ouch," laughed Nikkiti. "He will make a fine warrior one day."

Thomas came and stood next to his future wife. "Nikkiti—"

Before he could say anything, she stood back, her eyes wide. "Thomas, I did not recognize you. How wonderful that you are wearing your tunic. You look very much like Kokee. You look very handsome." She glanced at Kokee and back to Thomas.

Thomas sighed, bathing in her acceptance. He took her hand and kissed it, smiling.

"Nikkiti, Chepi has taken his first steps today," he said, like a proud uncle.

Odina put the baby on the ground "Baba . . . walk to Nikkiti," she said. He stood on wobbly little legs, looking up at everyone. He glanced at Nikkiti and suddenly fell over, bursting into tears.

Nikkiti picked him up, whispering to him. He stopped crying and whimpering softly, molding himself to her as his eyes started to close.

Thomas was in awe. She was a natural at so many things and would make a wonderful mother.

He watched as she stroked the baby's forehead and wondered whether, as his wife, she would ever hold her husband with such love and tenderness.

***

Thomas entered Opechancanough's yehakin. It was dim and warm from the glowing fire. "Ah, Thomas, come in. Thank you for coming. I see you bear the native attire. It suits you well," said the old man. He was stripped of his mantle and headdress and wore only simple breeches and moccasins. Thomas could see the scars of war on his wrinkled brown skin. He was old but tough, and his presence of authority dominated the room, no matter the informality of his words.

Thomas bowed his head. "It is an honor to wear this tunic and to be here," he said. "But I'm curious as to the purpose of our meeting."

Opechancanough paused and looked at Thomas with seriousness in his eyes. "I am aware that Kokee has spoken to you about the future of the Powhatan tribe. The years have taken their toll on this old body, and the time will soon come when the next world beckons me. The gods have sent a message that leads me to believe that you and Kokee will be my successors as werowance.

Thomas nodded but sensed interruption or opinion was not appropriate.

"I received the message of your destiny before you arrived in Virginia, and it was a momentous day when you finally arrived. I wanted to observe you and get to know you better. Although you are the son of the great Pocahontas, you have been brought up to know only the ways of the Longcoats. It is natural that your loyalties are divided. I am aware that this will be difficult for you, as you have been shown to be a man of depth."

Uncertainty

Thomas nodded. "You are very perceptive, Uncle. I was brought up by my father's parents and have lived the life of an Englishman until now. However, my heart has always been with my mother's family. In coming to this beautiful country, it was my wish to do my best to continue the work of my parents in bringing English and Powhatan together to develop this land. However, as I have explained to Kokee, while I am honored to be considered, I do not feel I would be the right man to lead this tribe. Kokee knows the history, culture, and needs of the Powhatan Nation. Kokee is destined to take this role."

Opechancanough's eyes bore into Thomas. "I have seen your passion for peace, and I have seen how well you have integrated with the tribe." He threw a log onto the smoldering fire. Sparks rose into the air as the flames surrounded the wood. "You may feel unease at the responsibility this role bestows. You may be worried that you cannot do what might be expected of you. But if you were certain, you would not be the man for the job. Uncertainty is a gift sent from the gods. It makes one ask questions of oneself. It ensures against those who rule with blind power and selfishness without taking counsel from the wise."

Thomas listened intently. His heart was racing. He saw himself and Kokee in his mind's eye, and the feelings of fear, joy, and excitement mingled with dread as he remembered Lizzie, John, and Francis. Could he make it work? Could he have it all? There was only a glimmer of hope that he could.

Opechancanough continued in a low, somber voice. "You asked me what the purpose of this meeting is . . . Well, having made up my mind that you are the man I hoped you to be, today, I wanted to ask you to take on this role officially." Opechancanough looked directly at Thomas; his tone was dark. "However, this morning, something happened to spark *my* uncertainty . . ."

Thomas sat up straight. "What is that, sir?" he asked, eyebrows drawn.

"Askook has told me that you are not to be trusted. He says you are telling everyone that he burned down your barn and killed your chickens." His face was stern and disapproving.

Thomas's face drained of color. He was silent as he processed what had been said. Askook could not get away with this.

"Sir," he stuttered. "I do have suspicions about Askook having burned down the barn, but I have confided only in a trusted few about my fears as, unfortunately, I have no concrete evidence to back up my beliefs. It is no secret that Askook disapproves of Longcoat occupation, and my connection to the tribe has, at the least, unsettled him. He has made his hatred of me known on many occasions." He stopped and looked into the fire, organizing his thoughts. Opechancanough waited patiently for him to resume.

Thomas looked up at the old man. "Unfortunately, in this matter, it is my word against Askook's. I have to rely on the fact that as an honorable man who embraces the concept of uncertainty, and knowing the characters of the individuals concerned, you will at least concede that you cannot be certain about my guilt, any more than you can be certain of Askook's innocence." Thomas looked at Opechancanough with an air of confidence.

Opechancanough nodded, his knurled brown face relaxing into a smile. He chuckled and nodded his head. "My son, your response is the response of a leader."

Thomas could feel the tension in the room leaving as Opechancanough continued.

"When I can no longer bear the mantle of werowance, my spirit will rest easily should you decide to take on my role jointly with your brother. In the coming months and years, the gods will reveal what you must do." He put his hands together and bowed. "You will know with certainty when the time comes."

Forty-Eight

My Enemy's Enemy

Askook watched as Thomas left Opechancanough's yehakin. He walked in front of Thomas, barring his way. "Well, Longcoat boy, how did your meeting go?" he sneered, a vein in his temple throbbing.

Thomas looked at him coldly. "The meeting with my uncle went very well, thank you." He walked around Askook, but before Askook could draw breath to retort, Thomas suddenly turned to face him, confronting him with raised eyebrows. "Askook, I have been meaning to ask you about your friend, Rowtag. I have not seen him recently."

Askook's face momentarily flashed panic. "Rowtag? You stupid Longcoat," he shouted. "Rowtag went up country, hunting. What is it to you?" Thomas could see the frightened bully coming out in Askook. His guilt spilled over his bravado and was plain to see on his face.

Thomas was still devoid of emotion as he stared at Askook. "Pocahontas sees what mortals cannot see. The wind and the trees speak to her, showing her truths no other could know. I am the son of Pocahontas." He looked to the sky.

Askook's eyes opened wide. He stared at Thomas, his breath quickening, unable to utter a response.

Thomas nodded slowly. "I had a dream, Rowtag . . . the chickens . . . the fire. Strangely, your face floated above them—your face. Askook, remember, the spirit of Pocahontas lives on, and I am of her blood. I see you when others cannot. I know all about you—you cannot hide."

Askook pulled himself up to his full height, trying to maintain his dignity in the face of threat. He was sweating and breathless. "You have no proof that I had anything to do with Rowtag's death or your fire. You have no evidence."

Thomas pursed his lips and nodded. "So Rowtag is dead, is he?"

Askook's threshold of sanity was surpassed. His face turned red, and he lurched towards Thomas, fists held high. Thomas deftly sidestepped, and Askook landed on the ground shouting obscenities.

Thomas walked away, shouting over his shoulder, "Be careful, Askook. Pocahontas is watching you." He reached for her pearls in his pocket, and her smile lit the sky.

***

Askook watched Thomas leave and staggered to his yehakin, glancing around to ensure no one had seen the altercation. His head was thumping with insistent voices competing with one another, flooding him with conflicting demands. He lay in the silence, trying to block out the overpowering noise until he could take no more and was propelled into the world of the gods. "Please . . . no!" he shouted, flailing his arms in the air.

As always, in this alternative world, his father greeted him with a sneer. "You useless squaw," he taunted. "Get on your knees!"

Askook fell to the floor, looking up at his father. "Father, please, I have tried. I want to please you. I want you to be proud of me." He had tears in his eyes, and his mouth trembled.

"Look at you, you sniveling half-wit. How can I call you my son?" the voice shouted.

"Please, do not hurt me. I will do better next time," Askook whispered.

The voice boomed louder as Askook covered his ears and crouched in a ball on the ground.

"You are the savior of the Powhatans. You must destroy the Longcoat invaders. It is your mission. If you do not do this, you know what your punishment will be . . ."

Askook's mind drifted back to the last time he had been punished. He was five years old.

His father stood over him, shouting words of encouragement as he tried to complete his task of tearing the wings from a bird.

He looked into the beady eyes and felt the bird's heart trembling in its tiny chest. He stopped, a tear running down his face, and let the bird fly away.

His father growled, grabbed his arm, pulled it out of the socket, and threw him against the wall like a rag doll. Taking a thorny stick, he thrashed and thrashed. Askook felt the searing pain until his mind went black.

The pain vanished as he lay bleeding. He could no longer feel. This was the gift that his father bestowed.

From that day, no feeling existed unless it was self-inflicted and he had control over it.

The voice of his father returned in the present moment. "I will plague you until the day you die if you disobey me," he snarled.

Askook lay on the ground, squeezing his eyes shut and holding his hands over his ears until the voice faded.

As he came back to consciousness, he reached for his hunting knife. Pointing the razor-sharp tip at the skin on his arm, he slowly and deliberately cut into the flesh as he had done so many times before. He paused to relish the familiar sensation and sight of the crimson droplets as they fell to the ground.

He sighed. He was alive; once more, he had been saved from his incompetence.

***

Askook spurred the horse on. He had to meet with the filthy Fitzgerald Longcoat. He could fake respect. He had done so with Opechancanough for years. His goal had been made clear, and he would not fail. He would prove to his father that he was worthy of his love. He would finally be recognized as the greatest warrior that ever lived.

As he approached the outer gates of Jamestown, the guards shouted to him from the towers above the gates. "Who goes there?"

Askook replied, "I am a relative of Thomas Rolfe, and I come on an urgent peace mission. I must meet with Sir George Fitzgerald urgently," he shouted.

He heard them talking but could decipher nothing of what they were saying apart from "Rolfe" and "peace pact." Then a guard appeared. "Dismount and hand over your weapons," he said.

"I have no weapons," he lied, touching the small knife that was tucked beside his groin. No Longcoat would search a Powhatan in such an intimate location.

"Enter!" the guard shouted. "Hold your hands up!"

Askook did as requested and, true to form, was frisked lightly as if he were a piece of rotten fish unfit to be touched. The guard nodded.

"Go on, then. Present yourself at the gates of the triangle." The guard looked him up and down and spat on the ground. Askook's head throbbed with hatred, but his veneer of subservient inferiority held fast as he dug his finger into the wound on his wrist. The excruciating pain reminded him of his mission.

He rode through the outskirts of Jamestown, noting the neat, small houses the invaders had hastily erected. His hatred was fueled by seeing land once owned by Powhatans now despoiled by filthy gold-digging foreigners. He noted meager attempts at cultivating crops that were dying of neglect. They would undoubtedly be banging on the door of the Powhatans when their hunger pangs started to gripe again.

As he came to the gates of the fortified triangle, there was another guard to deal with.

"What is your business?" he bellowed.

"I come to see Sir George Fitzgerald on urgent peace business," he called.

"What is your name?"

"I am a relative of Thomas Rolfe; my name is Askook. Thomas has sent me with a message for Sir George Fitzgerald. It is very important, and I must deliver it as soon as possible. Lives could be lost if you do not let me enter. Please, sir, I am begging you to be quick." Askook's face was earnest.

The guard was not convinced. "I have no orders to expect a Powhatan visitor."

Askook could feel his anger rising and squeezed the wound on his arm, diverting energy from rage to pain. "Sir, perhaps you would consult with your superior. The peace pact negotiated by Thomas Rolfe decrees Powhatan and English to be friends. I come as a friend. If I am not allowed entry, this friendship and the peace process itself could be damaged."

The guard looked around furtively, thinking through his next promotion. "Come in, then," he conceded, opening the gate. He frisked Askook almost at arm's length as the previous guard had done. Askook smiled to himself at their incompetence. They did not deserve to win this land, and he would ensure they recognized this when the time was right.

He looked around. "Where do I find Sir George?" he asked—false respect on his face.

The guard pointed to a long wooden building that stretched almost the whole length of one side of the triangle.

He had never visited Jamestown before, and he was surprised at the bustling activity, curious to see the large ships tied alongside the dock. He started walking past the church and towards the center of the small town. He had gone to great lengths to ensure his appearance was spectacular. He had "borrowed" Opechancanough's mantle, which made him feel superior, and his red pucceen-painted face gave an air of menace. People stopped and stared at him; a small child hid his face in his mother's skirts. That was the reaction he wanted. When he saw fear in people's eyes, he felt soothed, relieved that he was not the one who was afraid.

He approached more guards at the entrance to the wooden barracks.

"State your name and your business," the guard shouted.

"I am Askook; I come on behalf of the Great Opechancanough at the request of Thomas Rolfe. I wish to speak to Sir George Fitzgerald urgently on a matter crucial to the peace process." Lying came so easily to Askook that he almost believed it himself.

He was taken down a dark corridor. The guard opened a door, and Sir George looked up from scribbling in a large ledger.

"Who the hell are you?" Sir George snapped.

"My name is Askook, and I come to discuss a mutually beneficial proposition. However, as it is extremely delicate and concerns the peace pact, we must talk in private." He looked pointedly at his companion.

"Smith . . . I can take it from here," Fitzgerald barked at the bewildered guard.

"Well, Mr. Askook, I am curious. You had better sit down." Fitzgerald sat back in his chair, looking down his nose as if Askook was dog excrement on the sole of his shoe. "Your name has never been mentioned to me by either Opechancanough or Thomas Rolfe. I can see no reason for discussing a delicate issue with you."

Askook unobtrusively poked his wrist and felt the energy. "I am one of Opechancanough's most prized warriors. I have his ear over others. My father died while saving his life, and from that day, he has regarded me as more than a son. He tells me everything, and he listens to my counsel."

Fitzgerald raised his eyebrows. "How nice for you. But I still do not see why you are sitting here talking to me."

"You and I have one thing in common . . ."

Fitzgerald shook his head with a snigger, "I very much doubt that, my man."

Askook stood up. "Hatred of Thomas Rolfe," he growled.

Fitzgerald's eyes narrowed and a smile spread slowly over his face.

Forty-Nine

Sarah

Thomas was in the fields checking the tobacco plants. He had learned much about cultivation from Lizzie, the boys, and the Powhatan workers who helped tend the fields daily. He was a good plantation owner; his workers liked and respected him. Today, everyone was topping the plants to make the leaves branch. It was a tedious but necessary job in the process of maximum production. Thomas worked alongside Lizzie, John, Francis, and ten Powhatan workers. They laughed and chatted as they worked. John and Francis worked together, avoiding their brother. Thomas had not sought their forgiveness, hoping that things would work through in time.

He looked up to catch his breath, wiping the sweat from his brow, and through the trees, he caught a glimpse of a horse and cart with a woman and child approaching the house. He stopped and walked closer. He was not expecting anyone. Then he recognized the bright auburn hair and green jacket. It was Sarah Fitzgerald and George.

He made his way to the house and arrived just as they were pulling up outside the front door.

"Heathen!" shouted George as he jumped from the buggy, running over and throwing himself at Thomas.

Thomas struggled to keep his balance, laughing. "George, you will floor me if you're not careful. You've grown since I last saw you."

George hugged him, burying his face in Thomas's coat as if he did not want to let him go. Thomas put a hand of comfort on his hair, sensing that something was not right with the lad.

Sarah came over, smiling. "It is good to see you, Thomas."

Thomas noticed her hollow cheeks and the sadness behind her smile.

"Come in, both of you," he said. "The others are working, but I can fix you a cup of broth." He led them up the steps to the kitchen.

Thomas indicated for them to sit down.

"The plantation looks like it is thriving, Thomas," Sarah said, "and your house is lovely." she looked around. "I hear you will be married in a few months, too. Congratulations."

Thomas nodded. "Yes, I am marrying Nikkiti from my mother's tribe."

"I am sure she must be very lovely, Thomas. She is lucky to have you."

Thomas looked serious. "Yes, Nikkiti is very special. We have been spending a lot of time together over the past few weeks, thinking about our future and the future of our families."

She noted his matter-of-fact response, and a flicker of sorrow crossed her face. "The important thing is that you love and respect one another," she said.

He looked away for a split second, breaking eye contact. "And how have you and George been?" he asked, knowing the question was more loaded than casual.

She pulled George close to her on the sofa and hugged him. "I cannot lie. We have some challenges, Thomas. But we are surviving. George's father has exacting standards, but we are managing . . . are we not, George?"

George looked at the floor and silently nodded.

"I see," said Thomas, uncertainty in his voice. He did not want to pry or put her on the spot in front of George, but he could see from her physical appearance and George's apathy that all was not right. "Well, it is lovely to see you both. Would you like some refreshment?"

Sarah shook her head. "No, thank you, Thomas. We cannot be too long. Sir George does not know we are here."

Thomas tensed. "I see. Tell me, Sarah, is there something wrong that you have come here without your husband knowing?"

She looked at George. "Why don't you have fun with that lovely dog while I talk to Thomas? Maybe she would like to go outside and you could throw a stick for her?"

George nodded and went over to Waba, who was lying on a mat in a corner of the room. "What is her name, Heathen?"

"She is called Waba. Sadly, she had an accident a little while ago, and she can no longer run like she used to. She likes to wander around and sniff. I am sure you and she could have a great adventure outside. Oh—and she loves her ears fondled," said Thomas.

George called her name, and Waba looked up at him with large brown eyes. She wandered over to him and gently nuzzled him as George encouraged her towards the door. She hobbled but was full of enthusiasm for an adventure with her new playmate.

When they had disappeared, Thomas turned towards Sarah. She looked at the floor; her once feisty spirit transformed into a meek and frightened shadow.

"I have been thinking about my husband's child," she said. "I was ashamed and hurt when everything came to light. That poor girl and innocent baby were victims of my husband's cruelty."

"You have nothing to be ashamed of, Sarah," said Thomas.

"I know logically it's not my fault, but I feel that if things between us had been better, it would not have happened. I cannot stop thinking about that girl and her baby."

Thomas was touched by her concern; his eyes were soft. "Odina is being well looked after by her family. Chepi, her baby, is thriving and has even taken his first steps."

"Chepi is George's brother. I have been trying to give my husband another son since we arrived in Jamestown. Unfortunately, I have failed . . . and now my husband sees little point in my existence and uses me only as a punching bag for his frustration. That is why he sleeps with other women, and that is why I feel guilty."

Thomas got up and sat next to her, brows drawn. "Sarah, I am so sorry. I heard some rumors but did not want to interfere for fear of making things worse. Now I know I must do something."

"No, Thomas, you must not do or say anything to Sir George. He is evil, and you will be hurt, and anyway, it *would* make things worse for George and me.

"My main concern is for George. I keep him away from his father so he is not physically hurt. I know he does not understand why his father seems to dislike him, but I am doing my best to keep his spirits up. That is part of the reason we are here today. You are so good with him, and he loves you."

Thomas paused, shoulders hunched. "If I cannot help protect you and George, what can I do, Sarah?"

She looked at him intently. "I would like to meet with Odina and Chepi. George has a brother, and I think he should have the right to visit him. I also want Odina to know that there will never be any hard feelings between her and me. I know she was taken advantage of, and

I want her to know that."

Thomas shook his head. "That is a tall order, Sarah. It is a big risk for you. Sir George would be furious if he ever found out."

"To be honest, Thomas, I am willing to risk it for something so important. I am past caring about Sir George. Things between us could not be much worse. But I want his son to grow up knowing his brother and seeing that Powhatans are not heathens. I want him to be the start of the new generation—someone who does not judge a person by the color of their skin. You have taught me this, Thomas, and I want George to learn this as well."

"So you want me to take you to Werowocomoco?"

"Yes. I would like us to arrange a meeting. I know Sir George is going on an expedition next month that will take him away for a few days. Perhaps we could do it then?"

Thomas had a bad feeling in his stomach. He looked at her sunken eyes pleading with him. "Be careful what you wish for, my lovely Sarah."

Fifty

Two Sons, One Father

They had spent many hours together talking about the future. She was animated about the importance of their forthcoming marriage but, as yet, had shown no signs of closeness. Thomas's attempts at snatched moments of brief intimacy—a touch of her cheek, an arm around her waist, or taking her hand—were accepted rather than relished. She never overtly rejected him and was always amiable, but he knew something was missing. Maybe love would grow.

Of late, his mind had wandered to thinking of Jane, a pointless and painful exercise that always left him feeling a hunger that would never be satisfied. He had promised Nikkiti that Jane would never be in his thoughts, but this was proving difficult, as he had no replacement affection to focus on. He had overheard the gossip about how well the organization of Jane's wedding was progressing. Soon, Jane would be another man's wife.

He sat with Nikkiti in a yehakin, drinking a warm liquor made with fermented berries. She smiled and told him about day-to-day activities in the tribe. He listened intently to her tales of human stories that, although different in cultural context, were no different from those of Jamestown. He pondered how gossip was universal. People were so similar, yet minor differences made for war and destruction. He sighed, caught up in his thoughts, his eyes glazed as her words drifted above him.

"So, how are things at Varina?" she said, looking at him with her large brown eyes. "Are John and Francis being more grown up about our marriage yet?"

He was jolted back to the moment and shook his head. Anguish flashed across his face. "It will take time, but at least they have started speaking to me again. They love you. They think I am a traitor."

"They do not know you then. One day, because of you, there will be no bad feelings between our families. They should be as proud of you as I am."

She knew exactly what to say, but why did she not take his hand? Why did she not pull him closer to show him in gestures rather than mere words that she cared for him? He looked at the ground.

There was a moment of awkward silence.

"Sarah Fitzgerald and George visited the other day," he said.

Nikkiti's eyebrows rose. "That poor woman. How is she?"

"She's not good. She had a complicated relationship with her husband even before his indiscretion. Now, she feels guilty for what happened to Odina, even though it had nothing to do with her. She wants to meet with Odina and Chepi so that George can meet his brother and she can make amends."

Nikkiti's eyes were wide. "A noble gesture, but I do not know what Odina would feel about that. It might be too much for her. Odina is terrified that the Longcoats will come and take Chepi away."

"I know Sarah; she would never do that."

"I am sure you are right, Thomas, but we must go slowly with Odina. She understandably holds hate in her heart for Sir George."

He nodded, frustration clawing at his chest as he focused on Nikkiti's beautiful face. They were like brother and sister discussing the problems of others rather than two people about to be married.

Pausing, he sighed and reached over and took her hand. She was startled by the sudden intimacy and jumped back.

Realizing her unintentional rejection, she moved closer to him, lowering her eyes. "I am sorry, Thomas," she said and took his hand in hers, smiling with soft eyes.

He frowned. "Is there something wrong, Nikkiti?" he asked.

"Nothing at all, Thomas; you startled me. I love spending time with you. When we are married, there will be so much that we can do." Her eyes were bright as she gripped his hand with mock excitement.

He bathed in her presence, straining to tame his hunger for more.

***

Odina had grudgingly agreed to meet with Sarah. She trusted Nikkiti and Thomas; they had saved her, and she owed them. But what did this lady dressed in Longcoat finery want from her? She felt defiant toward Sarah.

When "Sir," as she had been instructed to call him, had bedded her, she had no time or choice to think whether or not he had a wife. He was a man who was never refused. A few black eyes and countless bruises later, her stomach had started to swell, and a new life began. She became a mother. She would protect Chepi with her life.

"My name is Sarah," the pretty lady said, "and this is my son, George." Sarah crouched down beside her little boy, looking adoringly at him.

Odina's eyes opened wide. She had not expected a child to be involved.

Sarah continued, her eyes soft. "We want nothing from you, Odina. Our sons are brothers, so perhaps we can try to be friends for their sake."

Odina lowered her eyes, her mind in a whirl. Her gorgeous little Chepi was her world. She could not imagine being without him. Yes, this little boy was Chepis's brother, but what did that mean? Sarah was older, more worldly wise, and more beautiful than she was, none of which mattered. Odina could not see Sarah's heart, and this was what she needed.

George watched Odina shifting in her seat and looking away as if she wanted to be elsewhere. He saw the fear in her eyes, and he knew what fear felt like. He could not bear for this lady to feel about him and his mother the way he felt about his father. He pulled away from his mother and walked towards Odina.

"I would like to be your friend," he said. He held out his hand, looking at her with hope in his eyes.

Odina took his hand, and her motherly instincts took over. A child was a child, Longcoat or Powhatan, free of the prejudices of culture. She smiled weakly. "What is your name, my new friend?" she said.

"My name is George Fitzgerald the Second," he said proudly.

Odina flinched, recognizing the name of her abuser. She let go of his hand but continued to look at him. "My name is Odina," she said. "I am pleased to be your friend."

George beamed at her. "Why is your skin dark and your hair so black?" he said.

Sarah sprang forward. "George, you must not comment on people's appearances," she spurted, red-faced. "It is very rude."

Odina ignored Sarah. "Well, George, my new friend," she said. "My mother and father come from the Powhatan tribe, and all of my family have the same skin color and dark hair. I wonder why you have yellow hair, blue eyes, and pale skin?" She raised her eyebrows.

George tilted his head to one side, thinking. "Well, Odina, my mother and father have the same skin color as I do. My mother's hair is red and my father has hair a bit like me. So we are different from your family." He paused, a puzzled look on his face. "Does that mean we cannot be friends?"

Odina's face was serious. "I know you already have a friend with dark skin, don't you?"

George frowned. "Do I?"

Odina nodded her head. "Thomas has dark skin, does he not?"

George's eyes opened wide. "Yes, of course, I forgot the color of his skin," he said, "and he is my best friend. I remember when I first saw him, that I thought he was different, and I called him 'Heathen.' But now I know he is not different at all. I still call him Heathen, but he does not mind." He put his head to one side, pausing to consider her words. "But big people only have friends with the same color of skin. Maybe you do not want to be my friend."

Odina laughed. "You are much smarter than 'big' people. Come sit with me," she said.

He sat next to her and looked up at her with innocent eyes.

"I have a little baby with pale skin like yours. He is the most precious thing in the world to me. I love every part of him. Not all big people hate difference. But you are right. Some big people are not wise. They do not know the truth."

"What is the truth, Odina?"

"The truth is that skin is only a covering for the heart. It does not matter what color it is. A person's heart is what matters."

George looked confused. "But you cannot see a person's heart," he said.

"Sometimes you can," she said. "You can look into their eyes, and you can see their heart. For others, you can see their heart by getting to know them. You must listen to what they say and watch what they do . . . and it takes time."

George looked into her eyes. "I can see your heart . . . and I know you are a good person," he said. "My stomach is telling me."

"You are very wise, my new friend. When you meet someone, look into their eyes, listen to what they say, watch what they do, and listen to your stomach. Do not judge by the color of their skin. There are good people and bad people of all colors in the gods' universe." She hugged him.

George pursed his lips. My mother is a good person," he said. "You can trust her." He looked at the ground. "My father is a bad man. He hurts my mother, and he hurts me."

Odina's face bore the hurt of many beatings. She hugged her new friend but knew she could not protect him from such a man.

***

Sarah and Odina sat together as Sarah held Chepi. They smiled, talked, and cooed at the baby as George played with Chogun. Odina's defensiveness had been lifted as she began to get to know George. She opened herself to his mother bit by bit when she realized her motives were noble. Over the course of the day, they had become firm friends who shared abuse from a man whom neither would speak of.

For the first time in many months, Sarah felt at ease. The surroundings were foreign, but the people were warm. Although she stood out with her auburn hair and pale skin, she felt more at home here than she ever had with her husband. She looked over at George, and her heart burst with happiness to see him playing games, chasing his companion, ducking and diving, and being a child—something his father had never permitted.

Sarah's only regret was that it was almost time to return to the reality of her life in Jamestown.

Thomas sat on the stump of a fallen tree, waiting to take Sarah and George back to Jamestown. He had spent time with Nikkiti, but she had to finish her chores, so she left him and he sat enjoying a moment of peace.

As he looked up at the blue sky, pondering how his life had gone so far, he heard voices whispering in the wind.

"I cannot get used to you being engaged to him," a man's voice said.

A woman responded, "It is difficult, but we must put our feelings aside for the sake of the tribe," said a woman's voice, continuing, "He must never know that we have been lovers. He is a good man, and I will make him a good wife. You and I cannot be. I am promised to Thomas by the gods and I will be a peacemaker second only to Pocahontas. This was your mother's legacy, and I must carry it forward, Kokee."

There was silence. The man said, "You seem to find this easy . . . Maybe you never truly loved me?"

"Of course I love you, Kokee, but I have a duty. You must accept this. We cannot meet alone any more."

Thomas knew the voices. He walked away. Now he understood.

Fifty-One

Unhealthy Alliance

Askook looked at Sir George, a respectful façade hiding the pure hatred he felt for this man who had invaded his country. "The time is right for us to act," he said.

Not used to being told what to do, Sir George looked down his nose at the impudent heathen. "I will decide where and when we act," he spat. The stupid heathen had no idea that the end of peace would be the end of his tribe. The poor idiot was going to shoot himself in the foot and probably end up dead. So be it.

Askook smiled. He believed himself to be a master of manipulation. He knew that to be successful, he had to swallow his pride and take his time. Sir George was consumed with a love of himself and a hatred for Thomas Rolfe, to the exclusion of reason.

This was a hatred that Askook shared. There was one difference, though. Askook knew how to play the game. Sir George was not aware there was a game. If peace were destroyed, the ensuing war would rid Virginia of the Longcoats . . . or so Askook thought. Askook nodded. "Of course, Sir George." He bowed and put his hands together. "Your knowledge of such things is far greater than mine."

Sir George preened himself, satisfied that he had the upper hand. "We must make sure that nothing can be traced back to us. Our alliance must remain a secret."

"You have my word."

Sir George continued, "So tell me what plan you have devised."

"I have a posse of warriors disillusioned with the peace process. They are willing to disrupt it at any cost. Unprovoked, they will attack your soldiers, and they will leave one who can report back to the governor. On their return to the tribe, they will tell Opechancanough that your soldiers attacked them and left them no alternative but to kill in defense. Both of our leaders will be angry, and peace will be compromised."

Sir George's mouth slowly formed into a grin. "So Thomas Rolfe will fail," he crooned.

"My lord, he will be disgraced."

"Well done, Askook; I will tell you when our soldiers are on special patrol . . . poor bastards. But they will be heroes sacrificed for a good cause. It is a privilege to die for one's country. Posthumous medals will be awarded to them. It is the least that I can do."

Askook got up from his chair. "I must go now." He bowed.

As Askook left, he looked back at Sir George. "It was nice to see your wife being so friendly with Odina and her baby son on their visit to Werowocomoco. I hope they had a nice time together." He smirked.

Sir George's face drained of color.

Fifty-Two

Bad Heart

Sarah stood like a shield in a corner of the room, sheltering little George, who trembled behind her. Her face was set, showing no emotion. If her husband knew how she felt, it would inflame his anger further. Her priority was to protect George.

"How dare you defy me and visit that whore! Thomas Rolfe was behind this . . . I know he was. You have been disloyal, and you have taken my son to a hive of debauchery. You stupid woman! Do you not understand that they are vermin? What if this gets out? I will be a laughingstock." He came towards her with his hand raised. She cowered, protecting her son. The blow landed on the back of her head, and she slumped.

George ran out from behind his mother, his small figure rigid, eyes flashing. "You are a bad man!" he screamed. "I can see your heart, and it is bad. You hurt my mama, and you hurt me. Thomas is nicer to me than you are. I hate you!"

Sir George's face contorted, and he picked the child up, throwing him against the wall like a rag doll. Sarah ran to her son and took him in her arms. The beaten tot looked at her with large, sad eyes, tears running down his cheeks. "Why does he hurt us, Mama?" he whispered.

Sarah could not contain her rage.

She looked at George's battered little body, kissing his head. She put him down gently and ran at her husband, her nails scratching his face like a wild cat. Blood ran down his face.

He grabbed her wrist, flinging her onto the floor. "You will never win, you stupid whore. I have arranged for your friend Thomas Rolfe's peace treaty to be shattered. He will be disgraced," he sneered.

In a daze, Sarah realized she had to find out what her husband was planning. He was proud of his evil schemes and often eager to share his "genius."

"You are not that clever," she shouted. "I don't believe you."

"It matters not what you believe, madam. Thomas Rolfe is finished!"

He scowled, kicked her in the stomach, and walked out of the room, leaving her lying on the floor winded and in pain.

Sarah knew, in her semi-conscious state, that she had to warn Thomas. She heard the key turn in the lock as she lost consciousnes

***

She felt someone shaking her shoulder. She looked up, unsure where she was. The face looking down at her was blurred. "Mummy, Mummy, wake up," he cried.

She blinked and pulled him to her, hugging him. "Are you alright, George?"

"Yes, my arm hurts, but I'm alright." He nodded slowly. "But I thought you were dead. I was so scared." He sobbed into her chest.

She held him tighter. "My sweet baby. Do not worry. I'm a little bruised, that's all." She hugged him again. But we must do something to get out of this room. We have to warn Thomas." She stood up, wobbly on her feet, and walked over to the door. She tried to turn the handle and pull. It would not budge.

George ran over to a small window. "Mummy, what about this window?

She went over and tried to open it. It was jammed.

She saw a tiny stool in the corner. "Stand back, George," she said.

She smashed the glass with all of her might. They stood and looked at the escape route, waiting for a second to see if anyone had been alerted by the noise. Nothing happened.

"George, let me line the window with pillows so you don't cut yourself . . . Go through, and I will follow you."

He carefully climbed over the pillows while she held his weight. Sarah reached through, took his hand, and she, too, avoiding the splinters of glass, squeezed through the opening. "We must get to Varina as quick as we can. We must warn Thomas that your father plans to disrupt the peace treaty."

Fifty-Three

Ambush

They stood on the banks of the James River. Ambrose Yeardley had a job to do. He was a handsome young man, large in stature, with blond hair and hazel eyes. He was well-liked among his men and respected among his peers.

His men were ready to go. They were personally chosen by him for the task ahead. They were young but well trained.

Governor West approached his nephew prior to his departure. "Good day, Ambrose. The weather is looking good for this mission."

"Not bad," he replied, smiling at his uncle. "One last mission before my wedding. I hope you and Aunt Anne are getting ready for the celebrations on my return?"

Governor West laughed. "Of course, my boy," he said. "You have found yourself a lovely girl there, Ambrose. I must say, you look the happiest I have seen you for some time."

"I can honestly say that my life has been transformed. This mission will be my last as a bachelor, and I will make sure it is successful."

Governor West nodded. "This mission will only take a week or so.

Thankfully, with Thomas Rolfe having built such a good relationship with Opechancanough, there should be no danger. There must be acres of fertile land further up the river, and the time is right for expansion. You need to seek it out."

"Yes, I agree, and there may be trade that we can do before the winter months. I will keep my wits about me, though. Those wolves are evil beasts if they are hungry."

"May God be with you, my son. We will look after Jane until you get back."

The men loaded up the kayaks with supplies. Their wives and children stood patiently waiting, while toddlers cried and struggled to get free, unaware of the solemn occasion. Wives with moistened eyes tried to focus on their children. Unspoken fears of previous missions that had ended in tragedy were hovering over the scene. It was a well-known fact that when an expedition set off, the rewards were great, but so were the losses. Many wives now wore black. But Thomas Rolfe had changed everything, and this was the first test of the peace he had negotiated.

The soldiers walked up and down, fidgeting and eager for the adventure. They had been trained for this, and the adrenaline pumped through their veins. Chances of a Powhatan attack were slim, but most secretly hoped for an ambush—a chance to prove their manhood, a chance to kill a heathen and live to tell the tale to grandchildren down the generations.

Jane stood demurely separate from the wives and children. The commanding officer's fiancée was a respected figure whose rank afforded her privileges. Ambrose walked towards her. "It will not be long before I am back. Think of me while I am gone, and light the fire for my return," he said as he embraced her.

She looked up at the tall figure towering over her—such a kind and gentle giant. She never failed to wonder how he would ever kill another human being. She hoped that God would protect him. He did not stir her like Thomas had, but she felt loved and protected. She was honored to be loved by such a gentleman. "My love, come back to me safe and sound," she clung to him.

He smiled. "I will be back before you know it," he said as he gently kissed the top of her head. After I leave, promise me you will go and stay with Lizzie for a while. She always cheers you up."

"I will go straight away." She took the locket from around her neck. "Take this with you. It has a lock of my hair inside. Think of me, as I will be thinking of you," she whispered. He took it from her. "You will be with me every step of the way," he said.

He looked over at the expectant assembled group. "I must go now, my love." Her small form melted into his last bearlike embrace.

He walked towards the kayaks laden with supplies, looking back and secretly winking at her.

There was a Powhatan guide for each kayak, and Ambrose's men distributed themselves equally between each one. Ambrose placed himself at the front of the first kayak.

It was a lovely morning. The sun sparkled on the water, and cotton wool tufts of small clouds streaked across the blue sky. The kayaks floated downriver for the first part of the journey, looking back as images of their loved ones standing on the pier became smaller and smaller.

The Powhatan guides led the way, and each man was on high alert for danger, whether man or beast. At last, their training was being put to the test, and they could prove that they were heroes. Adrenaline was flowing and spirits soared.

Ambrose clasped Jane's locket. The future was looking positive.

Fifty-Four

End of Peace

Thomas walked and walked with no particular destination in mind. How could he marry the woman his brother loved? His feelings for Nikkiti had grown, but how could he look at her, how could he caress her the way a man caresses a woman he loves, when he knew this secret?

Kokee's words repeated in his mind. *The love of my life is promised to another.* Thomas's mind churned as waves of despair washed over him. In marrying Nikkiti, he would further his mother's ambitions but crush the heart of the brother whom, in such a short time, he had grown to love. Would Kokee secretly hate him the way Thomas secretly hated Ambrose Yeardley? The quest for peace surely was not worth this agony. Opechancanough must be told. There must be another way.

He started walking towards the house. As he climbed up the wooden steps to the house, he heard a horse and carriage tearing down the driveway. He turned and immediately recognized Sarah Fitzgerald, her startling red hair flying out behind her as she spurred the horse to go faster. George clung on as the carriage bumped up the driveway, dust flying.

Sarah came to a sudden halt in front of the house, her face grimy and screwed up with anguish. She jumped down, pulling George with her, and they ran towards him. All thoughts of Kokee and Nikkiti were obliterated by the despair that accompanied his two friends.

"Thomas, we must speak with you!" Sarah's voice was urgent. "Sir George has lost his mind!"

Thomas rushed down the steps with open arms.

Her legs gave way as she walked forward. He rushed to her aid, gently holding her arm. "Sarah, my goodness. Take your time; let's get you inside." He supported her up the stairs, with George walking behind.

Sarah and George sat in the kitchen, breathless and staring. Thomas got water for them and sat down to listen. "What has happened?" he said, eyebrows drawn.

"I have so much that I want to tell you Thomas, but before I tell you about what has happened to us, there is something that you need to know . . ." She closed her eyes and paused to take a breath. "Sir George let it slip that he plans to sabotage your agreements for peace with the Powhatans. I do not know exactly what he will do, but he was very pleased with his plan. He wants to destroy you, Thomas. Is there anything out of the ordinary happening that could be open to attack? You must stop him before it is too late."

Thomas bit his lip, searching his mind to try and think what Fitzgerald's target could be. "Wait a minute . . . Ambrose Yeardley is starting his mission upriver sometime in the next few days—he might even have already gone. It's the only significant operation planned this year. But it's only an exploration of new territory for trade. What could he do to thwart that?"

Sarah shook her head. "I do not know, Thomas. It might not be that, but it's something in the near future."

Thomas's face fell. Ambrose Yeardley—Jane's fiancée. He paused, looking at the floor. He would do anything for Jane's happiness . . . even save the man he envied most. Jane's face flashed before his eyes, and his stomach turned.

"I think that could be it, Sarah—I cannot think of anything else," he said.

She grabbed his arm. "You must go and warn them, Thomas."

He looked down at her, anxiety on his face. "I will go, but first you must tell me what Sir George has done to make you run away like this."

Sarah recounted every sordid detail of the abuse that she and George suffered at the hands of her husband. "I never want to go back there." She looked at him. "I cannot go back there." The tips of her eyelashes sparkled with teardrops. "Thomas, I have been locked in that room all night, and I have been thinking about the future George and I will have. I cannot bear it any longer. Having met the Powhatans, I realize how civilized they are . . . ironic when the English call them 'heathens.'

"I know it might sound like I have lost my mind, but I would like to go live with the Powhatans, if they allow us to. If we're lucky, Sir George will not even realize we've gone—he cares so little for us."

He took her hand. "It would be a courageous thing to do, Sarah. Are you absolutely sure that is what you want?"

She paused, sighing. "I don't think I have many options left. Our life in Jamestown is not a life. To see George playing and being a child again with his little Powhatan friend made me realize the pressure we've been under. George never complains, but the coldness of his father hurts him terribly. I have to do something."

Thomas looked down. "I'll do all I can, but Sir George will cause trouble."

"Yes, I'm prepared for that. He doesn't care about me, but I recognize that George is his son, and he may try to force him back. But he has been so disinterested and distant from George, he would only try to get him back to repair his damaged ego—not for love for his son, because there is none."

She looked at George, who had fallen asleep, his head resting on her shoulder, and stroked the hair from his forehead.

"It seems that your mind is made up, Sarah. I will talk to Opechancanough. It is unusual for a white woman to live with the Powhatans, but he is a reasonable man, and he will understand your reasons. He will also be keen for George and Chepi to be together. I will help in whatever way I can to make this happen for you. At some point, though, Sir George will realize you are not coming back, and that is when trouble could arise. So you must stay hidden until we get you to a safe place."

"Thank you, Thomas; I knew wecould rely on you. But for now, you must go and warn Ambrose. That is your first priority. Make haste.

***

Governor West looked up from his desk as Thomas crashed through the door.

"I'm so sorry, sir, but I must speak with you. I have urgent news." He was red in the face and panting.

"Take a moment, Thomas. Catch your breath."

"Sir, I do not have time. I have it on good authority that there may be an attack on Ambrose's mission."

West stood up. "Good God, man, you must be mistaken. What about the peace treaty?"

Thomas stared down at his hands. Now was not the time to disgrace Fitzgerald. It would mean betraying Sarah and her plans to leave her husband. Fitzgerald believed Sarah to be under lock and key, and it was better that this belief remained intact until Sarah's position was secured.

"I believe there are factions among the Powhatans that are prepared to sabotage peace. Unfortunately, there are also those among us who are also against peace. Our traitors have divulged Ambrose's movements to make him an easy target for a Powhatan attack."

West sat down and looked straight at Thomas. "Who?" he shouted.

"Sir, I have no proof, but we must act now to prevent a tragedy. Nothing will have been lost if I am wrong except a few hours and men checking on Ambrose. If I am correct, and we do nothing, it could mean a massacre of innocent men. We can investigate the culprits and ensure justice is done at a later date."

West nodded. "Take what you need, Rolfe. Go after them and warn them."

"Thank you, sir."

"You are a good man, Rolfe. Your father would have been very proud of you. When you get back we will rout these traitors out. Things are difficult enough without having enemies within."

***

Thomas spared no time. His assembled group were heavy of heart, with no one waving them off and wishing them luck. Ambrose's group had a day's advantage, and Thomas would have to push his men to the limit to catch up. Without being told, Thomas knew that Askook had to be the instigator of this fiasco. Fitzgerald would have been a willing but stupid accomplice to this evil plan.

The going was tough. Ambrose's men had the advantage of time, taking a leisurely trip peppered with breaks and rest. Thomas could not afford such luxury. They rowed for hours and hours, their arms nearly at breaking point. Eventually, as darkness fell, they were forced to make for land and set up camp. Wolves howled as they prepared a fire. Guards were posted, watching for the slightest movement indicating a pack was surrounding them. Luckily, the fire and smoke kept the beasts at bay.

"We must get some rest, lads, as it will be an early morning for us. We have to make up the time if we are to catch up with Commander Yeardley."

"But sir, we are exhausted," said one of the soldiers.

"I know, Sergeant Green , but we need to travel more hours in the mornings and evenings if we are to get to Commander Yeardley to warn him. It is the only way. Luckily, he is only one day ahead, so if we push ourselves, we should get to him by tomorrow evening."

"Yes sir," he said, dragging his voice.

They settled down for the night, designating several lookouts in different shifts. Thomas took the final shift to rouse the men at the crack of daylight to ensure an efficient start.

At dawn, they rose and continued the journey on land as Ambrose had done.

On and on, they trudged through mud and bramble. This was virgin land, most of which had never been trodden by man. The forest was brutal.

Then they heard shouting. A shot. More shouting.

"Quick men over there, it looks like we're just in time," shouted Thomas.

They ran through the trees until they saw a clearing in the distance. It was obvious that Ambrose had stopped to rest his men, as there was a smoking fire with embers still lit. The men stood, muskets drawn, looking around them as the sounds and colors of Powhatan aggressors flashed through the trees around them.

"We have surprise on our side," whispered Thomas. "They have surrounded Ambrose's men, now we must surround them . . . We must be quick, as they are getting closer, and Ambrose is a sitting duck."

They did as they were told. Once in place, Thomas took aim, raised his musket and fired. Surprise and relief flooded the faces of Ambrose's men, and panic flooded the faces of the Powhatan aggressors when one of their warriors fell to the ground.

"You are outnumbered, Askook!" Thomas shouted. "We will kill every last one of you if you do not retreat."

"Kill us, and the peace pact will be broken," screamed Askook.

"Go home, Askook. Be prepared, though. Opechancanough will carry out the appropriate punishment when I inform him of your betrayal."

Thomas signaled for his men to advance towards Ambrose's encampment. They formed a circle, muskets pointing towards the Powhatans hiding in the trees. Realizing the danger of being associated with Askook's plan, the warriors melted into the trees.

Thomas, smiling, turned to shake Ambrose's hand but was met with the long faces of his men. Ambrose lay on the ground with a Powhatan arrow through his heart, a silver locket in his hand.

Fifty-Five

Bad News

The journey back to Jamestown had been arduous. A beloved officer was lost. They carefully transported his body, dreading to imagine the heartbreak of his future bride when she discovered his fate.

Thomas was numb. In the past few days, his world had tumbled around his ears. His future marriage, his relationship with his brother, peace negotiations, Sarah's happiness, and now Jane's happiness had all been thrown up in the air. He did not know where everything was going to land, and his head was bursting with the pressure of trying to solve it all. Maybe nothing could be solved.

He had made a mess of everything. How arrogant to imagine that he was the great Peacemaker waltzing into a situation that was so complex even the great leaders had not solved it. And how could he think for one moment that a beautiful Powhatan girl wanted to marry him because she loved him? As for saving Ambrose, he had done his absolute best . . . or had he?

As he made his way back to Varina, he could see Jane's carriage, and his heart rose and sank simultaneously. He walked up the wooden steps with lead feet, dragging one leg after the other, going towards the door but pulling back at the same time until he was forced to open the large wooden door.

What seemed like a crowd of people sat around the fire, but through blurry eyes, he only saw Jane. He looked from her to the floor, his face lined with the devastation of what he had to say.

Before he opened his mouth, they knew.

John jumped from his chair, leading Thomas to sit by the fire. Lizzie ran to get him some ale. He sat and stared at the floor.

Jane fiddled with her fingers in her lap, tears silently running down her face.

Lizzie handed Thomas the ale, which he took, nodding appreciation but still unable to speak.

Sarah came over and crouched down in front of him. "What happened, Thomas?"

He looked past Sarah towards Jane. "I am very sorry to say that although we managed to avert a complete massacre, Ambrose was fatally injured."

Jane's silent tears fell steadily, and Lizzie put her arm around her friend to comfort her. Thomas was frozen to the spot. Jane was crying for another man, and he failed to quell a horrible resentment welling up inside him. He was ashamed. Ambrose had been a decent young man, brave to the last, whose life had prematurely ended. If he had been ten minutes earlier maybe he could have saved him. It was his fault that Jane's life had been ruined. Thomas tried to reason with himself as he stared at the floor.

He felt a small hand on his shoulder. "Do not be so sad, Thomas.

Bad News

Pocahontas will look after Ambrose," George whispered. Thomas looked up and lifted George onto his knee. "Such wise words, George."

Jane looked over at Thomas.

"Thomas, thank you for putting your life on the line to try and save Ambrose. I will be forever in your debt." Her eyes were red-rimmed, her face blotchy with tears.

Thomas continued staring at the floor. "Ambrose was one of the most respected and well-loved soldiers I have ever known. He died a hero, and you can be proud."

"Did he suffer?" she whispered.

"No. His death would have been instantaneous. Your locket came out of his pocket as he fell. I have it here for you." He lifted George off his knee, walked over and put the locket in her hand.

Everyone else in the room was silent. It was as if there were only two people in the world.

She looked at the locket and broke down sobbing, her shoulders quivering with distress.

Thomas put his arm around her, his heart breaking.

"I need to go back to my parents, Thomas. They are the only ones who can help me through this terrible time."

He released his hold on her. "I can take you there, Jane. Please, at least let me do that for you."

"No" she whispered. "I would rather Lizzie accompany me."

"Of course," he said, lowering his head.

***

After Jane left, everyone at Varina remained somber. Her tragedy, plus Sarah's uncertain future, dampened everyone's mood. Even little George, while happy to be out of his father's clutches, was disoriented and unsure where his future lay.

Sarah sat staring into the fire, her mind in a whirl. George quietly modeled animals with flour and water, his eyes glazed as if in another world.

Thomas, twiddling his fingers, forced his thoughts away from Jane. With everything that had been going on, he had avoided the subject of Sarah and George's future, but he had to address it for her sake. Fitzgerald was not one to let things lie for long, and they needed to act before he got the upper hand.

Thomas got up and sat next to Sarah on the sofa. He took her hand and looked into her eyes. "Sarah, as much as I do not want to, I think we have to think about your future," he said.

She was startled out of her thoughts. "Yes, I must address it; I know that, Thomas." Her face was downcast. "I have stayed here too long already. Sir George must realize I have gone. It is only a matter of time before he figures out I am here. At present, you are the only ones who know that I have left."

Thomas took both of her hands in his and stared into her eyes for several seconds. "Are you positive that you want to live with the Powhatans?"

She nodded and looked down.

Thomas nodded. "We must get you both out of here as soon as possible. If he knows you are here and decides he wants to take George, you could both be in danger. I will meet with Opechancanough tomorrow and explain the situation. He does have a soft side."

George looked up and sidled over to his mother. "Are we in danger, Mother? Will Papa find us? I don't like Papa; he has a bad heart."

Sarah hugged George and kissed the top of his head. "Don't worry, my little man; Thomas will protect us."

"Will we go and live with Chogun? I like Chogun. And my little brother Chepi is funny. He keeps falling over . . ." He smiled, then his face changed as a memory came into his mind. "But I do not want to go back home to Papa. He hurts me." He hugged his mother, cementing himself to her.

Thomas looked at George. "Remember our secret? Pocahontas is always there. She looks after us both; you don't have to worry."

Sarah gave Thomas a quizzical look.

"Sarah, George and I will make sure everything turns out well. We have a special friend to help us . . . don't we, George?"

George released his hold on Sarah, smiled, and nodded. "Yes, we do," he said.

Fifty-Six

Another Chance

As Thomas approached the quioccosan after the disastrous ambush, it seemed as though the whole world had changed. He had to meet with Opechcancanough to secure a future for Sarah and George, and to ascertain the damage done to the peace process by Askook and Sir George.

The Powhatan attack was a severe breach of the agreement. Would Opechancanough believe the truth, or would false tales of Longcoat aggression incite him to fury?

Opechancanough sat waiting for him. His face was stern as he looked into the embers of the fire. Thomas slipped in and quietly sat opposite, waiting to be addressed. His heart was pounding.

The silence was broken as Kokee entered the quioccosan, nodded to Thomas and bowed to Opechancanough. Thomas was surprised to see Kokee but relieved that he would have his brother's support.

Opechancanough raised his eyes. "The gods are not pleased."

Kokee sat forward. "We have tried to make peace, but the Longcoats are intent on war." Kokee looked at Thomas with sadness. "All of our warriors are safe, but they were cruelly attacked. It was an unprovoked assault as they were hunting. When our warriors defended themselves, sadly, a Longcoat officer was killed." He looked at Thomas, and the sadness in his eyes had turned to defiance as previous memories came into his mind. "We have given them so many chances. I believe that whatever we do will not be enough for them. Perhaps, as others have said, they are determined to steal our land, and negotiations are pointless."

Thomas's heart sank. This was not the brother he had come to know and love. This was a Powhatan warrior addressing him as the enemy. Kokee had not given him the chance to speak. He looked at Kokee with pleading eyes, but he looked away. Kokee had made his mind up.

Thomas took a breath. "This was a serious incident, but please do not rush to conclusions."

Kokee's eyes flashed. "No one is rushing to conclusions, Thomas. The facts speak for themselves. The English broke the peace pact." Sweat was breaking out on Kokee's forehead.

Kokee had always wanted peace. It had been his reason for being. He had instilled Thomas's desire to carry on their mother's work and they had been so close. Thomas pondered recent events. Suddenly it came to him. The thing that had changed their relationship was a broken heart.

Thomas's impending marriage to Nikkiti was integral to peace. If peace was abandoned, there would be no need for the wedding. Kokee had tried to keep his feelings in check, but the recent incident must have tipped him over the edge. Conscious or not, his hatred of the English was surfacing for so many understandable reasons.

Without Kokee on his side, peace was all but lost. However he had to try.

He took Pocanontas's string of wedding pearls from his pocket.

"I have looked at these pearls every day since she was taken from me. When I was old enough to understand her story, my only goal was to do her bidding. She came to me as she came to you, Kokee, giving us courage and giving us a cause to strive for. It is you, Kokee, who reignited my enthusiasm for her legacy."

Opechancanough and Kokee were silent, staring into the fire, absorbing Thomas's words.

"Since arriving in Virginia, I have given my heart and soul to the cause of peace between the Powhatan and the English. I have an allegiance to both. I have come to love my Powhatan family." He looked at Kokee, but Kokee continued to stare into the fire.

"Immediately prior to this attack, I found out about this cowardly plan to destroy attempts at peace. It was not a military operation but a deliberate attempt to sabotage our efforts to end this war. It was a conspiracy between Askook and Sir George Fitzgerald, both of whom detest me enough to crush everything I have been working for. Neither wants peace, for their own selfish reasons, so they conspired to create a false incident which would force war on us all.

"I tried to stop it as soon as I knew about it, but I was too late. Governor West did not authorize this attack and it was not authorized by you, Opechancanough. Please do not let the views of two deranged men ruin a peace that, if nurtured, could last for generations." His eyes were focused on the two Powhatans before him, even though neither met his stare.

Opechancanough raised his eyes to look at Thomas. "I have never doubted your loyalty to us or your dedication to peace," he said. His rheumy eyes betrayed his tiredness. "Askook has a special place in my heart. He believes in the sovereignty of his people, as did his father, to whom I owe my life. I do not believe he would deliberately contrive such a plan; you must have been misinformed of his contribution to this fiasco."

The old man seemed to visibly shrink under the weight of conflicting loyalties. Thomas's heart sank to think that Askook was winning, not because of truth or integrity but because of a split-second decision made by his father many years ago.

Opechancanough looked at the young men in his presence. "For years, I have wrestled with the problem of Longcoat invasion. I have listened to the gods and done their bidding as I thought fit. From kindness to aggression, from friendship to war, it has been impossible to resolve anything in the long term. I hoped that your coming, Thomas, would make the difference."

Thomas was bursting to interject. "But this time, it was working! This time, only the petty jealousies of two men caused it to fail."

Kokee shook his head. "My brother, I wanted to believe that we could do it. I wanted to be able to say to Pocahontas as I lay sleeping that we had realized her dream."

Thomas's eyes were sparkling. "But we can, Kokee." Thomas noticed Kokee's aggression diminished as he spoke about their mother. For a second, they reconnected. Thomas was desperate not to lose the momentum. "Governor West knows what happened. He is prepared to keep the peace going . . . we are almost there. Even if I have been misinformed about Askook, this was a single event. It does not have to determine the future."

Opechancanough smiled. "Your enthusiasm makes me feel young again, Thomas, but while this is a single incident, I cannot believe there will not be others. I have come to the end of my tether. You were our last chance, and you have done all you can. The truth is, we are not just fighting each other; we are fighting within our own communities. I am tired of trying . . . we are fighting the instincts of human beings to be cruel to anyone of a different color or culture. The stupidity of human nature is a mountain that is too high to climb."

Thomas looked at the ground. "It is indeed a high mountain, but it is worth the climb." He looked up. "One more meeting. I am begging you . . . one more meeting?"

***

Nikkiti sat outside the yehakin, sewing a suede tunic. As he approached, she smiled and put her handiwork down. "Thomas," she said, her face lighting up. He took in the image of this beautiful girl, so full of honor and principles that she would forsake her own desires for the good of her people.

He crouched down, pecked her on the cheek and sat beside her.

"I see you're very busy," he said.

"I am sewing tunics for our wedding, but I am never too busy to talk to you." She smiled as she turned to face him.

He looked into her eyes. "Nikkiti, I feel like the luckiest man alive to be marrying you . . ." He paused, and she looked expectant.

Her eyes changed as the silence became meaningful. She looked at the ground. "You have come to tell me that you do not want to marry me because now Jane is free; you want to marry her." She looked up at him, her face flushed, eyebrows drawn. "I heard that her fiancée was killed, and I was waiting for you to be honest with me. I thought it might take a little bit longer."

Thomas drew back in horror. "No, Nikkiti. What I have to say has nothing to do with Jane."

Nikkiti looked chastened. "I can tell that there is something serious in your heart, Thomas, and you are hesitant to tell me, so it must be bad. If it is not about Jane, what is it?" Her eyes softened, and she put out her hand to touch him gently.

"I overheard you and Kokee talking," he whispered.

"We talk all the time, Thomas." She laughed. She looked at him and dropped her head when he did not smile.

"Nikkiti, you and Kokee should be together. You love one another."

She sighed. "I am sorry that you heard us, Thomas. The fact that we care for one another is not important. What is important is peace. Opechancanough was right to announce my betrothal to you. He and the gods know it will cement the union between the English and the Powhatans."

Thomas looked away, his mind racing. "But you cannot marry me if you love Kokee."

She looked at him, her eyes wide. "You are marrying me when you are in love with Jane."

"That's not the same thing. I care for you and will be honored to be your husband."

"And I you. I care for you, Thomas, and more importantly, we will be instrumental in cementing peace. I love Kokee, but I have accepted that we are not meant to be, as you accepted that you and Jane were not meant to be. We have a duty, and we are willing . . . unless you have changed your mind?"

Thomas shook his head. She was a woman of intense determination and principles, but he had not realized how single-minded she was until now. "What about Kokee? How can I cuckold the brother that I have found after all these years? Kokee has become my dearest friend and one of my most loved relatives. It breaks my heart to think of my deliberate betrayal of his feelings."

"One man's feelings are as nothing compared to the peace of a nation," she said, her eyes flashing.

"Did Opechancanough know that Kokee and you had feelings for one another when he presented you to me?"

"He knew we had always had a friendship, but not in the way of lovers."

Thomas looked at her steadily. "And you omitted to tell him?"

Her face showed no emotion. "I could see how much I could do for peace, following in the steps of Pocahontas," she said. "I am destined to be famous like her."

Thomas looked away, trying to understand the psyche of the woman he was marrying. While her dedication to the cause was honorable, it was also shocking in its ruthlessness. He suddenly wondered if she was capable of loving anything but the cause.

Nikkiti's face took on an expression of aggression he had never seen before as her voice rose in anger. "I can see what you are thinking, and if you break off this marriage, I will ensure you are disgraced. You can forget any cozy plans of leading the Powhatans with Kokee when Opechancanough departs this world; you will be shunned forever."

He could hardly believe what she was saying. There was only one thing that he could do.

Fifty-Seven

Dismantling The Dream

As he walked away from Nikkiti, he saw Kokee in the distance stacking wood with Chogun. They were laughing and playing. Now and again, Kokee would lurch at Chogun, pretending to throw a log in his direction. Chogun laughed and ducked.

Kokee, his strong but gentle brother, would be a good husband for a girl who truly loved him. His heart sank when he thought of Nikkiti, the girl Kokee had fallen for. She had never hidden her willingness to sacrifice in the quest for peace, but Thomas had not realized that her heart was frozen to all but her obsession. She was not capable of loving anything but the cause.

He caught Kokee's eye and waved. Kokee saw him and waved back. It was not the enthusiastic greeting he used to receive, but at least he was smiling, so Thomas walked towards him.

"Kokee . . . Chogun!" he shouted, "Do you need any help?" He smiled.

"Help from a scrawny Longcoat?" Kokee shouted. Thomas was relieved that the banter between them had not been completely destroyed. There was hope yet that their relationship could be salvaged.

Kokee put the log down and looked over at his brother. "So . . . you have been talking about the wedding with Nikkiti, I presume."

Thomas's face was solemn. "Yes, I have. And I need to talk to you as well."

"Talk with me? The great peacemaker wedding will be in a few weeks, will it not? There is nothing to talk about."

Chogun jumped forward. "Yes, we are chopping enough wood to make a huge fire . . . and all the squaws have been talking about how much venison we will need to feed all the Longcoat visitors. Will George and Sarah be coming too? I hope so . . . we have such fun together. It will be so exciting!" His eyes were starry, and he jumped up and down, pretending to dance.

"Whoa, whoa . . . I'm still not sure what you're saying, Chogun, but I think you need to calm down."

At that moment, Cleopatra's voice could be heard calling from a distance.

Kokee looked at Chogun. "Cleopatra is calling you for dinner, you rascal. You had better go quickly. You know what she is like." He clapped him on the back. "Come back after dinner, and we can finish some of these logs."

Chogun rolled his eyes. "Do I have to?"

Kokee shrugged his shoulders. "Yes to both things," he said, winking at him.

Chogun dropped the log he was holding. "If I must, but I want to know everything you talked about when I was not here."

Kokee made a shooing motion with his hands, and the lad reluctantly turned and jogged towards Cleopatra.

"Now, Thomas, what do you want to talk to me about? Opechancanough agreed to meet the Longcoats again; I do not think there is much more to discuss . . . unless it has something to do with your wedding." He sat down on one of the logs.

Thomas sat next to Kokee. "It is to do with the wedding. There is not going to be a wedding."

Kokee flushed but said nothing, staring at the ground, trying to hold on to thought and feeling.

Thomas looked straight at him, his eyes unflinching. "You love Nikkiti, do you not?"

Kokee slowly raised his eyes to meet Thomas's gaze. He nodded his head.

The two brothers sat in silence for several minutes.

Thomas sighed. "Kokee . . . I had great respect and fondness for Nikkiti and believed I could grow to love her, but I would never have agreed to marry her if I had known your feelings for her."

Kokee's face was drawn. "It is true, I have loved Nikkiti forever. We have been talking about our children since we were children. But recently, she has grown distant. She talked of nothing but peace. And when you arrived, and Opechancanough put it to her that she could marry you, she became obsessed. She changed, Thomas. It was like I did not know her any more. I tried to reason with her, but she was determined, so I had to go along with it and try to be happy for you both."

Thomas pursed his lips. "But you would never be truly happy, Kokee. I've been in the same position . . . I understand. That is why I've told her that I cannot marry her. She doesn't have feelings for me. She only wants the glory of following in the footsteps of our mother. Even without your involvement with her, I've come to realize that our lives together would have become unbearable. I've told her that she must tell Opechancanough that she no longer wishes to marry me. That way, she will not feel the shame of rejection. If she does not do this, I will reveal the truth."

Kokee stared at him. "She would be publicly humiliated."

Thomas nodded. "That is why she must say that it is her own decision. I can manage being the rejected party."

Kokee ran his fingers through his thick, dark hair. "What a mess," he said.

Thomas smiled. "It was a mess. But I hope that you and I can reestablish our relationship. I must admit, sacrificing my relationship with Nikkiti is easier than sacrificing my relationship with my brother."

The two brothers embraced.

The sound of a child's voice pulled them apart. "What am I missing?" cried Chogun.

Kokee laughed. "Well, I think you are going to have to learn a bit more English and get a bit older to understand what went on here," he said.

Chogun's face went red with frustration. "I knew if I went, I would miss something. I hate being a child!"

Thomas took his hand and pulled him forward, looking at him. "I know you understand a little bit of English, so I will give you some exciting news . . . George and Sarah are coming to live at Werowocomoco."

Chogun's face lit up as he turned to Kokee. "Is he saying that George and Sarah are visiting?

Kokee smiled. "No, he is saying they are coming to live here, Chogun."

Chogun jumped up and down. "My best friend is coming. I am so happy!" he shouted.

Fifty-Eight

Home

The journey back to Varina seemed endless. He longed to be in the kitchen supping ale, surrounded by his family. He felt that Werowocomoco's warmth was steadily growing dim, and he was starting to feel like a stranger among the inhabitants again.

While tensions with Kokee were resolved, they were not completely eradicated. Nikkiti was hostile, and Opechancanough's favor was fading alongside the hope of peace. Yes, another meeting would occur, but both sides were weary, and the human instinct for war seemed to overshadow common sense. He sighed as Varina came into view and he anticipated the warmth that lay inside.

As he opened the door, Waba darted at him, whimpering and pawing at him. Lizzie and Sarah were at the kitchen sink, and John and Francis played with George. Nothing had changed . . . but everything had changed.

George looked up and ran towards him. "Heathen!" he shouted. The others looked around, and even John and Francis grinned with delight to see him. George grabbed him by the hand and dragged him to a chair beside the fire. Waba lay next to him, her large brown eyes gazing up with unadulterated devotion. He caressed her velvet ears.

They all gathered around. "So what happened, Thomas?" said Lizzie. "Was Opechancanough angry about the attack? Did he believe you when you told him it was a conspiracy?"

Thomas looked at all the expectant faces. "There will be another meeting," he said. "But I'm unsure if it will succeed this time."

"Why not, Thomas?" said Sarah.

"It's a long story," he said. ". . . And Nikkiti and I have decided not to marry." His voice was emotionless.

Everyone looked around, unsure how to react.

John was the first to speak. "I know we've had our differences, Thomas, but I am truly sorry," he said, looking at the floor.

Francis followed. "Yes, I am, too," he whispered.

Thomas gave them a weak smile. "Thank you. It was a mutual decision, and it's the right one, but these things are never easy."

Lizzie walked over to him, put her arm around his shoulder, and hugged him. "I'm sure you know what you're doing, Thomas. We're all here for you."

Thomas felt a tugging at his jacket. "Heathen . . . Heathen . . ."

Thomas smiled. "What is it, George?"

George's face was puckered with worry. "Do we have to go back and live with Father? If you're not marrying Nikkiti, we cannot live with Chogun." Tears started rolling down his cheeks.

Thomas pulled him forward and hugged him. "Don't worry, George. My not getting married does not affect you. I've spoken to Opechancanough, and he would be happy to have you live with Chogun and Chepi. You are Chepi's big brother, after all."

George pulled away, a huge grin appearing on his face. "Am I a big brother?"

"You are indeed," said Thomas.

George screwed up his face. "How can he be my brother? Brothers live together with the same mamas and papas."

Thomas looked at Sarah. "Most of the time, that is true. But sometimes it is different. Kokee is my brother, and we grew up in different families."

Sarah came closer. "Don't worry about how; just enjoy being Chepi's brother. We will have a whole new family that will love you."

George frowned. "And you're sure father will not make me go back to live in Jamestown?"

Sarah shook her head. "No, George. Your father understands that we have a new family now."

George's face lit up. "Then I must go and finish the carving I was doing for Chogun," he said.

His mother hugged him. "Yes, you go along and do that, George. I'm sure Chogun will love it."

George ran out of the door, excitement on his face.

"Hold on George, we're coming to help you" shouted Francis. The two boys followed him.

Thomas looked at Sarah. "Sir George is highly unpredictable. Now that Opechancanough has agreed that you can live there, we must get you to Werowocomoco immediately, as Sir George may come looking for you. He will be less keen on following you to the Powhatan Nation, so you will be much safer there. We have had a breathing space while the focus has been on Ambrose's death, but whatever he thinks of you, I cannot believe that he will not feel the shame of your having left him. It is dangerous for you and George to be here for too much longer."

Sarah nodded. "We are ready to go, Thomas."

They heard footsteps pounding up the steps to the front door, and

John bounded in, followed by George and Francis.

"There is a group of men thundering towards Varina," panted John.

"Yes," said Francis. "We could not see at that distance who it is . . . but whoever it is has something serious on their mind. I would not be surprised if it is Sarah's husband."

Thomas moved quickly. "Sarah, George, you will have to hide. We do not have time to get away before they arrive." He looked around, panic in his eyes. There is a cellar under this room. Pull back the carpet quickly!" he shouted.

They pulled back the threadbare carpet to reveal a square cut out in the floor. Thomas pulled it up and revealed stairs going down into the darkness.

"You must take a candle down, as it is very dark down there."

Sarah and George did as they were told, faces strained, staring ahead of them.

George looked up at Thomas as he descended. "Thomas, please do not let my father take me away."

"He will not find you down there, George. You must be as quiet as a mouse, though." Thomas put his finger to his mouth for silence. George nodded.

"I will not make a sound, Thomas, I promise."

Thomas put the hatch down and replaced the carpet, putting the dining room table over it.

He sat down at the table as if he had been there for hours, looking up with fake surprise as the door burst open. Sir George Fitzgerald stood armed and flanked by three of his men.

Thomas jumped up. "How dare you enter my house like this!" he screamed. His face was red with a mixture of fear and anger as he stood on the carpet, imagining Sarah and George crouching like escaped convicts in the space below.

Sir George stood his ground with hands on hips. "Where is she?

Where is that bitch? She has stolen my son!"

"I assume you are talking about your wife? I have no idea where she is. If you were any kind of husband, you at least would know where your wife is."

Sir George's face turned puce with rage. He turned to his three companions. "Search the whole house; I know they're here. She can rot in hell for all I care, but I want my son and heir."

Thomas stood in front of him. "I shall be reporting your intrusion to Governor West. On top of your conspiracy with Askook, this will not go down well, Sir George."

"You have no proof of anything . . . your word against mine. I have years of service. You're just a novice from Norfolk. I know who West will believe."

Thomas could take no more; in the heat of the moment, his will to win against Fitzgerald overcame common sense. "Even your wife knows the truth. She knows exactly what happened."

Fitzgerald exploded. "What has that whore been saying? She must be here. I will kill her if I find her!" he screamed. He turned to his three henchmen, "Tear this place apart . . . leave no stone unturned!"

Thomas sat down at the table, his feet on the carpet covering the hatch. "They're not here, George. She left hours ago."

"*Sir* George to you. When I find her, she will regret ever having been born."

The intruders stomped around the house. They ran up the stairs, and Thomas heard slamming doors and heavy footsteps overhead. Eventually, Sir George came down, followed by three sheepish soldiers.

"She must have escaped. I will find her, and I will kill her. She cannot be allowed to steal my son and spread vicious rumors about my integrity."

Thomas glared at him. "She has more integrity in her little finger than you have in your whole body."

Sir George lurched towards Thomas, his fists primed.

Waba emerged from the shadows, fangs gleaming and growling with menace in her eyes. She limped, but was still capable of inflicting pain on anyone who did not take her seriously.

Sir George stepped back. The soldiers raised their pistols.

Thomas stood up. "I want you to leave my house now, or there will be serious consequences."

The soldiers lowered their pistols, uncertainty on their faces.

Sir George stood his ground. "I am leaving of my own accord. You do not order me around. This is a waste of my time. That bitch is hiding somewhere, and I will find her." He glared at Thomas. "I will also make it my priority to ensure Governor West is cognizant of your scheming, you bastard heathen."

He marched out of the house, nose in the air, giving Waba a wide berth.

Fifty-Nine

The End Of The Legacy

He should have been happy as he approached the Powhatan village to introduce Sarah and George to their new life. There was to be another peace meeting, and Kokee and he were on good terms again. Why did he feel dread in the pit of his stomach? Had the world changed, or had he changed? Or maybe reality was overpowering hope. The encounter with Sir George had been unsettling, and Thomas knew there was bound to be more trouble.

When they met this time, embracing Kokee brought more emotion than at any other time he could remember. As he felt the brotherly hug, he wanted to capture the closeness. Kokee represented the Powhatan part of his life; for some reason, he felt it slipping away, even as he clung to him in greeting.

Kokee released him. "Welcome, brother," he said as he searched

Thomas's face, sensing an intensity in his demeanour.

Thomas nodded and smiled. "I have brought Sarah and George, two of my greatest friends," he said as he turned to them. "George, Sarah, this is my big brother, Kokee."

George came forward and bowed. "I am pleased to meet you, Kokee," he said, holding his hand out. "I am a big brother too. My little brother is called Chepi."

Kokee took his hand and shook it. "Pleased to make your acquaintance, George. I know your little brother well, and I have heard all about you from Chogun, as he is a very good friend of mine. He says you play a wicked hide and seek."

"Chogun is my best friend," replied George." He turned to look around him. "Where is he? Can I go and play with him?"

Sarah came forward. "I think we should go and see Odina and Chepi first. We'll be sharing a yehakin with them. Would you like to see where you'll be sleeping?"

George's face lit up, and he jumped up and down. "Yes!" he screamed. "I'll be sleeping in a yehakin. Can I have clothes like Chogun? I would much prefer to be Potan than English."

Sarah laughed. "It's Pow-a-tan, and let's take it one step at a time, George."

Kokee took George's hand, and they all walked towards one of the outer yehakins. As they entered, Chogun ran towards them. "George!" he shouted.

Odina was sweeping the floor, and Chepi toddled around, moving from bunk to bunk with his unstable gait. He turned to look when the visitors entered, falling on his bottom and laughing.

George looked around the yehakin. It was quite dark, but the light from the open door filtered through. There were four bunks lining the walls. Animal skins hung from the rafters, and it smelled of the smoke of the now extinguished fire. It was a smaller space than the yehakin he had been in when he met Odina, but it was cozy and comforting. His eyes were wide. "Where do you sleep, Chogun?"

"I sleep in the yehakin next door," he said. "So we will be able to see each other a lot."

Odina walked over to Sarah and hugged her. "Welcome, Sister; I have made bunks for you and George."

Sarah was overwhelmed. For the first time in many months, she felt safe. She looked at Thomas and silently said, "Thank you."

He nodded, relieved. Sir George would be unlikely to come to Werowocomoco to find Sarah. It would jeopardize his career if he made an unauthorized visit, endangering the peace negotiations, shaky though they were. For now, Sarah and George were in the best place. Thomas's next task was to make arrangements to meet with Governor West to try to repair the relationship between the Powhatans and the English as soon as was practicable.

Everyone turned towards the entrance as the door opened and Nikkiti appeared. Thomas flushed and looked at the ground.

"Everyone is waiting to welcome you and George, Sarah," she said. We are all assembled on the green. Opechancanough will arrive soon, and we are roasting venison in your honor." She put her hands together and bowed her head. As she left, she caught Thomas's eye and glared icily in his direction. He felt the glare as if it were a physical assault, discomfort flooding his body. He looked away.

Odina picked up Chepi, who struggled to escape her clutches. "Oh no, you don't, my little rascal. We are going to the green for a celebration," she said. Kokee took the struggling baby from Odina and put him on his shoulders. Chepi immediately stopped squirming and smiled triumphantly at his young mother.

Odina smiled at Kokee. "You are very good with little ones, Kokee."

"To me, they are what matter," he said.

Everyone filed out of the yehakin and walked towards the green space, which stood in the middle of the village. Chogun chased George, and they laughed and pushed each other, oblivious to the sense of occasion.

When they arrived, Sarah looked around at her new extended family. They had dressed up in ceremonial clothes and smiled at her in welcome. Thomas stood by her side. "I hope you will be happy here, Sarah. It will be a very different life for you."

She nodded. "I am pleased to be somewhere different. I would not have survived if I had stayed in Jamestown. I could not have done it without you, though." She smiled up at him.

They all sat down on long tree trunk seats that surrounded the fire in the middle. Drums started to sound, signifying the entrance of Opechancanough.

The great leader appeared, flamboyant in his full Powhatan regalia. His magnificent headdress touched the ground. The colors of the feathers were exquisite. Everyone stood in respect. He raised his hands, palms downwards, signaling for them to be seated.

As Opechancanough started to speak, Thomas noticed a movement in the side of his vision. He turned to see Nikkiti walking to the back of the crowd. Someone had just arrived on horseback and was jogging towards her. He squinted to see who it was.

Askook. Thomas's heart sank. Where had Askook been, and what was he doing talking to Nikkiti?

Nikkiti had made it clear that she had turned from friend to enemy. If revenge was what she wanted, allying with his greatest adversary was the most traitorous thing she could do.

Their eyes met over the crowd.

Sixty

A Final Score

The celebration was in full flow. People were dancing, eating venison, and rejoicing. Sarah and George had never witnessed such joy and were overwhelmed to be a part of it. The colors, the smell of fire and roasting meat, and the sounds of drums filtered through the surrounding forest. This was the joy of human interaction not experienced in the world of the English gentry.

Strong fragrant tobacco was passed from person to person, and many were feeling the hallucinogenic properties starting to engage, throwing arms about in wild abandon. Laughter filled the air.

Thomas looked around at the people he had come to love.

Chepi, on Kokee's shoulders, laughed with glee as Kokee danced with Odina. She looked adoringly at him. Perhaps there was a spark of romance between them? Perhaps his brother had started to move on from his feelings for Nikkiti, at last realizing his childhood crush had more important goals for herself.

Sarah was in animated conversation with Opechancanough, who was explaining the traditions and celebrations of the Powhatan tribe. She was nodding and smiling, and the old man was in his element, his hands gesticulating to illustrate his vivid descriptions.

George and Chogun darted in and out of the crowd in their own childish world, their faces shining in the light of the roaring bonfire.

Thomas searched the crowd but could see no sign of Nikkiti or Askook. Could they be plotting against him? Both were now enemies; together, they could be a formidable force.

He walked around the green, casually searching. Then he saw them.

Askook and Nikkiti were talking to none other than Sir George Fitzgerald, who was flanked by four soldiers. Thomas's heart sank. Of course . . . Askook had told Sir George that Sarah was here. What better way for him to curry favor with the English and simultaneously destroy Thomas's hope for harmony?

Thomas started walking towards the plotters. As he approached, Sir George caught sight of him. "Thomas Rolfe," he growled, "this is your fault. She would never have come here of her own volition." He raised his hand and pointed his finger at Thomas. "You will pay for this, you filthy heathen. I have come under the authority of the British Government to retrieve my wife and son. The fact that you did not reveal their whereabouts when I visited your plantation shows where your allegiance lies and is tantamount to treason. Governor West is fully apprised of the situation and, at last, has realized who you really are . . . a filthy heathen!" He turned towards his soldiers, who stood to attention. "Arrest this man!" he bellowed. His face was red with sweat, his beady eyes sparkling.

The soldiers scrambled around Thomas, pinning his hands behind his back and binding them tightly. Fitzgerald pushed past as he charged towards the center of the celebrations.

Thomas had no time to warn Sarah. He found himself being shoved in her direction, as he was forced to follow Sir George into the now-intoxicated melee of gyrating and howling bodies.

The crowd parted as Sir George rammed through, oblivious of those knocked to the ground by the force of his fury.

Opechancanough and Sarah were still deep in conversation, unaware of the approaching storm.

Kokee heard the commotion and looked through the throng. He caught a glimpse of Sir George careering through the crowd with Thomas following, hands bound, and knew something momentous was about to happen.

He took Chepi down from his shoulders and gently passed him to Odina.

"Take Chepi and hide," he whispered. She felt the fear written in his drawn eyebrows.

"What is going on, Kokee?" she gasped, her eyes darting around. She pulled Chepi into her chest.

"Just go as quickly as you can. Sir George is here. I sense there will be trouble." He darted towards the musicians, commanding them to cease playing so the situation could be laid bare.

When silence replaced the cacophony of sound, the celebration stopped as if the revelers had turned to stone. They looked to Opechancanough through bloodshot eyes, stunned by the sudden end of the celebration.

Opechancanough and Sarah stopped their conversation, suddenly aware that the center of attention was on them. Sarah's eyes opened wide, and she shrank back with terror when she caught sight of her rampaging husband. She shouted for her son. "George! George!"

George came careering towards her, and she reached out and pulled him tightly to her, glaring at her husband.

Opechancanough looked calmly around, his wise old eyes taking in every element of the scene before him. "Sir George Fitzgerald, I believe. To what do we owe this vulgar interruption of our festivities? I was not aware that we were due to meet. There has been no communication with Governor West." His voice was calm, with an undertone of menace.

Sir George stood before Opechancanough. Faced with the old man's presence of authority, he realized the danger he had put himself in. He felt for his gun and looked to his companions for backup.

Behind him, the soldiers stood, guns trained. Tension hung in the air like thick fog.

Kokee stood at the other side of Opechancanough, and to his dismay, Odina returned minus Chepi and came and stood next to him. Her face was ugly with hatred as she stared at her abuser. "He will never take my child," she growled under her breath with clenched teeth. "I will make sure of it."

The crowd waited, murmuring, bobbing up and down and straining to see Sir George's next move.

Sir George stood tall. "Sir, I come on a matter of urgency. My wife has been led astray by this man." He turned and nodded at Thomas. "I would like to escort her and my son back to where they belong. I do not wish to cause trouble, merely to take back what is mine." His voice shook.

Opechancanough sighed and looked at the ground, shaking his head.

"Sir George, Thomas Rolfe is a man I would trust with my life. Far from kidnapping, he has rescued two of your wives with your children, and brought them to safety following your abusive behavior."

Sir George's face turned scarlet. "Sir, I—" he shouted.

Opechancanough held his hand in the air for silence. "Before you say something that you may regret, Sir George, I suggest you untie Thomas Rolfe and order your companions to put their guns away so we can have a civil conversation."

Sir George hesitated, his eyes darting from Opechancanough to Sarah to Thomas and back again. A determined look crossed his face, and he took a step towards Sarah. Little George darted in front of his mother.

"Leave my mother alone! Go away. You have hatred in your heart," he shouted.

It was as if his son had lit a touch paper. Sir George roared with anger. "You ungrateful little bastard!" He launched himself towards the lad, his fist poised to punch the little boy.

The brave George Fitzgerald the Second stood protectively in front of his shrieking mother, waiting for the blow to land on his small body.

Everyone gasped as Sir George's hand seemed to freeze in midair. There was a silence that seemed to go on and on before Sir George dropped to the ground like a felled tree, staring up at the sky, blood dripping from his mouth.

Odina lowered her bow, the arrow having been discharged directly into the heart of her abuser, as she had imagined so many times.

The four soldiers trained to respond instantly pointed their guns and fired in Odina's direction. The crack of the guns filled the silence. Kokee had darted in front of her as soon as he saw the guns raised. Thomas watched, powerless, as the bullets entered the body of his wonderful brother.

Chogun rushed to his friend and threw his body over him. "Kokee . . . Kokee," he cried. "Do not leave me." His tears fell on Kokee's bloodied body.

Kokee looked up at him and smiled, remembering how he had thrown himself over the body of his father.

His eyes closed as he drew his last breath.

Sixty-One

Aftermath

The next day, Thomas stood looking up at the body of his brother placed on a scaffold, as was Powhatan tradition. Kokee was wrapped in animal skins, and his possessions and jewels were placed around his body.

The celebrations of the day before had turned into the nightmare that was now taking place. It was the same location, the same people, but the singing and dancing had been replaced with solemn reflection and relentless wailing.

Thomas's head was filled with the pain of loss as the reality of what had happened filtered through the continual vision of Kokee falling on the ground. The sudden transference from vibrant life to stagnant death happening in seconds destabilized him. He was empty. No vision, no hope, no thoughts of the future. He vaguely heard the sound of Opechancanough's voice droning on in Algonquin, but nothing permeated his pounding head.

Nikkiti and Odina, united in their grief for the man they had both loved, held hands, staring at the ground. Manitou stood quietly next to Nikkiti, her canine sensitivity reflected in her soulful brown eyes. She understood the significance of what was happening more than the hundreds of howling human mourners.

Chogun was nowhere to be seen. His broken heart was too raw, and his young spirit too damaged to face the body of his best friend.

As the ceremony finished and the mourners dispersed, Thomas felt a small hand clutching his, breaking his trance of grief. "I'm sorry, Heathen," whispered George. "You're not a little brother any more."

A small light filtered through Thomas's darkness. "That's the strange thing, George. Even though I am sad, deep down, I know that I will always be a little brother. Kokee will always stay in my heart."

George grinned. "He's with Pocahontas, isn't he?"

Thomas nodded. "Maybe next time she visits us, Kokee will be with her."

Sarah stood next to George and reached out to Thomas. "What will you do now, Thomas?" she said.

"So much has changed, Sarah." He looked to the spot on the ground where Sir George had died and up to the platform that held Kokee's body. "With Kokee gone, I am not sure I will be able to carry on my work here. I will meet with Opechancanough to see if anything can be salvaged, but I am not holding out a lot of hope . . . and to be honest, my heart is no longer driving me on." He hugged George. "Take good care of your mother, George, and keep opening your heart to the spirits," he said. He turned to Sarah and gave her a peck on the cheek. "Be happy, Sarah. Life is too short to dwell on the past; you must look to the future and enjoy these wonderful people."

She smiled and nodded, a tear glistening in her eye.

He walked towards Opechancanough's yehakin with legs like stone.

Opechancanough sat in his full regalia, a broken man. He stared at the fire, briefly looking up as he heard Thomas enter.

"I have tried, Thomas," he said, "but I cannot try any more. There are some Longcoats and some Powhatans who would willingly seek peace, but alas, there will always be those who are greedy, selfish, and hungry for war who will sabotage attempts at peace. You were right about Askook, and he will be severely punished, but even if he changes his ways, there are others who will stand up for what he believes. We cannot change the reality of human failings."

Thomas nodded, his face displaying the emotions of the tragedy they were both facing.

"I fear war is inevitable," he whispered. "I will rally my warriors to wipe out the Longcoats. If I do not do this now, the numbers will increase and there will be too many to defeat. This war will be greater than the war that killed your father in 1622, and I intend to return the land to the people who are native to this country. I welcome you into the Powhatan tribe to fight with us and win with us. However, you must choose between us and them. You can no longer be a part of two worlds."

Thomas stared at the fire, memories of his visits to the Powhatan village flitting through his mind, glistening his eyes with joy and sadness.

However difficult it was, he had to acknowledge that morally his loyalty must be to Lizzie and the boys. He did not belong here. It was a foolish dream.

"I am honored, sir. However, my sister and brothers need me at Varina." He bowed his head and put his hands together at his heart. I hope that maybe one day we will meet again in peace . . . if not in this life, in the next life."

Opechancanough's face softened; he closed his eyes and bowed his head in acknowledgement.

Aftermath

Thomas left the yehakin and walked toward his horse. He took one last look at the Powhatan village before turning in the direction of Varina.

***

On the long ride to Varina, he had plenty of time to reminisce about his time in Virginia. The highlight had been meeting Kokee . . . and Jane. Both relationships had been fleeting but unforgettable.

Now he had to concentrate on the plantation and his English family. He was no longer torn between two cultures, but the grief of the loss of his Powhatan identity would take many moons to resolve, if ever. He felt Pocahontas's pearls in his pocket. She would always be with him, no matter what happened.

He climbed the steps of the plantation house and opened the door.

Everything was the same. The fire burned in the grate, the stew bubbled in the pot, and Waba lay fast asleep on the rug. Francis and John sparred with each other in the corner and Lizzy peeled the potatoes.

One other person stood with her back to him, her long blond plait hanging to her waist. She turned, and when she saw him, she ran to him, throwing her arms around him. He buried his head in her shoulder as they both wept.

He felt the pearls in his pocket. Now he understood real peace.

Epilogue

Thomas Rolfe

Thomas married Jane Poythress in 1645 in Henrico, Virginia. They had one daughter who was also called Jane. Thomas became a Lieutenant in the British army and defended against Native Americans in the 1646 war. He is said to have died in 1680 (although the actual date is unconfirmed) and was buried in Charles City County, Virginia, United States.

His daughter Jane, married Col. Robert Bolling (1646-1709) and she died in childbirth. Her son was Col. John Fairfax Bolling.

It is understood that Edith Bolling Wilson, wife of Woodrow Wilson, was a descendant of this family. Robert E. Lee, Confederate General and Martha Washington may also have ties to this family.

Opechcancanough

Opechcancanough, true to his word, continued the war with the colonists and launched a bloody attack in 1644. About 400 colonists were killed, but the Powhatan were ultimately defeated and the war was over by 1646 as the English were better prepared and had greater numbers.

Opechcancanough was finally caputured in 1646 at the age of 90-100 years old and paraded through Jamestown in disgrace. While imprisoned, he was shot by one of his guards and died.

Following Opechcancanough's death, Necotowance became paramount chief, and signed a treaty that decreed that the tribes became tributaries to the King of England, paying a yearly tribute to the Virginia governor.

Also by Sue Wright

Tempest, Bermuda 1609

The story started here, with John Rolfe, Thomas Rolfe's father.

The tale of a young man leaving his tragic past behind and setting out to fulfil his dreams in the New World.

Passionately in love with his new wife, and looking forward to a new start as they boarded the ship to Jamestown, nothing could have prepared them for the tragedy that was to come. On a tumultuous sea where rivalries, politics and racial discrimination were rife, John's beautiful lover, to protect a closely guarded secret, makes a tragic error of judgement. It would change everything.

Peacemaker's Dream - The story of the first true lady of America

The story continues with Thomas's mother-Pocahontas.

She was young, smart and principled.

They were out to get her. She never gave up... and neither did they.

In a story based on fact, you will discover the heart wrenching account of the struggles of a nation under siege unprepared for the sophistication of its invader. Their most effective weaapon was a young girl who has mistakenly been portrayed as a cartoon character in modern culture.

The record is now being put straight about the life of Thomas Rolfe's mother, how she met John Rolfe and the sacrifices she made.

You will cry at her loves and losses, you will smile at her mischief, but you will finally know the truth.

Her legacy was her two sons and the continued drive for peace.

www.ingramcontent.com/pod-product-compliance
Lightning Source LLC
Chambersburg PA
CBHW020516080526
44583CB00013B/621